Fiscal Decentralisation, Local Government and Policy Reversals in Southeastern Europe

William Bartlett
Sanja Kmezić • Katarina Đulić
Editors

Fiscal Decentralisation, Local Government and Policy Reversals in Southeastern Europe

palgrave
macmillan

Editors
William Bartlett
London School of Economics and Political Science
European Institute
London, UK

Katarina Đulić
Faculty of Economics, Finance and Administration
Belgrade, Serbia

Sanja Kmezić
University of Graz
Graz, Steiermark, Austria

ISBN 978-3-030-07142-4 ISBN 978-3-319-96092-0 (eBook)
https://doi.org/10.1007/978-3-319-96092-0

Softcover re-print of the Hardcover 1st edition 2018

Cover illustration: Hemis / Alamy Stock Photo

This Palgrave Macmillan imprint is published by the registered company Springer Nature Switzerland AG
The registered company address is: Gewerbestrasse 11, 6330 Cham, Switzerland

Preface

This book arose out of a project generously funded by the Regional Research Promotion Programme (RRPP), which is funded by the Swiss Agency for Development and Cooperation, Federal Department of Foreign Affairs, from 2014 to 2016. The overall research programme was coordinated and operated by the Interfaculty Institute for Central and Eastern Europe at the University of Fribourg (Switzerland). The initial project involved a study of fiscal decentralisation in Montenegro and Serbia with research teams from the two countries led by Sanja Kmezić and Katarina Djulić (members of the European Research Academy Belgrade (EURAK) think tank in Belgrade) and mentored by Will Bartlett (from the London School of Economics and Political Science - LSE). The project was subsequently widened through a follow-on grant from the RRPP, which enabled researchers from other countries in the region of the Western Balkans and the former Yugoslavia to meet together in a series of workshops in 2016 to 2017 of which this book is the result. This research network has become a Working Group of the LSEE Research Network on Social Cohesion in South East Europe, hosted at the LSEE research unit at the European Institute of the LSE.

Interest in the relationship between central and local government in the successor states of former Yugoslavia and in Albania was visible from the start of the transition process. The imperative of the transformation from socialist to capitalist economic relations required a reduction in the power of the central state in the economy, while at the same time the process of democratisation emphasised the importance of strengthening the powers and responsibilities of local government. In Bosnia and Herzegovina, Kosovo,[1] and Macedonia[2] fiscal decentralisation and the devolution of political authority have also been proposed as a means to defuse ethnic tensions. This points to a fundamental property of decentralisation, namely that it brings decision-making responsibility to the local level, where local preferences can influence public policies and public expenditures. As public policies become more responsive to local needs, it could be expected that social welfare at local level would increase.

Few social scientists have studied the issue of decentralisation in this region, despite the important consequences of different governance arrangements for economic development and social cohesion. In addition to its academic merit in this regard, the project and the associated research network have made a great effort to draw policy lessons based on the evidence that has been accumulated and to reach out to policy makers to disseminate the findings of the research aiming to have an impact on policy making in this field.

Almost 30 years after the start of the transition process in the region, the balance between central and local government has still not reached a stable arrangement. The findings from the research analysed in the chapters below identify the "to-and-fro" nature of policy making that has led to several policy reversals that have played out through various phases of centralisation, decentralisation, and back to centralisation again. This process has revealed the nature of the gaps between legislated intentions and actual implementation of policies and the increasingly authoritarian tendencies of central governments. It has also led to a new understanding of the importance of decentralisation for inclusive local economic development and for democratic societies capable of defusing ethnic tensions. As the region moves forward, slowly and hesitatingly, in its process of European integration, the resolution of many of the issues that face the local governments in the region and addressed in this book is likely to become even more important in the future.

London, UK — William Bartlett
Graz, Austria — Sanja Kmezić
Belgrade, Serbia — Katarina Đulić

Notes

1. This designation is without prejudice to positions on status, and is in line with UNSCR 1244 and the ICJ Opinion on the Kosovo Declaration of Independence.
2. The name for the country is recognised by the UK government, but it should be noted that the name is currently under negotiation between the government of the country and Greece, with provisional agreement at the time of writing as "Republic of Northern Macedonia".

Contents

Notes on Contributors

Anto Bajo is a senior scientific advisor at the Institute for Public Finance and a full professor at the Faculty of Economics, University of Zagreb, Croatia, where he is Lecturer in Public Finance and Public Sector Financial Management. His area of interest is managing public sector finances and fiscal impact of structural reforms.

William Bartlett is a visiting senior research fellow at the LSEE Research Unit at the European Institute, London School of Economics and Political Science, UK. He is a coordinator of the LSEE Research Network on Social Cohesion in South East Europe. He is the author of the book *Europe's Troubled Region: Economic Development, Institutional Reform and Social Welfare in the Western Balkans* (2008), and has published over 100 articles in refereed journals and book chapters. He has carried out consultancy and research projects for the European Commission, the European Parliament, the Council of Europe, the European Training Foundation, the United Nations Development Programme (UNDP) and the United Nations International Children's Emergency Fund (UNICEF).

Halko Basarić has been working for more than 20 years as a consultant for USAID and World Bank local governance and local finance reform projects both in Bosnia and Herzegovina and internationally. He holds a master's degree in Public Policy from the Central European University, Budapest.

Adem Beha is a lecturer at the Department of Political Science, University of Pristina, Kosovo. He is the author of the book *Between Stabilization and Democratization: Elections, Political Parties and Intra-Party Democracy in Kosovo* (2016).

Nina Branković is an expert in policy development and political analysis. She is a PhD candidate at the University of Zagreb. She holds a master's degree in Public Policy from King's College, London. Her academic and research interests include innovation policy, political economy and education for development.

Boštjan Brezovnik is an associate professor at the Faculty of Law University of Maribor, Slovenia. He teaches courses on public administration and local self-government. His research interests also include public finance and fiscal decentralisation, public procurement, public services and regional development. He has participated in a number of international research projects.

Katarina Đulić is an associate professor at the Faculty of Economics, Finance and Administration in Belgrade, Serbia. She is also a co-founder of European Research Academy Belgrade (EURAK) and has carried out numerous consultancy projects for the International Finance Corporation, USAID and the Austrian State Secretariat for Economic Affairs (SECO) aimed at governance and public financial management reform.

Mateja Finžgar is a PhD student at the Faculty of Economics and Business of the University of Maribor, Slovenia. Her doctoral research project focuses on the international comparison of the different fiscal decentralisation systems. She has published several scientific papers in the field of fiscal decentralisation.

Mijat Jocović is an assistant professor at the Faculty of Economics of the University of Montenegro, Podgorica, Montenegro. He is a researcher and a consultant on various projects funded by international development agencies.

Jadranka Kaluđerović is a professor at the Faculty for International Economics, Finance and Business of the University of Donja Gorica (UDG), Montenegro, and the Director of the Institute for Strategic Studies and Prognoses (ISSP), the first economic think tank in Montenegro. Her research interests include macroeconomics, business cycles and economic policies.

Sanja Kmezić is a lecturer at the Karl Franzens University of Graz, Austria. She is a co-founder of the non-profit think tank EURAK, Serbia, and has worked as an advisor on various international development programmes aimed at local government and public administration reform.

Lejla Lazović-Pita is an assistant professor at the Faculty of Economics of the University of Sarajevo, Bosnia and Herzegovina. She holds a PhD from the University of Bamberg, Germany. Her academic and research focus is on public finance.

Marjan Nikolov is President of the think tank Center for Economic Analyses (CEA) in Skopje, Macedonia, and was a lecturer at the International Slavic University, where he was Lecturer in Local Government Finance. He holds a PhD in Economics from the University of Ljubljana and an MSc in Economics from the University of Reykjavik.

Žan Jan Oplotnik is Professor of Finance at the Faculty of Economics and Business, University of Maribor, Slovenia, where he is also the vice-rector for Finance. He is the co-author of more than 100 scientific papers published in national and international journals, and scientific books.

Marko Primorac is an assistant professor at the Faculty of Economics and Business, Zagreb, Croatia. He is an affiliate of the international CESifo Research Network and was a member of the Commission for the Development of a New Local and Regional Government Financing Model by the Ministry of Finance, Croatia, in 2017.

Elton Stafa is a PhD candidate in Statistics, and a senior expert at USAID Albania and the Network of Associations of Local Authorities of South-East Europe. He has contributed to the development of Albania's Public Finance Management Strategy and to municipal finance legislation. He has been an advisor to the Albanian Finance Ministry.

Anton Vukpalaj is Assistant Professor of Political Science at the University of Pristina, Kosovo. He is author of the book *Ex-Yougoslavie, de la guerre a la justice* (Former Yugoslavia, from War to Justice) published by Michel Houdiard Editeur in 2010.

Merita Xhumari is Professor of Public Policy at the University of Tirana, Albania. She has participated in several international research projects focusing on social policy and local governance issues. She is the author of the textbooks *Process and Institutions of Social Policy* and *Pension Trajectories in Western Balkans 1990–2010.*

List of Figures

List of Tables

1

The Political Economy of Decentralisation and Local Government Finance in the Western Balkans: An Overview

William Bartlett, Sanja Kmezić, and Katarina Đulić

Introduction

The countries that emerged from the ruins of former Yugoslavia in the 1990s present a unique laboratory for the analysis of economic, social, and political change. Along with their counterpoint, Albania, which had a far more centralised system under communism, they have traversed armed conflicts, partial transitions to market economies, varied paths of democratisation, EU accession and pre-accession processes involving deep institutional change and most recently the spillover from the

W. Bartlett (✉)
London School of Economics and Political Science, European Institute, London, UK
e-mail: w.j.bartlett@lse.ac.uk

S. Kmezić
University of Graz, Graz, Austria

K. Đulić
Faculty of Economics, Finance and Administration, FEFA, Belgrade, Serbia
e-mail: kdjulic@fefa.edu.rs

W. Bartlett et al. (eds.), *Fiscal Decentralisation, Local Government and Policy Reversals in Southeastern Europe*, https://doi.org/10.1007/978-3-319-96092-0_1

Eurozone crisis, which led in most cases to deep recessions, high levels of unemployment, deep fiscal gaps, and dangerously high levels of indebtedness. Each of these challenges has brought the issue of the distribution of powers and resources between the central state and lower tiers of governance to the fore. Although the Yugoslav successor states shared a common economic, historical, political, and social background, each has tailored its policies towards financing local government in accordance with its specific context, while Albania began from a different, more centralised, set of initial conditions. This book analyses the political economy of fiscal decentralisation in these countries over the last quarter century. Its aim is to identify the variety of decentralisation approaches that have been adopted and to explain the reasons for their differences and similarities, rooted in different combinations of political and economic interests. In this respect, the book contributes to the body of literature on the political economy of post-communist transition as well as to the literature on the role of fiscal decentralisation in post-crisis Europe.

This introductory chapter provides a general overview of the political economy of decentralisation and presents the structure of the book. It provides a methodological umbrella for the analytical approaches applied in the country case studies, emphasising the political economy drivers of decentralisation reforms that have taken place over the whole transition period from 1990 to 2016. It argues that decentralisation has attained only partial success in addressing the specific policy objectives of democratisation, balanced economic development, and post-conflict reconciliation of ethnic communities. It also guides the reader through the main arguments discussed in each chapter of this volume, situating the eight case study countries into the wider discussion of the political economy of decentralisation in the post-communist transition process.

Decentralisation in the Successor States of Former Yugoslavia and in Albania

In former Yugoslavia, decentralisation led to increased regional inequalities that were only partially corrected by regional development policies and fiscal transfers from the centre (Flaherty, 1988). Fiscal responsibilities had become highly decentralised by the end of 1980s, and economic elites in each Republic carried out investment projects that were in their own interest rather than the collective interest, causing duplication of productive facilities and a reduction in macroeconomic efficiency, which damaged economic performance (Kaiser, 1990). With the break-up of Yugoslavia, most of these problems disappeared since there was no longer a single political entity responsible for regional redistribution. Instead the problems of revenue and expenditure assignments, of meeting diverse preferences of population sub-groups, of designing effective policies of fiscal redistribution between regions and municipalities, of imposing hard budget constraints and preventing local debt accumulation shifted to the erstwhile republics themselves which had become countries in their own right and now had to deal themselves with the thorny problems of the most appropriate level of decentralisation and the most appropriate territorial design.

In the Yugoslav successor states, the transition from socialist to market-oriented economies has led to a deep transformation of both economies and political institutions. The first stage of transition from socialist republics with a high level of devolved powers involved an initial centralisation as part of the process of state-building (Bartlett, Maleković, & Monastiriotis, 2013). As the transition progressed, political decentralisation reduced the dominance of central state institutions over their emerging markets, and to assist democratisation and empowerment of citizens at grassroots level. Independence of the Yugoslav successor states also triggered a wave of constitutional and administrative reforms bringing about new territorial organisation. One group of countries (Slovenia and Croatia) created a large number of local governments, raising questions about diseconomies of scale, the cost of bureaucracy, and the optimal number of municipalities. A second group of countries (Bosnia and Herzegovina, Kosovo, and Macedonia) adopted territorial-administrative reorganisation as a method of defusing ethnic tensions in a post-conflict setting, at least partially under the oversight of international peacekeeping forces. A third group of countries (Montenegro and Serbia) were reluctant to engage in redefining their territorial-administrative organisation because they wished to avoid an escalation of ethnic tensions and potential fragmentation of their territories.[1]

While the book focuses on the successor states of former Yugoslavia, the case of Albania is included as a comparative example of a country that began the transition process from a different set of initial conditions, namely an almost complete centralisation of political and economic power in the hands of the state. There, decentralisation accompanied democratisation from the start of transition in the early 1990s.

The Political Economy of Decentralisation in Transition Countries

Proponents of decentralisation have argued that it has beneficial effects on efficiency. The Oates theorem, now also known as the first-generation theory of decentralisation, suggests that decentralisation has the property that it brings decisions closer to the population that votes on them, and so different jurisdictions can choose the mix of services that most reflects the preferences of the local populations (Oates, 1993, 1999). This creates allocative efficiencies and raises overall welfare compared to a centralised allocation of services. The effect is reinforced when voters are mobile and can choose which jurisdiction they wish to live in, with an appropriate combination of taxes and services (Tiebout, 1956). This aspect of decentralisation is known as the problem of expenditure assignment. However, regions or municipalities with greater economic potential can raise more taxes at lower tax rates and provide better quality services than others, creating a pressure for the migration of populations from poorer to richer regions. This effect is quite typical in the Balkans, as in many developing countries, where capital cities have become centres of attraction for both labour and capital, leading to large and growing regional disparities, in an inversion of the optimising Tiebout effect. Thus, decentralisation of responsibilities for expenditure on local public services can create problems of horizontal imbalance, as fiscal decentralisation can bring about inequalities between jurisdictions that have different resource endowments (Prud'homme, 1995). This was arguably the problem that afflicted the federalised former Yugoslavia.

In response to this, redistributive policies must be carried out by the central government through fiscal transfers, and this requires that the central government should control a large proportion of tax revenues. This aspect of the problem is known as the revenue assignment, and can give rise to vertical imbalances between the central and local government if the resources reallocated through government grants are insufficient for local government units to carry out their assigned expenditure responsibilities so that they experience difficulty in supplying the required level of local public services.

This perspective has been criticised under the so-called second-generation theories of decentralisation which argue that political actors are not benevolent and have their own self interesting mind when making decisions relating to the appropriate distribution and uses of public financial resources between different levels of government (Oates, 2005, 2008; Weingast, 2009, 2014). The focus of the second-generation theories is less on the optimal level and extent of revenue and expenditure assignments, but rather on the political interests that lie behind the actual level of assignments achieved. For example, there is no guarantee that the redistributed resources will be used to address income inequalities within jurisdictions, and will not be captured by local elites for their own benefit. Thus, rather than viewing imbalances between local government expenditure assignments and the revenues that are allocated to carry out as an accidental deviation from an optimal plan, the second-generation theories investigate the political interests and incentives that might cause such an imbalance to come about. These issues are closely related to the way in which local governments are elected and whether central governments have the power in practice to override local government decisions.

The second-generation theory is also more sceptical about the use of government grants as redistributive or equalising devices in the face of decentralised jurisdictions with different levels of wealth. Under the first-generation models, direct grants are seen as an efficient solution to the distributional imbalances that might be brought about by decentralisation, capable of being adjusted by elaborate formulas to the specific characteristics and needs of differently composed municipalities. The second-generation models however see the dangers of perverse incentives at work, as municipalities may overstate their needs in pursuit of rent-seeking gambits, or divert the grants to uses that benefit local elites rather than the general welfare (Bardhan, 2002).[2] Hard budget constraints may be difficult to enact in a political economy in which local politicians support the central government and may borrow to excess in an effort to attract local voters to their cause, leading to a build-up of local indebtedness. In addition, patronage networks may be particularly strong at the local level, where personal connections are visible and votes for the local ruling party can translate into privileged access to resources such as public sector jobs (Kleibrink, 2015). Moreover, strong party networks connecting central and local party machines provide channels linking central government subsidies to local governments in which the ruling party has majority control (Gunay & Dzihic, 2016). Considerations such as these give analysts pause for thought when considering the benefits of decentralisation, which may be potentially very real where local preferences are diverse as in situations of ethnic polarisation, especially following periods of conflict like that which have taken place in some of the successor states of former Yugoslavia.

The book discusses the outcomes in the successor states of former Yugoslavia by elaborating on these two approaches. The separate chapters discuss vertical and horizontal imbalances, and the principal agent relationships between central and local governments, highlighting the political connections and divisions between the two levels of government that provide insights into why these relationships are so problematic. The chapters in this book discuss how the different countries in the WB6 have dealt with these dilemmas. These centre-local government relations are especially relevant in the context of clientelistic forms of capitalism that have developed in the Western Balkans and Albania during the transition process, in what can increasingly be called systems of political capitalism, in which business interests and political establishments are closely interconnected. In the context of the economic crisis that spilt over into the region from the global and eurozone economies since about 2009, these interconnections have favoured the recentralisation of political power, the drift towards more authoritarian and illiberal forms of government, and the reversal of decentralisation policies that had gained ground after the democratic turn in the region in 2000.

Europeanisation and the Political Economy of Decentralisation

The armed conflicts of the 1990s had delayed the EU membership perspective (with the exception of Slovenia, which joined the EU in 2004) giving rise to a new characterisation of these countries as the "Western Balkans".[3] This was a region in which democratisation had been stalled or incomplete, turning it into a super-periphery within the European economic space, characterised by political turmoil and instability, pervasive clientelism and an unattractive business environment for local economic development (Bartlett, 2009). However, following the Thessaloniki Declaration of 2003, the process of EU integration and the accompanying request for the creation of new subnational structures to absorb EU assistance funds provided a further motive for reform of centre-local relations. During this period, political and fiscal decentralisation took great strides forward, while EU assistance funds also supported the development of new administrative structures at regional level. Yet, although Slovenia was the first country from the region to become an EU member state, and therefore could have been expected to been most strongly influenced by the support for local government capacity to absorb cohesion funds and regional funds, empirical research has shown that in Slovenia the early impact of cohesion funds on central-local relations was relatively weak with the main role in allocation of EU resources maintained by the central government authorities (Andreas & Bache, 2009), while in Croatia some greater impact in empowering local government institutions in the pre-accession period could be observed (Bache & Tomšić, 2009). It may be that the lack of impact of Europeanisation on strengthening local democracy in the region and the weak capacity of local governments to fully absorb EU assistance funds have been due to the top-down nature of such assistance. Where local governance reforms have been designed with local concerns in mind they seem to have been more effective (Pickering, 2010), Chap. 3 by Anto Bajo and Marko Primorac focuses on the process of decentralisation in Croatia. They show that the decentralisation policy in Croatia was carried out in the absence of a coherent long-term strategy, creating an excessive number of small and weak local government units, which are neither financially self-sufficient nor capable of providing effective public services. The path of fiscal decentralisation has been marked by three main phases. The first phase involved administrative and territorial decentralisation, the second phase was characterised by fiscal decentralisation, while the third phase has involved recentralisation under the influence of the consequences of the economic crisis. As Croatia became closer to EU membership, intergovernmental fiscal relations began to focus on achieving a more balanced economic development through fiscal equalisation. With this in mind, the chapter emphasises the role of instruments and methods of fiscal equalisation. Although the intensity of fiscal decentralisation has gradually increased, the fiscal autonomy of local government units is still limited or non-existent. A more suitable decentralisation policy would prove beneficial not only for fiscal reasons, but also for improving the capacity for absorbing EU funds.

Chapter 2 on Slovenia by Boštjan Brezovnik, Mateja Finžgar, and Žan Jan Oplotnik focuses on vertical imbalances in local government financing. After Slovenia achieved independence, the introduction of democratic local self-government required a radical change from the previous system. The former communes had been designed to carry out the deconcentrated duties of the state administration, but were too large to fulfil the role of self-governing municipalities. Therefore, in 1993, 212 new municipalities were established. These were based on historical developments, traditions, and political compromises rather than a rational assessment of local needs and duties that they should perform. Thus, Slovenia still lacks an efficient network of municipalities. The chapter examines the disproportion between municipal functions and the funds needed to support them. It shows that resources that are allocated to municipalities by the Constitution and the law and are insufficient and not adequately aligned to their responsibilities. Slovenia became an EU member state in 2004, since when it has benefited from EU funding from the regional development funds and the cohesion funds, mitigating some of the problems of vertical fiscal imbalances. The Financing of Municipalities Act, adopted in 2016, provides for fiscal equalisation based on a formula that allocates a per capita lump sum to individual municipalities, taking into account other criteria based on demographic and geographic characteristics of municipalities.

Crisis, Policy Reversals, and Local Government Debt

A stronger role of local governments required greater financial resources at their disposal. Thus, an essential part of the decentralisation process involved strengthening the fiscal autonomy and capacity of local municipalities. Decentralisation was an integral part of the political transition to democracy in the successor states of former Yugoslavia (albeit following an initial period of recentralisation in early 1990s linked to state-building) as it mirrored the process economic transition that aimed to reduce the power of the central state through privatisation (Bartlett et al., 2013). In the early 2000s, fiscal decentralisation took off in the Yugoslav successor states and Albania and led to the redistribution of an increased share of total government revenues and expenditures to the local level in up to the onset of the global economic crisis, as detailed in the chapters in this book. However, following the spillover of the global financial crisis and the ensuing Eurozone crisis to the region from about 2009 onwards, financial instability has pushed many countries into policy reversals involving a return to greater fiscal centralisation (Kmezić, Djulić, Jocović, & Kaludjerović, 2016). Local governments have been under a double-sided squeeze. On the one hand, the impact of the crisis has led to worsening economic and social conditions, and hence created additional pressure on local government expenditures for poverty reduction measures encompassing social protection, housing, community support, and so on. On the other hand, local government revenues have been adversely affected by falling tax revenues, and by the temptation for central governments to pursue their policies of fiscal consolidation and budgetary austerity by "raiding" local government budgets. Such raids have taken the form of transferring additional expenditure assignments to local authorities, while at the same time squeezing central government transfers to local government revenue accounts. This has provoked deep imbalances between the increased local expenditures required by delegated competences on one hand, and the reductions in the revenue base in response to the crisis on the other. These imbalances between functional and financial decentralisation have tended in several cases to undermine local public service delivery, municipal capital investment, and local economic development; in other cases they have led to increased local government debt, potentially threatening the overall financial stability of the countries concerned. Three of the countries, Bosnia and Herzegovina, Montenegro, and Serbia, were particularly hard hit by the economic crisis leading to the growth of debt in local municipalities.[4]

Chapter 4 on Serbia by Sanja Kmezić and Katarina Đulić addresses the political economy of decentralisation in Serbia from 1990 until 2016. It describes the major changes that occurred in territorial, administrative, and political decentralisation, focusing on fiscal decentralisation, and analyses the effects of changes to the regulatory framework on local government revenue and expenditure from 1990 to 2016. Three phases of fiscal decentralisation are identified. The first phase, from 1990 to 2000, was characterised by a highly centralised and authoritarian governance of public services. The second phase, from 2000 to 2008, featured the decentralisation of powers, expenditures, and revenues within a wider process of democratisation and strong economic growth. The third phase, from 2009 to 2016, has seen a recentralisation of public revenues, due to the consequences of the economic crisis that hit the country in late 2008. During this phase, the shares of local government revenues and expenditures in GDP fell, while the system of local government financing suffered from instability, a lack of predictability, and legal and financial uncertainty. More than a dozen significant legislative changes affected local government revenues, leading to huge reductions in local government budgets. A continuous transfer of new mandates to local governments caused their expenditures to increase beyond their revenue capacity. This in turn led to an accumulation of debts and dramatic reductions in local government capital budgets that compromised the delivery of local public services. Additionally, the secrecy surrounding local government fiscal data has undermined the evidence base for policy-making and has led to a lack of transparency and to weak oversight of the financial system.

Chapter 5 on Montenegro by Jadranka Kaludjerović and Mijat Jocović also focuses on the issue of volatile municipal revenues. Until the beginning of the 2000s, the state administration system was extremely centralised, and municipalities were marginalised, even in terms of financing their own policies. In 2003, the government reformed the state administration on the basis of a Public Administration Reform Strategy. Due to the simple organisational structure of public administration and the fact that some complex and financially demanding functions such as education and healthcare are not the responsibility of local government, fiscal decentralisation has been relatively straightforward. Yet, more than a decade after the process of fiscal decentralisation was initiated aiming to increase the efficiency of public finances at the local level, municipalities face high debts and arrears. The chapter identifies two distinct phases of municipal financing. In the first phase (2003–2008), the state adopted legislation that strengthened the role and fiscal autonomy of local governments. Municipalities took advantage of the economic boom experienced in this period to increase their expenditure on the basis of revenue growth, both actual and projected. However, during the second phase (2008–2015), the government imposed several centralising policies, abolishing some sources of municipal revenue in an attempt to reduce the fiscal burden on the business sector. The chapter shows how revenues were hit by a decrease in economic activity and municipalities began to accumulate arrears and debts. Montenegrin municipalities are currently in a very difficult and challenging financial situation, which can only be solved with the involvement of both local and national tiers of government.

Chapter 6 by Halko Basarić, Nina Branković, and Lejla Lazović-Pita deals with the case of Bosnia and Herzegovina, focusing on the issue of increasing local public debt. The chapter analyses intergovernmental fiscal relations, focusing on the position of local governments over the past 20 years. It identifies three main phases in the process of fiscal reforms and shows that expenditure assignments across both main political regions (or "entities"—the Federation of Bosnia and Herzegovina and Republika Srpska) are similar, even though these entities differ in their constitutional organisation. During the three phases of decentralisation reforms, the assignment of expenditures did not change in either entity, while the assignment of revenues changed in different ways. Indirect tax revenues, which make up the largest share of local government revenues in both entities since 2006, declined after the onset of the crisis triggering fiscal stress at the level of local governments. To overcome the volatility of revenues, local governments began to borrow more from 2009 onwards leading to increased local public debts.

Local Governments in Transition and the Political Economy of Ethnicity

According to the first-generation theories of decentralisation, municipalities in which populations have more homogenous preferences should be able to deliver more effective public services. The Oates theorem proposes that in such cases if the provision of services is decentralised, then they will be more accountable to local preferences, and different municipalities can choose the mix of services they prefer. When societies are ethnically riven, this might suggest that ethnic representation in local governments would be an important part of a solution to ethnic conflict. On the other hand, the second-generation theories point to the dangers of allowing political economies to develop in which the self-interest of central and local politicians overrides efficiency considerations. In this perspective, ethnically divided local government systems may reinforce the tendencies towards local patronage networks (Brancati, 2006). Clientelistic relationships between members of ethnic groups and political parties may be empowered to influence the distribution of resources between central and local levels with little regard to efficiency, but rather to reward the ethnic elites within divided societies. This latter seems to have been the case in the examples of ethnic conflict riven societies in the Western Balkans, such as Kosovo (Burema, 2013; Gjoni, Wetterburg, & Dunbar, 2010) and Macedonia (Lyon, 2015; Nikolov & Brosio, 2015). The chapters in this book explore these ideas in greater depth.

Chapter 7 by Marjan Nikolov examines the evolution of decentralisation in Macedonia in the post-independence period. Since its independence in 1991, the country has experienced three distinct periods of decentralisation. In the first period, following independence power was concentrated and centralised to ensure macroeconomic stability and the only competencies municipalities had were in the area of communal services. In the second period, laws were introduced that defined the system of local government finances and the budget process. The third period began in 2005 following the Ohrid Framework Agreement (OFA) that brought a period of internal armed conflict between Macedonians and Albanians to an end, and a new Constitution was adopted. It was marked by significant ethno-political influences on the efficiency of the delivery of local public services. The chapter presents the process of territorial organisation during the three periods of decentralisation reforms and the trends in revenues, expenditures, and horizontal equalisation. It also examines the impact of the economic crisis on local governments, their borrowing dynamics, and the role of EU pre-accession and structural funds. The analysis shows that the EU assistance had little impact at the local level. The chapter reflects on the policies adopted during decentralisation in post-OFA Macedonia and shows that they were not well matched to the level of local development. The analysis shows that ethnic fragmentation has had a negative impact on efficiency of public services in ethnically fragmented municipalities.

Chapter 8 on Kosovo by Adem Beha, Anton Vukpalaj examines the process of decentralisation and the system of local government financing in Kosovo, covering two distinct phases of local government reforms from 2001 to 2008, and from 2008 to 2015. The chapter describes the system of local government system established by the United Nations Mission in Kosovo (UNMIK). Since the creation of new municipalities in 2001, local government was regulated by UNMIK without endorsement of the Assembly of Kosovo. Until 2008, new municipalities depended exclusively on central government funding, although larger municipalities began raising own-source revenues based on municipal assembly regulations. Following the unilateral declaration of independence in 2008, new laws were passed to implement the political, territorial, and fiscal reforms agreed during the UN-mediated final status talks between Kosovo and Serbia. Difficulties were encountered in the creation of new municipalities with Kosovo Serb majorities due to the resistance of Kosovo Albanian political parties and the challenges of economic and fiscal sustainability of these small and predominantly rural municipalities. The chapter identifies the failure of the central government to allocate sufficient funding for new municipal competencies, and weak trends of own-source revenue collection as key challenges of fiscal decentralisation in Kosovo. It questions whether decentralisation can be an instrument for ethnic conflict resolution in an environment in which local authorities are heavily dependent on central government grants.

Albania: Struggling with the Legacy of Extreme Centralisation

Chapter 9 by Elton Stafa and Merita Xhumari on Albania, with a previously highly centralised system of governance, provides a contrast to the chapters on the countries that emerged from former Yugoslavia. The chapter begins with an overview of the process of decentralisation focusing on patterns of change in decentralisation reforms undertaken over three periods (1990–1997, 1998–2008, and 2009–2015) aimed to improve the effectiveness and efficiency of public administration and the quality of public services through various reforms to the administrative and territorial system as well as the financing of local government budgets. In 2015, a new Territorial and Administrative Reform has introduced new local governance reforms. It offers an unprecedented opportunity for stronger local governments, more and better local services, and a more balanced development. Yet, this opportunity may be lost, unless it is accompanied by changes and improvements in the financial instruments available to local governments to deal with the challenges they face and fulfil their increased responsibilities. Ideally, these changes would be reflected in comprehensive fiscal decentralisation reform that would improve local finances and local fiscal autonomy by addressing a number of systemic weaknesses and policy-induced distortions, provide tightened public finance management rules, define a clear strategy for eliminating local payment arrears, and ensure an open and inclusive dialogue between central and local governments. The chapter emphasises the need to strike the right balance between territorial-administrative reforms that have already taken place and the pending reforms in the area of fiscal decentralisation.

Conclusion

Overall, the chapters provide a panoramic view of the process of fiscal decentralisation in the Yugoslav successor states and Albania. They show how each country has been affected by the economic crisis, often leading to fiscal stress and large build-ups of debt. They illustrate the relative weakness of processes of Europeanisation, although the influx of funds to the new EU member states has mitigated some of the worst effects of the economic crisis on local government budgets. Problems in managing interethnic relations illustrate that the hopes of the first-generation theories of fiscal decentralisation that decentralisation would bring government closer to the people, and address the conflictual nature of different preferences related to ethnicity, have been largely unfounded in the region. Instead, the analyses point to the relevance of the second-generation theories of fiscal decentralisation that emphasise the role of political interests at both central and local government levels in influencing the outcomes of fiscal decentralisation. The forces or clientelism, patronage networks, and democratic backsliding have diminished the effectiveness of local governments, and underpinned the ability of increasingly authoritarian central governments to raid local government budgets as a means of shifting the response to the economic crisis to the local level. Local government debt build-up, largely hidden from public view, and popular dissatisfaction with the deteriorating quality of local public services are likely to increase the risks of political instability, which in turn may bring about a revival in the processes of effective and comprehensive fiscal decentralisation in the future.

Notes

1. Swianiewicz (2013) identifies a single Balkan typology of local government arrangements in which the scope of local government functions is relatively restricted compared to Central and Eastern European transition countries that joined the EU in 2004, but which have directly elected mayors. However, our typology provides a more nuanced view of the Balkan model of decentralisation.
2. For example, in an analysis of decentralisation in Serbia, it has been noted that: "municipalities which do pay attention to their current expenditure in order to leave more room for capital investment are not rewarded accordingly for their responsible behaviour, so the system creates, to a certain extent, perverse incentives for local self-governments to collect lower revenues and to tolerate inefficiencies" (Avlijas & Uvalić, 2011, p. 227).

3. Up until 2013 when Croatia became an EU member state this included Albania and all the Yugoslav successor states apart from Slovenia.
4. Fiscal policy was pro-cyclical in response to the crisis in most countries of the region, meaning that some governments, notably Montenegro and Serbia, failed to cut expenditure during the crisis despite nominal adherence to austerity policies, leading to a buildup of debt (Koczan, 2016). Part of this debt was built up at local level. General government public debt increased to high levels especially in Montenegro and Serbia to over 60% of GDP and over 70% of GDP respectively. Bosnia and Herzegovina, which was under an IMF Stand-By Arrangement for most of the post-crisis period, implemented austerity more rigorously and by 2015 the general government public debt was only about 40% of GDP (Bartlett & Prica, 2018).

References

Andreas, G., & Bache, I. (2009). Europeanization and multi-level governance in Slovenia. *Southeast European and Black Sea Studies, 10*(1), 29–43.

Avlijas, S., & Uvalić, M. (2011). Political economy of local level public sector employment: A case study of Serbia. *Southeastern Europe, 35*, 209–228.

Bache, I., & Tomšić, D. (2009). Europeanization and nascent multi-level governance in Croatia. *Southeast European and Black Sea Studies, 10*(1), 71–83.

Bardhan, P. (2002). Decentralization of governance and development. *Journal of Economic Perspectives, 16*(4), 185–205.

Bartlett, W. (2009). Economic development in the European super-periphery: Evidence from the western Balkans. *Economic Annals, LIV*(181), 21–44.

Bartlett, W., Maleković, S., & Monastiriotis, V. (2013). Decentralization paradigms in South East Europe: An introduction. In W. Bartlett, S. Maleković, & V. Monastiriotis (Eds.), *Decentralisation and local development in South East Europe*. Basingstoke: Palgrave.

Bartlett, W., & Prica, I. (2018). Debt in the super-periphery: The case of the western Balkans. *Third World Thematics*. https://doi.org/10.1080/23802014.2017.1438850

Brancati, D. (2006). Decentralization: Fuelling the firs or dampening the flames of ethnic conflict and secessionism? *International Organization, 60*(Summer), 651–685.

Burema, L. (2013). Decentralization in Kosovo: Defusing ethnic tensions or furthering ethnic isolation? In W. Bartlett, S. Maleković, & V. Monastiriotis (Eds.), *Decentralisation and local development in South East Europe* (pp. 100–117). London: Palgrave Macmillan.

Flaherty, D. (1988). Market and unequal regional development in Yugoslavia. *Soviet Studies, 40*(1), 100–124.

Gjoni, R., Wetterburg, A., & Dunbar, D. (2010). Decentralization as a conflict transformational tool: The challenge in Kosovo. *Public Administration and Development, 30*, 291–312.

Gunay, C., & Dzihic, V. (2016). Decoding the authoritarian code: Exercising 'legitimate' power politics through the ruling parties in Turkey, Macedonia and Serbia. *Southeast Europe and Black Sea Studies, 16*(4), 529–549.

Kaiser, R. J. (1990). The equalization dilemma in Yugoslavia. *Geoforum, 21*(2), 261–276.

Kleibrink, A. (2015). *Political elites and decentralization reforms in the post-socialist Balkans*. Houndmills: Palgrave Macmillan.

Kmezić, S., Djulić, K., Jocović, M., & Kaludjerović, J. (2016). *Fiscal decentralisation and local government financing in Serbia and Montenegro*. Maribor: Lex Localis.

Koczan, Z. (2016). Fiscal policy, business cycles and discretion: Evidence from the western Balkans. *Post-Communist Economies, 28*, 468–486.

Lyon, A. (2015). Political decentralization and the strengthening of consensual, participatory local democracy in the Republic of Macedonia. *Democratization, 22*(1), 157–178.

Nikolov, M., & Brosio, G. (2015). Efficient delivery of local public services in ethnically fragmented municipalities. *Lex Localis—Journal of Local Self-Government, 13*(3), 299–319.

Oates, W. E. (1993). Fiscal decentralization and economic development. *National Tax Journal, 46*(2), 237–243.

Oates, W. E. (1999). An essay on fiscal federalism. *Journal of Economic Literature, 37*(3), 1120–1149.

Oates, W. E. (2005). Toward a second-generation theory of fiscal federalism. *International Tax and Public Finance, 12*, 349–373.

Oates, W. E. (2008). On the evolution of fiscal federalism: Theory and institutions. *National Tax Journal, LXI*(2), 313–334.

Pickering, P. M. (2010). Assessing international aid for local governance in the western Balkans. *Democratization, 17*(5), 1024–1049.

Prud'homme, R. (1995). The dangers of decentralisation. *The World Bank Research Observer, 10*(2), 201–220.
Swianiewicz, P. (2013). An empirical typology of local government systems in Eastern Europe. *Local Government Studies, 40*(2), 292–311.
Tiebout, C. M. (1956). A pure theory of local government expenditure. *Journal of Political Economy, 64*, 416–424.
Weingast, B. R. (2009). Second generation fiscal federalism: The implications of fiscal incentives. *Journal of Urban Economics, 65*, 279–293.
Weingast, B. R. (2014). Second generation fiscal federalism: Political aspects of decentralization and economic development. *World Development, 53*, 14–25.

Part I

Europeanisation and the Political Economy of Decentralisation

2

Slovenia: Vertical Imbalance in Local Government Financing

Boštjan Brezovnik, Mateja Finžgar, and Žan Jan Oplotnik

Introduction

With independence and the introduction of parliamentary democracy, a new beginning became possible for local self-government in Slovenia in 1991. The new Constitution set out the fundamental political principles and social values through which the organisation of the state is defined, and within this great importance was attributed to local self-government.[1] In addition, a whole chapter of the Constitution was dedicated to local self-government, a relatively extensive text in comparison to the Constitutions of other countries. The text provides detailed regulations of certain key issues of local self-government that place strict limitations on the local self-government system in Slovenia, thereby establishing the

B. Brezovnik (✉)
Faculty of Law, University of Maribor, Maribor, Slovenia
e-mail: bostjan.brezovnik@lex-localis.info; bostjan.brezovnik@um.si

M. Finžgar • Ž. J. Oplotnik
Faculty of Economics and Business, University of Maribor, Maribor, Slovenia
e-mail: zan.oplotnik@um.si

W. Bartlett et al. (eds.), *Fiscal Decentralisation, Local Government and Policy Reversals in Southeastern Europe*, https://doi.org/10.1007/978-3-319-96092-0_2

foundations on which territorial, political, administrative (functional), and fiscal decentralisation can be built. The citizens of Slovenia exercise local self-government in local communities, which include both municipalities and regions (Šmidovnik, 1995). While the regions have not yet been established by the National Assembly due to a lack of political consensus, 212 municipalities have been established stemming from historical development, tradition, political compromise, geography, and other factors, rather than criteria of rationality in regard to the functions and needs they are supposed to carry out and meet. A municipality is defined as a self-governing local community and the guarantor of local self-government. It acquires such status upon establishment; the state founds it and determines its area by law, based on a preliminary referendum that expresses the will of the citizens residing in the area in question. The Constitution sets the criteria for the establishment of a municipality that form the elements of a local community. The area of a municipality comprises one or several settlements linked by the residents' common needs and interests, while its competences involve only those local affairs that it is able to govern independently and that concern its own residents. The state may transfer specific duties from state competences to a municipality, provided it earmarks the necessary financial resources. With these stipulations, the Constitution draws a clear line between the state and local self-government, yet past practices especially after Slovenia's accession to the European Union (EU) indicate that the distinction between original (local) and transferred (state) functions has become blurred. The state has transferred to the jurisdiction of local communities a number of competences, powers, and functions that are not local affairs by their nature; it has also not earmarked adequate financing for the performance of such functions. Although the Constitution does set certain principles for the financing of municipalities based on the idea of municipal self-financing, it is relatively easy, faced with excessive territorial and administrative decentralisation, to show that Slovenia is in fact a fiscally centralised state.

Fiscal decentralisation, one of the key issues related to the establishment and reform of the local self-government system, developed over three time periods. The first period lasted from the moment the Local Self-Government Act[2] and the Financing of Municipalities Act[3] entered into force in 1994 and the establishment of the first 147 municipalities in 1995, to the second wave of territorial decentralisation and the establishment of a further 45 municipalities in 1998 and the amendments to the Financing of Municipalities Act. In this initial phase, the so-called "guaranteed expenditure" of the financing system was established. During this period, municipal expenditures for financing the performance of urgent functions were covered from state budget funds within the scope of guaranteed expenditure. Such expenditure was determined by the Ministry of Finance and based on criteria set by the competent ministries. The second period of fiscal decentralisation began when legislators amended the Financing of Municipalities Act in 1998 and introduced the so-called "eligible expenditure" system that replaced guaranteed expenditure, which had proven inadequate due to the very high number of municipalities and the excessive transfer of functions to administratively weak municipalities even before Slovenia joined the EU. This phase ended in 2006 when a new Financing of Municipalities Act[4] ushered in the third phase of fiscal decentralisation. In the rest of this chapter, we will elaborate these policy changes along with other relevant issues of financing local self-government in Slovenia.

Territorial Organisation

Following independence, the introduction of local self-government was one of the most important functions of the new state, involving a radical change of the previous system. One of the central issues when introducing the new system of local self-government was the issue of the territorial formation of new municipalities (Grafenauer, 2000). Previously, the communes that carried out the deconcentrated duties of the state administration were too large to perform the role of classical municipalities. Perspectives on the new system of local self-government varied greatly among the political parties in the National Assembly, regarding both the content and pace of establishing the new system. Early in 1994, a referendum for the establishment of municipalities was carried out by the Referendum for the Establishment of Municipalities Act.[5] Two basic models for establishing municipalities were designed: a model of 163 municipalities with at least 5,000 residents and a model of 239 municipalities with at least 3,000 residents. Citizens' assemblies met all over Slovenia and the government prepared a proposal for referendum areas for the establishment of municipalities. After discussing the proposed documentation and numerous objections, the National Assembly determined that the referendum was to be carried out in 340 referendum areas.[6] The results of the referenda of May 1994 were not fully taken into account by the government. Of the total 339 referenda, 111 voted in favour of establishing a new municipality. Only 30 per cent of the eligible voters took part and were mainly from the proposed small municipalities. Given these results, the National Assembly adopted the Establishment of Municipalities and Municipal Boundaries Act[7] in 1994 and founded 147 municipalities, of which 11 were town municipalities. Later, in 1998, a further 45 municipalities were founded: 1 municipality was founded in 2002, 17 were founded in 2006, and 2 additional municipalities were founded in early 2011.

The National Assembly abided throughout by the constitutional provision that the territory of a municipality covers one or several settlements, all the while making arbitrary use of the constitutional and legislative provisions on the capacity to meet common needs and requirements of the residents and the fulfilment of other statutory duties in its area (basic school, primary healthcare, public utility equipment, postal services, library, premises for administrative activity, etc.), and especially the provision on the minimum number of residents that a municipality could have. Particularly, as regards the number of residents, it now holds true that this provision has become a legally provided exception, meaning that a municipality could exceptionally have fewer residents than the normal minimum due to geographical, national, historical, or economic reasons (the original text of the Local Self-Government Act did not stipulate the required minimum number of residents of a municipality; from October 1994 till August 2005, a municipality needed to have at least 5,000 residents, in August 2005, the act was supplemented by the mention that a municipality could not have fewer than 2,000 residents, and in August 2010, the exception that a municipality could have fewer than 5,000 residents was eliminated). The latter fact points to a politically inconsistent stance, as the required number of residents adapted to the political interests of the time.

Thus, 212 municipalities were founded in Slovenia; in 2015, 26 of these municipalities had fewer than 2,000 residents, 84 had between 2,001 and 5,000 residents, 48 had between 5,001 and 10,000 residents, 45 between 10,001 and 30,000, and 9 municipalities had more than 30,001 residents: out of which two—the City of Maribor and the nation's capital Ljubljana—exceeded 100,000 residents. Even though the number of residents per municipality (9,744 on average) places Slovenia well in the middle of the EU mean values, the state should establish municipalities by assuming the position that the territorial and population-related formation of municipalities should by all means be considered in relation to their functions, financing, as well as practical and organisational reality. This position is the only way that would allow municipalities to meet the needs of their residents in a sound, rational, and economical manner and to guarantee high-quality public service. That said, we should note that all Slovenian municipalities regardless of the size of their population have identical competences, from the smallest Municipality of Hodoš with 369 inhabitants to the City of Ljubljana with 287,347 residents in 2015.

The new territorial breakdown of Slovenia into municipalities has witnessed constant change since 1994 and has seen increases in the number of municipalities up to 2011. However, one should highlight the fact that the typical 'units' (renamed administrative units in the new arrangements) in charge of deconcentrated state functions on the local level have remained the same even after the new local self-government system was introduced and 147 municipalities were established (later increasing to 212 municipalities). This phenomenon shows that the state found it much 'easier' to establish or allow the establishment of and the modifications to a territorial area than it was the case for the formation of the units for the performance of governmental functions on the local level (Grafenauer & Brezovnik, 2011).

Organisational and Functional Aspects of Slovenian Municipalities

Upon the establishment of new municipalities, none of their functions, competences, or functional aspects were regulated. Therefore, in late 1994, amendments and supplementations to the Administration Act[8] were adopted, pursuant to which, in early 1995, the state took over all 'administrative duties and competences in the fields for which ministries have been established, as well as all other administrative duties of governmental nature, from the competences of the municipalities as provided for by law'. Starting on 1 January 1995, administrative units were organised that carried out state functions on the local level. In addition to that, a special Act on the Takeover of State Functions Performed until 31 December 1994 by Municipal Bodies[9] was adopted, in which competences were delimited by an exhaustive list of laws and competences enforced and performed until then by the municipalities and taken over by the state in accordance with the new arrangement. From then onwards, the operating area and the competences were set out or defined only in sector-specific legislation. The competencies of a municipality comprise local affairs that may be regulated by the municipality autonomously and that affect only the residents of the municipality. By law, the state may transfer to municipalities the performance of specific duties within the state competence if it also provides the financial resources to enable such (Article 140 of the Constitution of the Republic of Slovenia), but this has not yet happened. The basic criterion to determine the competence of municipalities versus the competence of the state is thus the (excessively limiting) constitutional provision that these are (all) local affairs that may be regulated by the municipality autonomously and that affect only the residents of the municipality. Such affairs are mainly those that are generally focussed on determining or ensuring normal living conditions for the residents. The criterion to determine the original duties of the municipalities is the obligation for a municipality to meet the needs and interests of its residents, which was/is at the same time the condition for establishing the municipality. Thus, a municipality was considered able to fulfil the needs and duties on its territory if the conditions stipulated by the relevant act were guaranteed (basic education, healthcare, municipal utilities, postal services, library, premises for administrative activity, etc.). Therefore, a municipality needed to be capable of ensuring 'material' goods and services for its residents. Nowadays, the original competences of Slovenian municipalities include all functions vital to everyday life and work of the people residing on their territories, which are indeed implemented in a significantly more rational and efficient way than they would have been under the central government. However, one has to note that due to the incessant identification of new 'original' municipal competences, the line dividing the original and transferred competencies is disappearing. One may also refer to this line as the separation of the two administrative systems—state administration and local self-government. Today, original municipal duties are set out in over 170 acts from virtually all areas of social regulation (Brezovnik, 2018; Grafenauer & Brezovnik, 2011).

In theory and in practice alike, one often begs the question whether the municipalities in Slovenia are actually capable of performing all of their original duties. That said, it should be noted that municipalities and other local communities are not formed based on rational criteria that would enable a preliminary assessment of whether they would be capable of performing their duties. It is often found that the size of numerous municipalities in Slovenia has been set in an irrational manner. The diversity among the municipalities and the inappropriate system of municipal financing have led to their inability to perform original duties (Brezovnik & Oplotnik, 2003). One of the options to resolve this issue would be to establish a second level of local self-government (regional), which would perform the duties that the municipalities would mostly be unable to perform. In this vein, we should note that until the end of 2006, the text of the Constitution defined regions as voluntary communities, the creation of which was left to the discretion of the municipalities and depended on the autonomous decision of the municipalities to integrate into regions for the regulation and performance of local affairs of broader importance. However, in the years after the adoption of the Constitution, both expert and political circles increasingly came to realise that the content of the constitutional provisions was a fundamental obstacle to the establishment of regions. When it turned out that the wording in the Constitution presented (too big) a hindrance to the adoption of appropriate legislation and to the establishment of regions comparable at the EU level, the activities aimed at adopting the Promotion of Balanced Regional Development Act[10] came to the forefront. The act was passed in 1999 and proved to be decisive as it enabled the drafting of regional development programmes and projects, thereby improving the options for acquiring resources from European funds within the framework of Slovenia's accession to the EU. The act established a special type of regionalisation, and its bases for the promotion of balanced regional development were statistical regions (12 regions) that served as functional territorial units for the implementation of regional structural policies and for the identification of territories affected by particular handicaps in development. Only as late as June 2006 did efforts to amend constitutional provisions on local self-government finally come to fruition, as the National Assembly adopted constitutional amendments that were supposed to boost decentralisation processes and provide better opportunities of balanced regional development throughout Slovenia, as well as affect the establishment of regions in particular. After discussion in the National Assembly, it called for a referendum on regional division according to the 12 + 1 model (12 regions + the status of the City of Ljubljana as a region). Voter turnout at the referendum held on 22 June 2008 was only 10.98 per cent, and the proposed breakdown into regions did not win support. Also, none of the proposed acts were adopted in the parliament, so that the efforts to establish regions proved to be unsuccessful during that term of the National Assembly; to this day, Slovenia remains unable to establish a second level of local self-government (Grafenauer & Brezovnik, 2011).

Based on the above-mentioned development, the logical consequence would be to merge municipalities. However, this development is an unrealistic expectation considering the difficulty of reaching compromises in Slovenian politics. Strong arguments in favour of mid-sized municipalities are also found in specialised literature where it is emphasised that one of the weaknesses of municipalities that are too small is insufficient expertise of leadership, which is very typical of Slovenian municipalities. In order for municipalities to effectively perform their duties, an effective administrative system employing an adequate number of public servants possessing the required skills, knowledge, and competences is key, while the most important element is an appropriate municipal finance system.

The Municipal Finance System

Pursuant to Article 142 of the Constitution of the Republic of Slovenia, a municipality is financed from its own sources. Thus, one of the fundamental constitutional criteria of local self-government is to ensure own sources for financing original municipal competences, that is, those that the municipality determines in its acts directly on the basis of its constitutional position and legal authorisation and those determined by the state. This ensures, in particular, the execution of public interests (governance) at the lower level in accordance with the constitutional principle of local self-government. Therefore, the degree of autonomy of local self-government, and thereby also its self-governance, depends on sufficient financial sources. Within the framework of its legislative function, the state adopts rules that regulate local self-government, as well as rules that regulate the financing of local communities. While Article 147 of the Constitution of the Republic of Slovenia stipulates that local communities impose taxes and other charges under conditions provided by the Constitution and law, the state never forewent its fiscal sovereignty in the past. Municipalities are limited in imposing taxes and other charges by the legislative framework, so that their rights related to the material basis for implementing local self-government are always derived from adopted acts or directly from the Constitution. Legislators should determine the material basis in accordance with the aforementioned Article 142 of the Constitution of the Republic of Slovenia, while the scope of the material basis should correspond to the duties that the municipality was performing within its operating area; the relationship between the revenue of a municipality and the constitutional and statutory duties it is supposed to perform should be appropriate. In its decision,[11] the Constitutional Court of the Republic of Slovenia emphasised this fact, stating that the municipal finance system must guarantee that the scope of funds made available to municipalities corresponds to what legislators have defined as sufficient to allow a municipality to ensure the performance of its constitutional and legal duties, which, however, is not guaranteed in practice (Grafenauer & Brezovnik, 2011).

The model used for the financing of municipalities comprises eligible expenditure, own-source revenues, and financial equalisation (Oplotnik & Brezovnik, 2006–2016). Costs that are taken into consideration when determining a municipality's eligible expenditure are those incurred by the duties it is required to perform based on relevant acts, referring to the following:

1. The provision of public services and implementation of public programmes in:

   - Pre-school education
   - Primary education and sports
   - Primary healthcare and health insurance
   - Social security
   - Culture

2. The provision of local public utility services
3. The regulation of municipal transport infrastructure and provision of traffic safety on municipal roads
4. Fire safety and protection against natural and other disasters
5. Spatial planning of municipal importance, environmental protection, and nature preservation
6. Payment of rent and housing expenses
7. Operations of municipal bodies and performance of administrative, professional, promotional, and development functions, as well as functions related to the provision of public services
8. Performance of other functions as outlined by the law

The average cost for financing the nominated functions is determined by the current expenses and transfers for these functions. It is distributed as a lump sum calculated using a methodology specified by the government following preliminary coordination with municipalities and their associations.[12] The lump sum is calculated by the Ministry of Finance based on the data submitted for the previous four years, taking into account the inflation rate. It is determined by the National Assembly as part of the national budget.[13] The formula for calculating eligible expenditure of each municipality takes into account its surface area (6 per cent), the length of municipal roads (13 per cent), the number of residents under the age of 15 (16 per cent), and the number of residents over the age of 65 (4 per cent), reflecting the specificities of each individual municipality. Altogether, these categories cover 39 per cent of municipal eligible expenditure. The remaining 61 per cent of eligible expenditure depends on the lump sum and the number of residents.[14]

Municipal revenues from income tax are calculated by the Ministry of Finance for each fiscal year using the formula:

$$R = A \times B \times (0.3 + 0.7 \times C).$$

where:

R is eligible municipal revenues;

A is the number of residents in a municipality;

B is the average eligible expenditure per capita in the country as a whole calculated using the formula: $B = T/P$, where T is the total eligible expenditure of municipalities for an individual fiscal year; P is the population in the country;

C is the diversity index calculated using the formula: $C = E/A \times B$, where E is the eligible expenditure of a municipality for each fiscal year.

If the calculated eligible revenue exceeds the calculated eligible expenditure of a municipality by more than 15 per cent, the surplus exceeding 15 per cent is decreased by 50 per cent.[15]

Municipalities are entitled to an overall share of 54 per cent of the income tax that was collected two years previously increased by the rate of inflation, based on the total assessed income tax of permanent residents in the municipality. Of this amount, 70 per cent is distributed to the municipality directly and 30 per cent is used for solidarity equalisation of municipal revenues from the income tax.

This solidarity fund is distributed to municipalities with revenues below their eligible revenues in order to bring the revenues from 70 per cent of the income tax up to the eligible revenues (R). The difference between income tax revenues and total municipal revenues from the income tax is used to provide an additional solidarity offset for municipalities where necessary. Financial equalisation funds from the state budget are distributed to municipalities that are unable to finance their eligible expenditure from their own revenues and revenues distributed through the equalisation mechanism.

Financial Sources of Local Authorities

Municipalities can be financed from their own resources to ensure the delivery of local public services. These financial resources determine the level of local self-government autonomy. The municipal finance system must provide municipalities with sufficient funds to perform their constitutional and legal functions. The government provides additional funds to municipalities that are unable to perform their functions due to their underdevelopment. This constitutional provision was one of the fundamental reasons for irrational territorial breakdowns witnessed in the past. Under the first Financing of Municipalities Act in 1994, all municipalities were provided with 'guaranteed expenditure', which later became 'eligible expenditure' in 1999. A new Financing of Municipalities Act was adopted in 2006. Due to the diversity of municipalities and the fact that all municipalities, regardless of their size, hold the same powers, it is impossible to devise a transparent and economically fair municipal finance model (Grafenauer & Brezovnik, 2011). Furthermore, the scope of municipal powers and functions has at least doubled since 1999. While municipal revenues increased from 4.6 per cent of the GDP in 2003 to 5.7 per cent of the GDP in 2015, municipal expenses (expenditure) increased from 4.8 per cent in 2003 to 5.8 per cent of the GDP in 2015 (see Table 2.1). Municipalities received €1,209 million in 2003, which increased to €2,226 million in 2015. However, these revenues were still not sufficient to cover the assigned functions.

The Local Self-government Act stipulates that local affairs of public significance are to be financed from own resources, government funds, and debt. Own municipal resources are (1) taxes and other duties and (2) revenues from property. The government provides additional funds to

Table 2.1 Population of municipalities in 2015

	Municipalities	Population	Municipalities (%)	Population (%)
<2,000	26	32,342	12.27	1.57
2,001–5,000	84	280,546	39.63	13.60
5,001–10,000	48	327,354	22.64	15.87
10,001–30,000	45	731,681	21.22	35.46
>30,001	9	691,154	4.24	33.50
Sum	212	2,063,077	100	100

Source: Republic of Slovenia, Statistical Office

municipalities that are unable to finance local affairs of public significance from their own resources.

Overall, municipal tax revenues remained relatively stable until 2005, barely increasing from 4.8 per cent of the GDP in 2003 to 5 per cent of the GDP in 2005 (see Fig. 2.1). After the introduction of the new Financing of Municipalities Act in 2006, municipal revenues began to increase, reaching 6.1 per cent in 2010. Thereafter, with the onset of the economic crisis, the share of municipal revenues in the GDP stagnated, and even fell slightly to 5.8 per cent of the GDP in 2015. The balance of municipal finances had a surplus in 2003, but after 2006, there was a huge deficit that reached −0.46 per cent of the GDP in 2008, and only recovered a sustained surplus in 2015. This was no doubt partly to the impact of the economic and financial crisis, which hit the country in 2008, along with the rest of Europe.

The largest part of municipal revenues comes from shared income taxes, which increased from 51.8 per cent of total revenues in 2007 to 52.5 per cent in 2010, before falling back to 46.1 per cent in 2015 (see Fig. 2.2). The next most important source of revenues is the category of fiscal transfers from the central government, which increased from 9.9

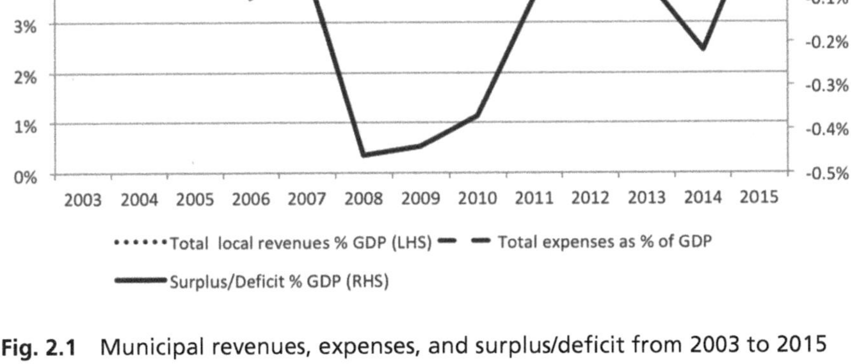

Fig. 2.1 Municipal revenues, expenses, and surplus/deficit from 2003 to 2015

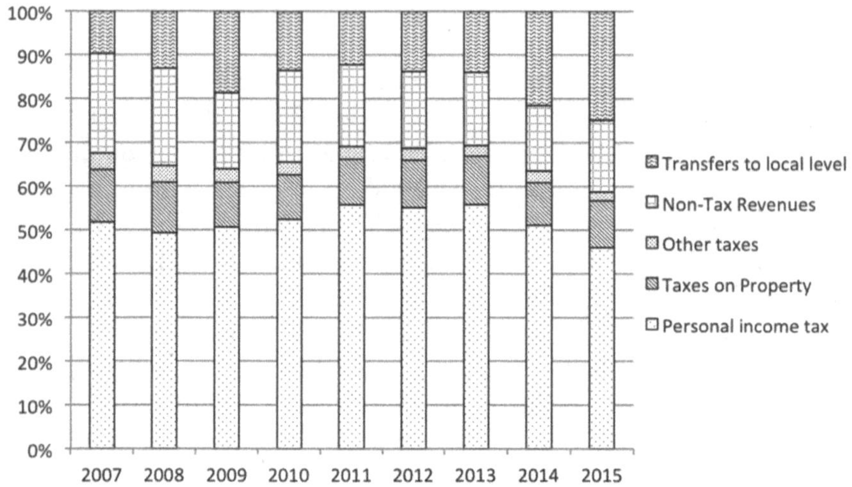

Fig. 2.2 Municipal budget revenues by financial source as per cent of the GDP from 2007 to 2015

per cent of total revenues in 2007 to 13.4 per cent in 2010 and then further to 24.8 per cent by 2015. This indicates the inability of the municipal finance system to effectively provide sustainable self-financing of local governments, as will be elaborated on further below. The third most important source of financing municipal revenues comes in the form of non-tax revenues, which fell from 22.6 per cent of total revenues in 2007 to 21.0 per cent in 2010, and further to 16.5 per cent in 2015. Revenues from property taxes remained fairly stable.

Tax Revenues

Municipalities are entitled to the following tax revenues:

1. Property tax
2. Inheritance tax and gifts
3. Tax on prizes from games of chance
4. Tax on real property transactions
5. Other taxes as specified by the law

Municipal revenues from the income tax increased from €516 million in 2003 to €885 million in 2007. In this period, municipalities were entitled to a 35 per cent share of income tax revenues. In 2006, the new Financing of Municipalities Act stipulated that the income tax share should increase to 54 per cent. Consequently, revenues from the income tax increased to €885 million in 2007 and to more than one billion euros in 2015 (Ministry of Finance, 2011, 2018). The property tax represents the largest tax source for municipalities. Municipalities reported revenues from the property tax in the amount of €142 thousand in 2003 (Bradaschia, 2012) and up to €235 thousand in 2015 (Ministry of Finance, 2018). Domestic taxes on goods and services decreased from €88 million in 2003 (Bradaschia, 2012) to €47 million in 2015 (Ministry of Finance, 2018). Non-tax municipal revenues consist of revenues from profits and property management, fees and charges, fines and forfeits, receipts from the sale of goods and services, and other non-tax revenues (Bradaschia, 2012). Revenues from municipal assets consist of revenues from leases and rents for land and structures owned by the municipality, revenues from capital investments, revenues from securities and other rights purchased by the municipality, and revenues from annuities, profits made by public enterprises, and from awarding concessions.[16]

Other non-tax revenues include fees and charges, fines and forfeits, revenues from the sale of goods and services, and other non-tax revenues. These revenues fell from €95 thousand in 2003 (Bradaschia, 2012) and reached more than €80 thousand in 2015 (Ministry of Finance, 2018).

Transfer Revenues

An optimal municipal financing model would be one in which equalisation payments made to all municipalities equal zero, meaning that municipalities become entirely independent of the state. In such a case, municipalities would be entirely self-financed and autonomous. In order to achieve this, the eligible expenditure of an individual municipality should equal the value of own revenues. However, eligible expenditure that exceeds own revenues requires financial equalisation, and some autonomy of the local community would be lost due to the direct transfer from the state budget (Brezovnik & Oplotnik, 2006).

Financial equalisation funds are allocated to a municipality that is unable to finance its eligible expenditure. Such a municipality is allocated financial equalisation funds from the state budget, equal to the difference between the calculated eligible expenditure and its revenues. In 2003, municipalities received €305 million in transfers, donations, and other non-tax grants from other levels of government, and prior to the reform of the municipal finance system in 2006, they received more than €430 million. After the reform in 2006, the amount of transferred resources fell to €176 million in 2007 and €251 million in 2008, but returned to the previous levels in 2009 (€386 million). However, the amount fell again in 2010 (€294 million) and 2011 (€252 million) and increased to €547 million in 2015 (Ministry of Finance, 2018). These data show that Slovenia never achieved the optimal municipal financing model. However, the reform decreased the volume of financial equalisation funds allocated from the state budget, raising the level of financial autonomy of the Slovenian municipalities (Bradaschia, 2012).

Borrowing

Another source of municipal funds comes from borrowing. Under Article 85 of the Public Finance Act, a municipality can borrow funds with the prior consent of the Ministry of Finance under the terms and conditions outlined by the Financing of Municipalities Act. Any debt transactions not approved by the ministry are considered void. A municipality can borrow funds if it is unable to balance its budget due to an uneven flow of receipts. In this case, the Public Finance Act stipulates that a municipality can borrow funds up to the maximum amount of 5 per cent of the last adopted budget; it is required to report loans and the repayment of debt principal to the Ministry of Finance. A municipality can only ask for loans that do not exceed the amount required to repay the principal of the municipal debt.[17]

Furthermore, a municipality can only take loans for investments planned in the municipal budget. A municipality that is included in the system of a single treasury account of the state can only borrow money from the state budget. In relation to the funds received from the EU budget for co-financing an investment, a municipality can borrow up to the amount of the funds granted for the period of receiving these funds. If, however, the implementation of the budget cannot be balanced due to an uneven flow of receipts, a municipality can borrow up to a maximum of 5 per cent of the level of expenditure of the last adopted budget. This restriction does not apply to municipal borrowing for the purposes of co-financing investments from the EU budget. A municipality can only borrow funds if the repayment of the loans does not exceed 8 per cent of the revenues for the year preceding the year in which the loan was granted, less any donations, transfers from the state budget for investment, and any funds received from the EU budget as well as any revenues of public utilities.[18]

Indirect users of the municipal budget, public agencies, and public enterprises that have been founded by a municipality, as well as other legal entities over which a municipality has direct or indirect control, can borrow funds and issue guarantees with the consent of the municipality, provided that these entities have secured funds for servicing the debt from non-budget sources. The consents issued are not included in the maximum volume of municipal borrowing. The volume of municipal borrowing has increased from €344 million in 2007, reaching €865 million in 2015, including the debt of legal entities at the local level, which means that the average debt per capita in 2015 amounted to €419. Municipal borrowing grew from 0.98 per cent of the GDP in 2007 and reached 2.2 per cent of the GDP in 2015 (Ministry of Finance, 2016). The reason for the extensive borrowing of municipalities in the period from 2007 to 2015 is the implementation of substantial investments, which, despite co-financing from the cohesion and other funds and the state budget, also required the participation of municipal funds. In this period, municipalities borrowed the largest extent in 2009 (€199 million) and 2010 (€134 million). This borrowing was a definite consequence of the financial crisis. Borrowing decreased in the following years and then rose in the 2014 election year, when municipalities borrowed €133 million. A drop of €74.8 million followed in 2015. With each new borrowing, new liabilities arise to repay debt for municipal budgets in the coming years. The volume of repayment of municipal debt in 2015 amounted to €80.8 million (Fig. 2.3).

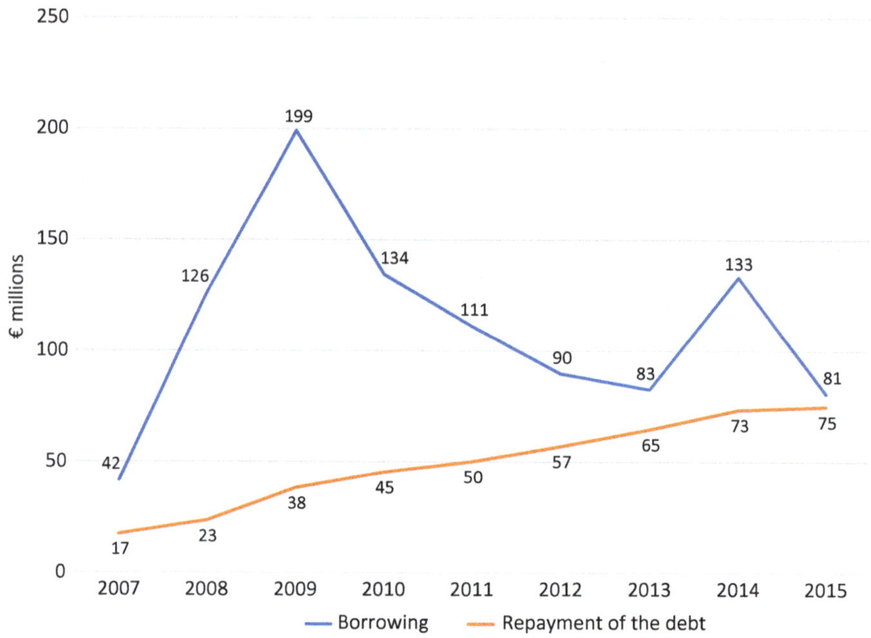

Fig. 2.3 Borrowing and repayment of municipal debt from 2007 to 2015

Analysis of the Effects of the Municipal Finance System

To what extent does the municipal finance system satisfy the principle of the proportionality of resources to functions? To what extent do financial means acquired through the eligible expenditure formula match the costs incurred by municipalities in the performance of their functions? Analysis of data for the period between 2003 and 2015 reveals that only about one tenth of the municipalities managed to cover their eligible expenditure from their own revenues before 2007. Since the changes in the law in 2007, the situation has improved, as only about half of all municipalities received funds from the financial equalisation mechanism, and these funds never exceeded 1 per cent of the total eligible expenditure. The other municipalities had surpluses of €83 million, which they were able to spend on development and investment. The underlying principles of local self-government were thus fulfilled during this period, with a high overall correlation between municipalities' own revenues and expenditures (Brezovnik, Finžgar, & Oplotnik, 2014).

Correlation was weaker at the level of individual municipalities. In 2007, expenditures of 30 municipalities were 10–50 per cent higher than 'permitted' by the eligible expenditure formula, and in 2008, their number increased to 47. In the same years, expenditures of 87 and 44 municipalities were 20–100 per cent lower than provided by the eligible expenditure formula. This development indicates a lack of municipal self-sufficiency. In 2009, there was a sudden change, as only 19 municipalities reported revenues greater than eligible expenditure, amounting to €12 million, while 191 municipalities required financial equalisation payments of €55 million. The proportion of self-sufficient municipalities fell to the level that was recorded prior to 2007, although the volume of equalisation payments did not achieve the previous levels. On the other hand, the increase in the volume of eligible expenditure was implicitly, via the calculated lump sum, also affected by the actual costs reported by municipalities, which increased by 21 per cent in the 2007–2011 period (Brezovnik et al., 2014). After 2011, the share of self-sufficient municipalities was stable, however, with a downward trend as it decreased every observed year. Then in 2015, the number of self-sufficient municipalities practically plummeted to just four municipalities (Ljubljana, Ankaran, Log-Dragomer, and Trzin). This trend also applies to the appropriate scope of funding, eligible expenditure, and revenue of municipalities in accordance with the Financing of Municipalities Act decreased by almost 8 per cent in the period ending in 2015, whereas municipal expenditures increased by 3 per cent, with the biggest increase being observed in the years 2010, 2011, and 2012 (no less than +3.6 per cent per annum). A minimal decrease of costs followed in 2013 and 2014 and stopped in 2015. In relation to the above, one should draw attention to the Fiscal Balance Act adopted in 2012, the purpose of which was to ensure the sustainability of public finance and to keep financial expenditure under control in the post-crisis period, due to which temporary measures were introduced that also impacted the operation of municipalities. The effects of the said act on municipalities in terms of decreasing current costs were much smaller than forecast, while certain solutions caused either time gaps of the expenses incurred or retrospective repayments. In aggregate terms, the current costs of municipalities increased in spite of the adoption of the aforementioned act. Additional financial compensation from the state budget was needed in

2011, 2012, and 2015, while there was no compensation in 2010, 2013, and 2014, when available income tax was sufficient to cover solidary financing. Eligible expenditures increasingly lagged behind reported current costs, already by 18 percentage points in 2016. In addition to that, in 2010, the Ministry of Finance issued rules on outlining the sub-programmes considered in identifying lump sums, which have been applied to budgets ever since. According to these rules, certain sub-programmes on which current costs and current transfers were incurred were excluded from the data used to calculate the lump sums for municipalities. This difference might have been small at first glance, but it constituted an automatic and 'silently introduced' decrease of the lump sum base by almost 1 per cent. During this period, the combined revenue of municipalities decreased on average by 0.7 per cent annually. A year-to-year comparison shows a steep decline of combined revenue of municipalities by almost 15 per cent in 2016 compared to 2015. The result would have been even worse had there not been an increase in income in 2014 and 2015, which most likely came from increased municipal investments, mainly from using EU funding for co-financing investments (end of the programming period 2007–2013 according to the n+2 rule). Data also highlight the impact of the economic crisis, as well as the constant deterioration of the ratios between costs and income or between financial sources and municipal duties, which constitutes an increased departure from and derogation of the proportionality principle (Brezovnik, Oplotnik, Padovnik, Finžgar, & Mlinarič, 2018).

These anomalies provide a reason to re-examine the system. It would be easier if the state covered all the costs of an individual municipality directly, thus ensuring a complete correlation between resources and costs. However, this would lead to a violation of the principles of autonomy and self-sufficiency. There would be a risk that costs would cease to reflect needs, but would instead grow in line with the ability of individual municipalities seeking to obtain the maximum possible revenues to 'adjust' their spending. Furthermore, such a method would poorly reflect differences between municipalities due to their diversity. Analyses have shown that Slovenian municipalities have very different needs with respect to the same functions and powers. This variety is shown through the breakdown of municipalities by their demographic and geographic characteristics, which also provides the basis for the calculation of eligible expenditure and is directly related to their costs.

Eligible Expenditure and Costs

Average eligible expenditure and reported costs were analysed in the search for answers to the questions raised above. This analysis revealed that municipalities spent €1.23 billion on average for the performance of statutory functions between 2007 and 2015, less in 2007 (€0.99 billion) and, interestingly, more in 2011 (€1.28 billion), 2012 (€1.34 billion), and 2013 (€1.32 billion), which occurred during the crisis. In the 2010–2016 period, Slovenian municipalities spent €1.31 billion on average for the performance of their functions. Per resident, the average yearly amount in this period was €639, and €689 in the case of urban municipalities (average burden increased by 7.8 per cent). That said, the average annual burden of municipalities with fewer than 5,000 residents (€654) was 2.2 per cent higher than the national average. Here, we must draw attention to an important anomaly in the municipal financing system, as urban municipalities are particularly underfinanced compared to other Slovenian municipalities. The gap between maximum and minimum costs per resident was wide, and the ratio between the lowest (Cerklje na Gorenjskem) and highest (Kostel) average annual current costs per resident was no less than 1:3.7. The majority of municipalities (188 municipalities or 89 per cent of the total) were placed in the interval of 25 per cent from the average, and just 17 per cent in the interval of 5 per cent from the average, which points to a great dispersion of municipalities. Municipalities covering large territories reported the highest average costs in this period (€743, 16 per cent above the average). Above average were also municipalities with above average road lengths (+7.1 per cent) and number of elderly residents (+7.7 per cent), while municipalities with younger residents statistically incurred lower than average costs (−6.7 per cent) (Brezovnik et al., 2018). Municipal costs increased by 3 per cent on average in the examined period, while eligible expenditure decreased by 4 per cent on average, which means than on a yearly basis, sources (according to the eligible expenditure mechanism) lagged 7 percentage points on average behind the reported current costs of Slovenian municipalities in the 2010–2016 period. During this time period, approximately 63 per cent of municipalities experienced increases in costs, and no less than 44 per cent saw their costs increase to over 25 per cent above the average. A similar percentage of municipalities (41 per cent) saw their eligible expenditure decrease by over 25 per cent in relation to the average. The average current costs increased the most for municipalities with a larger share of young people under 15 years of age (+3.2 per cent), current costs did not decrease in any of the examined groups, while the smallest increase was detected in municipalities that had a larger share of roads and elderly residents (+1.1 per cent). Eligible expenditure decreased most in municipalities with fewer than 5,000 residents.

Between 2010 and 2016, municipalities covered current costs by spending on average €1.315 billion, that is €639.43 per resident (arithmetic mean). Current costs account for 60 per cent of the overall budgetary expenditure structure. Annually, municipalities spent on average €811.5 million or 37 per cent of all expenditure on investment, which is €466.5 per resident. To repay debts, the average annual expense was €65.9 million or €36.8 per resident, a 3 per cent share in the expenditure structure. Loans and increase in capital share amounted to €6.9 million per annum on average, which accounts for 0.3 per cent or €2.4 per resident in the overall expenditure structure. Overall expenditures thus amounted to €2.2 million or €1,145 per resident. The increase in current costs in 2016 compared to 2010 is 3 per cent, while the overall expenditures decreased by 18 per cent, mainly due to the decrease in investment expenditures. According to programme classification, the observed budgetary expenditure categories revealed that by far the largest share of resources was allocated to education, namely 23.2 per cent, followed by 15 per cent of all expenditure earmarked for transport and transport infrastructure and communications, 11.4 per cent was intended for culture, 11 per cent for spatial planning and public utility activity, and so on (Brezovnik et al., 2018).

A significant portion of the costs comprises investment expenditures and investment transfers for the implementation of development functions. As will be demonstrated below, municipalities finance their investments predominantly by other financial sources, not state resources or resources acquired within the eligible expenditure mechanism, even though eligible expenditure should in accordance with its fundamental legal definition ensure an appropriate volume of resources to finance duties established by law, its calculation taking into account only current costs and current transfers. This fact, on the other hand, has a negative impact on the present-day and future financial sources of municipalities.

EU Funds and Capital Investments

Investments represent a direct form of performing municipal development functions. They involve the use of financial sources for the preservation and increase of municipal property in the form of public utilities (e.g. roads, pavements, public lighting, public water supply, sewerage, waste water treatment) or social infrastructure (e.g. schools, pre-schools, primary healthcare centres, cultural venues, libraries), land (e.g. industrial zones, residential buildings), equipment and gear (e.g. fire brigade vehicles and other equipment for protection and rescue), other tangible and non-tangible assets, as well as education, training, and improvement of the quality of living. The development functions of municipalities are set out in legislation, and the performance of such requires financial investments. The shortcomings of the existing investment system lie mainly in the fact that municipal investments are considered by the state as parallel, often less important activities of the municipalities, as if they serve their own purpose or as if they are a 'monument' to the municipal authorities erected during their term. Such an opinion may only be held by those who do not realise that, even today, many citizens of Slovenia do not have access to basic public utilities that would ensure quality living. Collecting rainwater or being dependent on wells that are drying up, or gazing worriedly into the skies to see whether torrential rainfall might render a gravel road so unusable as to hinder one's way to work/school/doctor's is a too often a cruel reality. It leads to personal anxiety and disappointment of the residents who are convinced, and justifiably so, that they are entitled as citizens, taxpayers, and human beings to basic conditions for normal living and development, regardless of their place of residence. Slovenian municipalities have largely managed to mitigate the consequences of the social and economic crisis precisely due to their investments. It was through municipal investment that many jobs were preserved and that many enterprises managed to survive. Local investment have also often enabled small local providers to acquire the knowledge and experience required to carry out projects in other environments and at other levels. Local-level investments ensure that the needs and interests of local communities are met and require proportionate financial resources, in compliance with the legislation and basic principles of the European Charter of Local Self-Government.

The analysis of municipal investments after Slovenia's accession to the EU, and particularly from 2010 till 2016, suggests that municipalities are extremely heterogeneous in terms of the average annual investment value per resident. The ratio between the municipality with the lowest investment value per resident (the City of Maribor with €175) and the municipality with the highest value (the municipality of Grad with €2,910) is 1:16.6, which reveals a highly varied investment capacity of municipalities, as well as very diverse development priorities of the different environments. In the specified period, all Slovenian municipalities combined had an average annual investment of €811.5 million, which equals €466.5 per resident (versus the current costs of €639 per resident, as mentioned above). Only 121 municipalities, that is, 57 per cent of all municipalities, fall within the range of 25 per cent from the average value of €466.5. Urban municipalities have average annual investments of €368 per resident, which translates to 21 per cent below the national average, and their share of investment from total expenditures, which amounts to 32.9 per cent, is below the national average. Municipalities with fewer than 5,000 inhabitants invest on average €517 per year, which is 10.8 per cent above the national average, while investments account for 41.3 per cent of their expenditure, that is, 1.6 percentage points above the national average.

During this period, Slovenian municipalities concentrated most of their investment on the field of environmental protection (22 per cent), mostly for wastewater treatment (a total of €966 million in the 2010–2016 period invested into sewerage networks and waste water treatment plants) as this sub-programme accounts for 77 per cent of investment resources in the programme classification area. This field is followed by transport

(20.4 per cent) and spatial planning with housing public utility activity (20 per cent); the supply of drinking water sub-programme, which accounts for 52 per cent of the programme classification area, had €593 million in investments in the said period. Education is next with 14 per cent, while investments in the field of culture and sports account for an 11.9 per cent share of municipal investments. These numbers also show the municipalities' need to build basic public utility structures (sewerage and treatment plants, aqueducts, and roads) and social infrastructure (especially schools and pre-schools).

Furthermore, 19 per cent of nationwide municipal investment occurred in municipalities with fewer than 5,000 inhabitants. Municipalities earmarked 23.5 per cent of total investment resources for investment into roads, which is 3 percentage points higher than the average in this field, 22.3 per cent for spatial planning with housing public utility activity, 18.5 per cent for environmental protection, which is 3.6 percentage points below the average of all municipalities, 14.3 per cent for education (investment into the structures and equipment of schools and pre-schools), and 8.5 per cent for culture and sports. An important difference lies in the comparison with urban municipalities. Urban municipal investment accounts for 29 per cent of all municipal investments, that is, an average of €239 per annum. In the examined period, urban municipalities allocated on average the biggest portion of their investment resources to the environment and natural heritage protection programmes (21 per cent, which is a good percentage point below the average share of all investments made by municipalities), followed by culture, sports, and non-governmental organisations (20 per cent, which is 8.4 percentage points above the average of all municipalities). The next categories are spatial planning and housing public utility activity with 18.25 per cent (slightly below the average of all municipalities), transport, transport infrastructure, and communications with 16.9 per cent (3.5 percentage points below the average share of all municipalities), and education with 13 per cent of investment resources. Urban municipalities are also above average in general administrative services and general public services with 3.3 per cent, whereas municipalities with fewer than 5,000 residents had a lower share than both urban municipalities and the average of all municipalities at 1.65 per cent. A wide gap between both types of municipalities was also present in the field of economy, for which municipalities with fewer than 5,000 residents earmarked just 3.4 per cent of all investments, while urban municipalities earmarked just 0.8 per cent. This comparison also highlights the different priorities for development and the gap in development. It could be reasonably assumed that the basic public utility infrastructure of urban municipalities was in better condition; therefore, they could allocate their investment resources to other areas (such as culture). Smaller municipalities devoted their resources mainly to investments for basic public utility areas, where there is the greatest need. This difference does not mean though that smaller municipalities do not need, for instance, new cultural centres, libraries, or sports grounds, but rather that their priorities were instead areas where there was greater need (roads, water supply, etc.).

After Slovenia's accession to the EU, municipalities financed their investments mostly through their own sources (58 per cent), that is, what remains from their own revenue both from income taxes and other own sources. Urban municipalities used a greater share (69 per cent) of own sources than the average, while this share is lower in the case of municipalities with fewer than 5,000 inhabitants, namely 54 per cent, which is 4 percentage points below the average. In terms of the share in the structure of sources, the use of EU funds accounted for 25 per cent. This information clearly points to the great importance of these funds for Slovenian municipalities in the past programming period. Slovenian municipalities used the greatest amount of these funds in 2014 (€349 million) and 2015 (€355 million). It was precisely in 2015 that the programming period 2007–2013 ended (realisation according to the n+2 rule), many investments were completed, and final payments were realised. The realisation of these investments and municipalities' successful disbursal of resources from various EU funds contributed to the improvement of the macroeconomic situation in Slovenia in 2014 and 2015. Even during the deepest crisis, municipal investments played an important role in the stabilisation of the economic conditions. Therefore, it makes sense to examine the discriminatory new financial perspective on investments that impacts municipalities, which was evident already from the amount of EU funds used in 2016 when Slovenian municipalities used less than €49 million from this source. We can only hope that the wrong (albeit rhetorically pleasing in terms of goals) orientation of Slovenian decision makers who consider municipal investments as public utility infrastructure to be unnecessary and counterproductive will not last long and that the appropriate amendments to the programmes will be made. EU funds were used predominantly in municipalities with fewer than 5,000 residents; a comparison shows that EU resources account for a 17 per cent share among urban municipalities, while they account for no less than 27 per cent among municipalities with fewer than 5,000 residents. On average, municipalities used this source of financing in a similar manner, namely by deviating +/−2 percentage points from the average. Net public borrowing accounts for a 4 per cent share in the financing of investments, a larger share (7 per cent) in the case of urban municipalities, whereas municipalities with fewer than 5,000 residents had an average share. Lastly, the investment resources of the state contribute 13 per cent to the financing source structure for municipal investments. This source is obviously more useful in the case of small municipalities than in the case of urban municipalities. One should once more emphasise the considerable non-homogeneity of Slovenian municipalities that also manifests itself in this area of examination (Brezovnik et al., 2018) (Fig. 2.4).

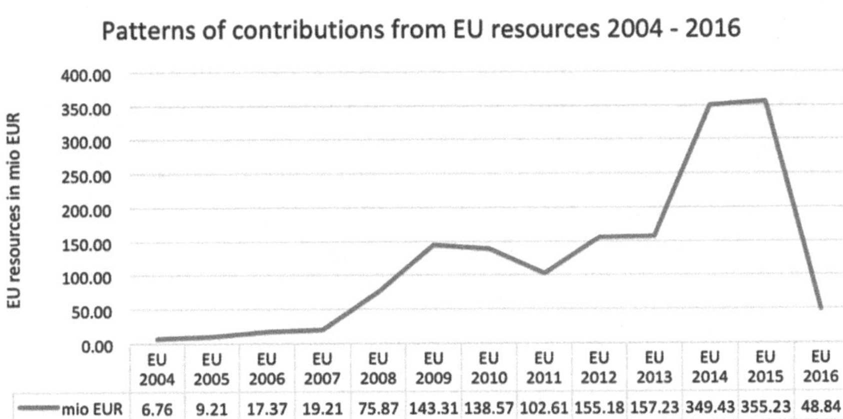

Fig. 2.4 Patterns of contributions from EU resources to municipal budgets during the 2004–2016 period, in EUR million

Conclusions

In spite of having carried out territorial, political, and administrative decentralisation, which began with the adoption of the new Constitution in 1991, Slovenia remains a fiscally centralised state. Following the introduction of the constitutional concept of fiscal decentralisation with the system of the so-called eligible expenditure based on self-financed municipalities in 1991, the resources allocated for the performance of municipal functions increased to 5.7 per cent of GDP in 2015, but did not follow the increase in municipal competences, which at least doubled during this period. Moreover, during the financial crisis, there was a departure from the proportionality principle, as the lump sum determined by agreement between the government and associations of municipalities (or by the law on budget implementation) deviated significantly from the calculated lump sum due to a decrease in income taxes. The state budget was unable to make up for the difference because of domestic conditions as well as international limitations (Government of the Republic of Slovenia, 2016).

Income tax, which is a shared tax, is the most important source of municipal financing, and this puts municipalities into a position where they are dependent on the state for financing. In spite of the constitutional concept of municipal financing based on the idea of self-financing with own sources, the state has not foregone all of its fiscal sovereignty and has not introduced a tax source over which the municipalities could enjoy full fiscal sovereignty. While the National Assembly adopted the Real Property Tax Act in 2013,[19] the Constitutional Court of the Republic of Slovenia repealed it in the following year. In the Local Self-Government Development Strategy 2020 adopted in 2016, the government committed itself to introducing a real property tax as the basic tax for local communities, but due to a lack of political consensus and the recentralisation of municipal financing this idea was abandoned.

In terms of the costs required for the operation of municipalities, an important factor in the financing system is the concept of eligible expenditure. Such expenditure is uniform for all municipalities, only taking into account the size of a municipality, not its particularities. However, there are certain discrepancies between the cost structure and the weighting values that are key to determining eligible expenditure, as analyses point to greater burdens that affect the budgets of municipalities with larger populations, especially in the case of urban municipalities. This will have to take into consideration if and when the financing system is reformed and more resources will need to be allocated to urban municipalities. The fundamental flaw of the system is therefore the current lump sum calculation system, which does not take into account real costs or standardised cost data, thus pushing Slovenia further from the principle of municipal financial autonomy. The analysis of the effects of the municipal financing system reveals additional distortions, which mostly reflect the large number of non-homogenous and administratively weak municipalities, the size of which has not been established in an rational way.

Another crucial deficiency of the system is evident in the financing of investments in those municipalities that are mainly financed by other means, rather than from state resources or resources acquired within the framework of the eligible expenditure mechanism. Prior to Slovenia's accession to the EU in 2004, regional development lacked coherence due to the inefficient investment financing system and the lack of a second level of regional self-government. Even though municipalities financed their investments from their own sources after Slovenia's accession to the EU, about one quarter of local budgets were financed from EU resources, demonstrating the sheer importance of these resources for Slovenian municipalities in the recent programming periods. With the realisation and co-financing from various EU funds, the contribution of Slovenian municipalities towards the improvement of the macroeconomic situation in Slovenia in 2014 and 2015 was very important. Even during the worst period of the crisis, municipal investments played a significant role in the stabilisation of the economic situation.

Over two decades after the beginnings of the decentralisation process, Slovenia adopted the Local Self-Government Development Strategy 2020 and committed itself to abiding by the principles of financial autonomy of self-governing local communities, of connection and proportionality between financial resources and the scope of municipal functions. Despite that, there is a lack of compliance with these principles. Having created many small municipalities that largely reflect political compromises, Slovenia has established a local self-government system that makes it impossible to create a transparent and economically equitable model of municipal financing, mainly due to the diversity of the municipalities and the fact that all municipalities, regardless of their size, have an identical jurisdiction.

In light of the foregoing arguments a logical policy would be to merge some of the smaller municipalities, which however may not be possible considering the difficulty in reaching the necessary political compromises. An alternative would be to establish a second level of local self-government as a development core in order to eliminate the deficiencies of the current system of local self-government and improve its capacity for absorbing EU funds.

Notes

1. Constitution of the Republic of Slovenia, Official Gazette, No. 33/1991-I. It should be noted that local self-government in Slovenia is guaranteed in Article 9 of the Constitution.
2. Local Self-Government Act, Official Gazette, No. 72/1993.
3. Financing of Municipalities Act, Official Gazette, No. 80/1994.
4. Financing of Municipalities Act, Official Gazette, No. 123/2006.
5. Referendum for the Establishment of Municipalities Act, Official Gazette, No. 5/1994.
6. Decree on Holding a Referendum for the Founding of Municipalities, Official Gazette, No. 22/1994.
7. Establishment of Municipalities and Municipal Boundaries Act, Official Gazette, No. 60/1994.
8. Administration Act, Official Gazette, No. 67/1994.
9. Act on the Takeover of State Functions Performed until 31 December 1994 by Municipal Bodies, Official Gazette, No. 29/1995.
10. Promotion of Balanced Regional Development Act, Official Gazette, No. 60/1999.
11. Constitutional Court of the Republic of Slovenia, Decision No. U-I-82/96, Official Gazette, No. 35/97.
12. The decree on the methodology for the calculation of the lump sum for the financing of municipal functions was adopted in 2009.
13. Article 12 of the Financing of Municipalities Act.

14. Article 13 of the Financing of Municipalities Act.
15. Article 38 of the Financing of Municipalities Act.
16. Article 54 of the Local Self-Government Act.
17. Article 85 of the Public Finance Act, Official Gazette, No. 11/2011, 101/2013, 55/2015—ZFis, 96/2015 ZIPRS1617, 13/2018).
18. Article 10.b of the Financing of Municipalities Act.
19. Real Property Tax Act, Official Gazette, No. 101/2013.

References

Bradaschia, N. (2012). *Finančni viri lokalnih oblasti v Republiki Sloveniji: magistrsko delo študijskega programa druge stopnje.* Maribor: Pravna fakulteta Maribor.

Brezovnik, B. (2018). *Pristojnosti in naloge slovenskih občin (s pregledom splošnih in posamičnih aktov ter aktov poslovanja občine): osma spremenjena in dopolnjena izdaja.* Maribor: Inštitut za lokalno samoupravo Maribor.

Brezovnik, B., Finžgar, M., & Oplotnik, Ž. J. (2014). *Financiranje slovenskih občin.* Maribor: Inštitut za lokalno samoupravo in javna naročila Maribor.

Brezovnik, B., & Oplotnik, Ž. J. (2003). Mednarodna primerjava sistemov financiranja občin. *Lex Localis—Journal of Local Self-Government, 1*(3), 1–38.

Brezovnik, B., & Oplotnik, Ž. J. (2006). Problematika sistema financiranja občin v Republiki Sloveniji. *Lex Localis—Journal of Local Self-Government, 4*(4), 91–121.

Brezovnik, B., Oplotnik, Ž. J., Padovnik, S. A., Finžgar, M., & Mlinarič, F. (2018). *Analiza sistema finaniranja občinskih nalog s predlogom metodologije za določitev povprečnine.* Maribor: Pravna fakulteta Maribor.

Government of the Republic of Slovenia. (2016). *Strategija razvoja lokalne samouprave do 2020.* Ljubljana: Government of the Republic of Slovenia.

Grafenauer, B. (2000). *Lokalna samouprava na Slovenskem; teritorialno—organizacijske structure.* Maribor: Univerza v Mariboru, Pravna fakulteta.

Grafenauer, B., & Brezovnik, B. (2011). Vzpostavitev in dograjevanje novega sistema lokalne samouprave. In G. Virant & P. Kovač (Eds.), *Razvoj slovenske javne uprave 1991–2011* (pp. 79–96). Ljubljana: Uradni list RS.

Ministry of Finance. (2011). *Bilten javnih financ, 13*(1). Retrieved from http://www.mf.gov.si

Ministry of Finance. (2016). *Poročilo o zadolženosti občin in pravnih oseb javnega sektorja na ravni občin na dan 31.12.2015.* Ljubljana: Ministry of Finance. Retrieved from http://www.mf.gov.si

Ministry of Finance. (2018). *Bilten javnih financ, 20*(1). Retrieved from http://www.mf.gov.si

Oplotnik, Z., & Brezovnik, B. (2006–2016). Zakon o financiranju občin / ZFO-1/ (pristojnosti in naloge Municipality z uvodnimi pojasnili in komentarjem). In B. Brezovnik (Ed.), *Pristojnosti slovenskih občin*. Maribor: Inštitut za lokalno samoupravo in javna naročila Maribor.

Šmidovnik, J. (1995). *Lokalna samouprava*. Ljubljana: Cankarjeva založba.

3

Croatia: Instruments of Fiscal Equalisation

Anto Bajo and Marko Primorac

Introduction

Croatia has a territory of about 56,000 square kilometres and a population of 4.2 million inhabitants. Although set up after independence as semi-presidential country, a parliamentary system was introduced in 2000. The Croatian Parliament (*Sabor*) is a unicameral legislative body, whose members are elected every four years by popular vote. The "House of Counties", set up in 1990 as a second chamber, was abolished in 2001. The Prime Minister, who has four deputy prime ministers and 16 ministers other than deputy prime ministers, heads the Croatian

A. Bajo (✉)
Institute for Public Finance, Zagreb, Croatia

Faculty of Economics, University of Zagreb, Zagreb, Croatia
e-mail: bajo@ijf.hr

M. Primorac
Faculty of Economics and Business, University of Zagreb, Zagreb, Croatia
e-mail: mprimorac@efzg.hr

W. Bartlett et al. (eds.), *Fiscal Decentralisation, Local Government and Policy Reversals in Southeastern Europe*, https://doi.org/10.1007/978-3-319-96092-0_3

Government (*Vlada*). In general, the executive branch proposes legislation and the budget, executes the laws and guides foreign and internal policies. The judicial system in Croatia is three-tiered and consists of the Supreme Court, county courts and municipal courts.

Croatia adopted its Constitution in 1990 and proclaimed independence in 1991. The Constitution defines the units of local self-government and administration. The counties that were established in the new legal environment carry out the functions of both the government and self-government. The municipalities and cities (local government units—LGUs) hold self-governing functions. The new legislative framework introduced the first model for financing LGUs and began the process of fiscal decentralisation. Croatia is now administratively divided into 21 counties (*županija*) as units of regional self-government and 556 local government units—cities (*grad*) and municipalities (*općina*). Croatia's capital—the City of Zagreb—is counted twice (as a city and a county) due to its formal dual status. Zagreb has the status of a county and also performs tasks as both a city and a county.[1]

Local elections in Croatia are held every four years, with the first being held in February 1993. Local elections are pluralistic, with many small regional parties and independent local candidates running for county, city or municipal offices. However, there is a strong domination of two political parties: the Croatian Democratic Union (*Hrvatska demokratska zajednica*—HDZ) and the Social Democratic Party (*Socijaldemokratska Partija Hrvatske*—SDP). The electoral system is proportional, and candidate lists must pass a threshold of 5 per cent to qualify for parliamentary seats. Each LGU elects its own Municipal or City Council.

The chairperson recommends members of the executive authority of an LGU to the representative body, which selects the members by a majority vote. The executive authority, responsible to the representative body of the LGU, usually consists of heads of administrative sections for economy, social affairs, finances and budget, education, health and welfare and so on. Since 2009, citizens directly elect city mayors, county prefects and municipal leaders. Sessions of LGU representative bodies are open to the public.

In the initial phase of decentralisation, the financing of LGUs was bedevilled by several practical problems. The lack of reliable data about the fiscal capacities of LGUs hindered the establishment of a sustainable financing system. Without a clear image of the financial capacity of LGUs it was impossible to propose their own revenue sources, and LGUs could only be financed only through the intermediation of counties. Despite having a heavy tax burden, some LGUs still did not have adequate sources for self-financing.

The new model of local government finance accompanied by a tax reform was hindered by the destruction brought by the "homeland" war, which was unevenly distributed across the country, requiring asymmetric state intervention to deal with reconstruction of severely damaged areas. It was not possible to include such extraordinary financing needs within the regular LGU financing system. Under the circumstances, determining the level of fiscal inequalities and the extent to which the revenues and expenditures of certain LGUs were out of keeping with the national average could only be a matter for speculation.

To cope with these problems, the Law on the Financing of Units of Local Self-Government and Administration[2] (below referred to as the Local Government Financing Law) was passed. This law set up the current system of LGU finance in Croatia. However, the new territorial organisation and the new financing model soon revealed some shortcomings. Debates about the optimal design of the local government financing system started to include the question of fiscal equalisation, as well as the appropriate extent of devolution of taxes and tax sharing.

Due to the consequences of the war, the central government defined areas of special national concern (ASNC) in 1995 to support their development and encourage the return of the displaced population. The scope of LGUs under special financing arrangements expanded in 2002 when the SDP ruled in coalition with several other parties, with the introduction of hilly and mountainous areas (HMA) into this special scheme. Accordingly, the number of LGUs within the ASNC and HMA has increased to as many as 230 out of all 555 LGUs. The policy of granting preferential financial treatment to this selected group of LGUs is rather inflexible, and the status is not easy to lose. Therefore, most of the LGUs within the ASNC and HMA have maintained their preferential status.

Primorac (2014) has demonstrated that such an inflexible equalisation system based on geographical, historical and other non-economic criteria cannot adequately address the problem of horizontal fiscal inequality. Delving into the reasons for the lack of political will to improve the policy, Bajo and Primorac (2017) questioned whether the equalisation model might have been intentionally rendered ineffective for political reasons. More precisely, they found a positive and statistically significant relationship between the political alignment of central and local governments and the status of LGUs within the ASNC. Although the analysis covered only one year, the authors claimed that their results indicate that the fiscal equalisation system has been manipulated for political purposes.

When approaching accession to the European Union (EU), Croatia paid increasing attention to the issue of balanced regional development. This included the reform of the fiscal equalisation system in order to better identify areas that were experiencing economic difficulties in financing public services. Accordingly, the equalisation system was reformed in 2018 largely based on the suggestions of Primorac (2014) to take into account the fiscal inequalities among LGUs in a transparent and direct way, rather than through non-economic criteria. The design of the new equalisation system should contribute to preventing political interference in the equalisation process, although the reform needs time to fully show its effects.

The process of fiscal decentralisation in Croatia has been extensively researched, from the early works of Bajo (1999) and Ott and Bajo (2001) which laid the foundations for research in this field, to comprehensive studies produced a decade later when the availability of relevant data removed many obstacles for delving deeper into certain topics (Jurlina-Alibegović, 2010). Publicly available data have gradually enabled additional international comparative studies, such as that by Blažić (2004) and many others.

Territorial Organisation

Although its degree of fiscal decentralisation is questionable, Croatia is administratively decentralised. The 21 counties (including the City of Zagreb) constitute the second, intermediate, level of subnational government, that is, *regional self-government*, whereas cities (127 with the city of

Table 3.1 The structure of the Croatian subnational sector

Tier	Units (1992)	Units (2011)	Tier	Population (in million)	Units/million citizens	Units/1000 km^2 (2011)
Central government	1	1		4.3	–	–
Counties	21	21	II	4.3	4.9	0.4
Cities	70	127	I	3.0	42.3	2.2
Municipalities	419	429		1.3	330.0	7.6
Cities and municipalities	489	556	I	4.3	129.3	9.8

Source: Authors based on CBS (2013)

Zagreb) and municipalities (429) represent the first level of subnational government, that is, *local self-government* (Table 3.1).

The counties are responsible for matters of regional significance, particularly those related to health care, education, economic development, traffic and transportation infrastructure, physical and town planning, and the planning and development of the network of educational, healthcare, welfare and cultural establishments. Cities and municipalities carry out matters of local significance including housing, physical and town planning, child care, primary health care, preschool and elementary school education, communal economy matters, welfare, culture, physical culture and sport, protection and improvement of the environment and civilian protection and fire protection. Should they provide adequate financing, all LGUs may also carry out activities related to the jurisdiction of the counties. The municipalities, cities and counties enact statutes that regulate their internal organisation and structure and the way they work.

The administrative-territorial structure is highly fragmented, with many relatively small local governments that have weak fiscal and administrative capacities. Almost two thirds of municipalities have fewer than 3,000 inhabitants. Even though a city can host the county seat, and every place that has more than 10,000 inhabitants and represents a historic urban centre can become a city, almost half of all cities have less than 10,000 inhabitants (Table 3.2).

Croatian municipalities are small and are mostly home to up to 3,000 people (in two-thirds of municipalities), while almost

Table 3.2 Population of municipalities in 2011

	Municipalities	Population	Municipalities (%)	Population (%)
<1,001	37	27,321	8.6	2.2
1,001–1,500	49	62,122	11.4	4.9
1,501–2,000	71	125,659	16.6	9.9
2,001–2,500	63	139,421	14.7	11.0
2,501–3,000	56	155,295	13.1	12.2
3,001–3,500	29	95,459	6.8	7.5
3,501–4,000	35	131,194	8.2	10.3
4,001–4,500	15	63,341	3.5	5.0
4,501–5,000	21	98,803	4.9	7.8
5,001–6,000	24	130,497	5.6	10.3
6,001–7,000	13	85,702	3.0	6.8
7,001–15,000	16	153,938	3.6	12.1
Total	429	1,268,752	100.0	100.0

Source: Authors based on CBS (2013)

Table 3.3 Population of cities in 2011

	Cities	Population	Cities (%)	Population (%)
<5,001	18	59,681	14.2	2.0
5,001–10,000	42	296,726	33.1	9.8
10,001–15,000	30	372,587	23.6	12.4
15,001–20,000	8	132,465	6.3	4.4
20,001–30,000	11	272,599	8.7	9.0
30,001–40,000	4	142,466	3.1	4.7
40,001–50,000	5	223,937	3.9	7.4
50,001–60,000	3	172,306	2.4	5.7
60,001–70,000	1	63,517	0.8	2.1
70,001–80,000	1	75,062	0.8	2.5
100,001–200,000	3	414,774	2.4	13.8
>200,000	1	790,017	0.8	26.2
Total	127	3,016,137	100.0	100.0

Source: Authors based on CBS (2013)

one-tenth of municipalities have less than 1,000 inhabitants. Only 46 municipalities have a larger population of between 5,000 and 10,000 inhabitants, while only seven municipalities have over 10,000 inhabitants (see Table 3.3).

Most of the cities are also small, with 71 per cent having up to 15,000 inhabitants, while 18 cities have less than 5,000 inhabitants. Only nine cities have more than 50,000 inhabitants, and only four cities have more than 100,000 inhabitants.

The Genesis of Fiscal Decentralisation

Fiscal decentralisation began in 2001 when some LGUs took over certain decentralised functions. Prerequisites for introducing fiscal decentralisation were gradually implemented after 1994 through the processes of political and administrative decentralisation. Fiscal decentralisation and fiscal equalisation depend directly on the development of the LGU financing system. Bajo and Bronić (2004) divided the development of the financing system into two periods: the first from 1994 to 2001 and the second from 2001 onwards. Now, more than a decade later, it is obvious that the financing of LGUs has been significantly influenced by the global financial crisis, with long-term consequences also reflected in intergovernmental fiscal relations. With this in mind, it is possible to distinguish three characteristic phases of fiscal decentralisation in Croatia:

1. The first phase (1994–2001)—administrative and political decentralisation
2. The second phase (2001–2009)—fiscal decentralisation
3. The third phase (2009–now)—recentralisation and the post-crisis period

The First Phase: Administrative and Territorial Decentralisation (1994–2001)

The beginnings of decentralisation in Croatia marked the gradual implementation of political and administrative decentralisation from 1994 to 2001. The formal requirements for decentralisation were created by the Local Self-Government Financing Law, which specified the sources of LGU revenue. However, the basis for the implementation of decentralisation had been prepared earlier through the establishment of the legal framework for administrative and political decentralisation. The financing of LGUs in this period was mainly centralised and LGUs had limited autonomy in collecting the revenue and determining the purpose of the collected funds. This period marked the establishment of a legal framework that determined the distribution of fiscal and administrative powers between the central government and local government units. In 1995, ASNC were defined with the aim of supporting their development and encouraging the return of the displaced population (Bajo & Bronić, 2004).

The Second Phase: Fiscal Decentralisation (2001–2009)

Fiscal decentralisation began in 2001, when the counties and larger cities delegated authority for funding health, education, firefighting service and social welfare. Powers to finance material costs and part of capital investments were transferred to LGUs, while expenditures for employees and other expenditures remained within the competence of the central government (ministries). The financing of decentralised functions was taken over by LGUs with the largest fiscal capacities, the number of which increased over time. Since 2001, LGUs were permitted to impose a surtax on the personal income tax, up to a ceiling established by the central government. The maximum permitted surtax rate depends on the administrative status of the LGU and its population (Fig. 3.1).

The revenue from personal income tax has gradually been devolved to LGUs. This revenue is partly used to finance decentralised functions and

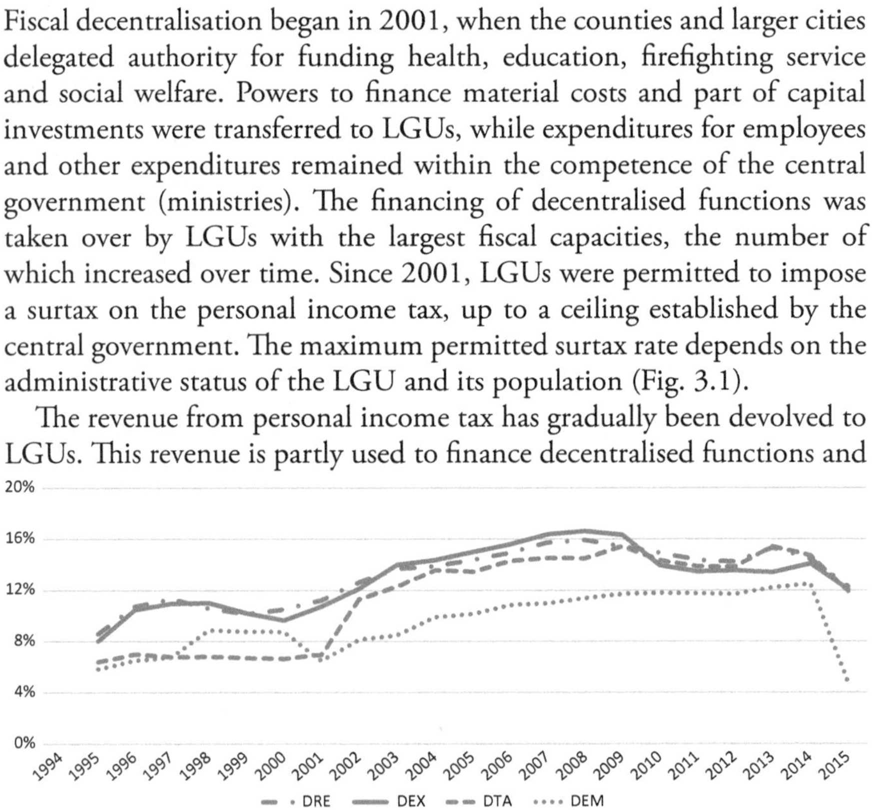

Fig. 3.1 Fiscal decentralisation in Croatia from 1995 to 2015. Source: Authors' calculation based on the data from the report on revenues and expenditures, receipts and expenses (Form PR-RAS) and the time series of Ministry of Finance's (MOF) data on revenue and expenditure of the consolidate general government budget for the years 1995–2015. Note: DRE—the ratio of the total revenue of local and general government, DEX—the ratio of the total expenditure of local and general government, DTA—the ratio of the total tax revenue of local and general government

partly paid into the fund for decentralised functions. With the reduction in the central government's revenue share from personal income tax, the scope for special financing of LGUs in the 45 hilly and mountainous areas has expanded. Since 2001, new criteria have been established for the allocation of current unconditional grants. These are allocated only to counties within the ASNC, which must pass on at least half of the amount to LGUs that are not direct beneficiaries of grants from the state budget (Bajo & Bronić, 2004).

Although Croatia is territorially, administratively and politically decentralised, it can still be considered a fiscally centralised country. The legislative framework for fiscal decentralisation established in 2001 triggered a steady increase in the extent of fiscal decentralisation until 2009, after which it diminished due to the financial crisis.

The Third Phase: Recentralisation and the Post-crisis Period (since 2009)

The coefficients for distributing tax revenues (especially personal income tax) have changed substantially over time, and since 2007 the system of local government financing has relied on personal income tax more and more heavily. Corporate income tax is fully retained by the central government, whereas personal income tax largely ceded to LGUs. The state directs a portion of revenues from the equalisation fund for decentralised functions to lower levels of government to ensure that the financing of decentralised functions meets the minimum financial standards. The scope of LGUs with special financing status has expanded, and now also includes LGUs on islands through the agreement on the joint financing of capital projects for their development. The system of state aid has introduced grants to municipalities and cities in the ASNC and hilly and mountainous areas as a compensation for the corporate income tax being passed on entirely to the central government.

In order to control the collection and spending of funds during the financial crisis, fiscal policy centralised both revenues and expenditures, while the revenues of the public sector in general have declined and the state has intervened on the revenue side of the budget, for example, by increasing the rate of value added tax to partially compensate for the decline in tax revenues. Unfortunately, this has not happened at local government level and so in 2015 only about 12 per cent of the general government budget was realised at the local level.

Decentralisation of Revenue

Taxes are the most important revenue source for LGUs, accounting for more than half of total revenue, while the second most important source are administrative fees and user charges accounting for over one fifth. Other categories of operating revenue have less significance; together with revenue from sales of non-financial assets they account for about one fifth of the total revenue of LGUs (Fig. 3.2).

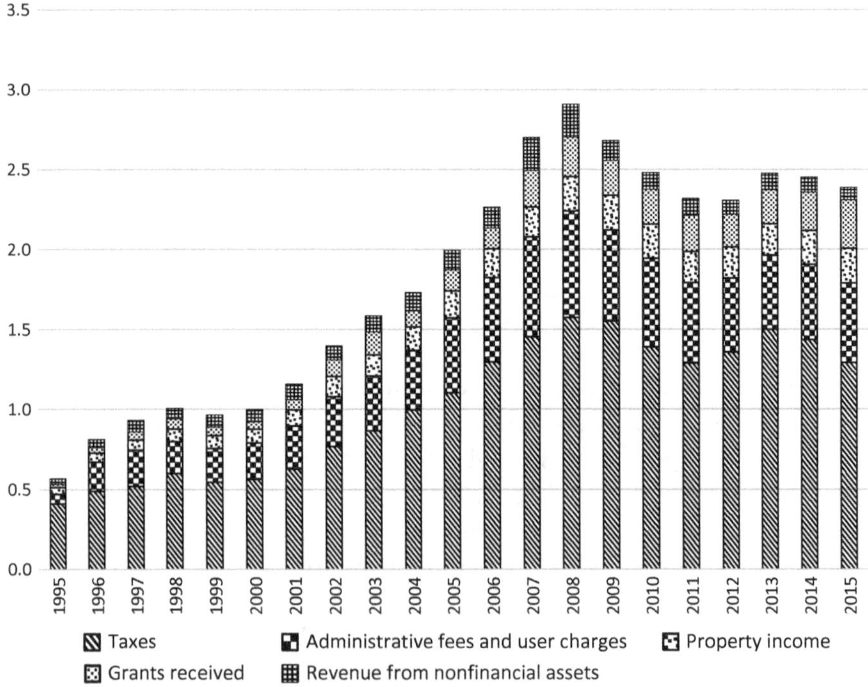

Fig. 3.2 Revenue sources of LGUs in Croatia from 1995 to 2015 (in EUR billion). Source: Authors' calculation based on the data from the report on revenues and expenditures, receipts and expenses (Form PR-RAS) for the years 1995–2015

The main sources of local government tax revenues are personal income tax (shared) and the surtax which accounts for almost 90 per cent of total tax revenues. The income tax became a particularly important source of LGU finance after 2007. Since then, the state has renounced the revenue from personal income tax, which is allocated to local governments through a comprehensive tax sharing scheme and a complicated transfer system. To compensate the resulting loss of revenue, the central government took over the revenue from corporate income tax, which was previously shared between the state, counties, cities and municipalities.

Since LGUs rely on personal income tax (PIT) as their main source of revenue, any changes to this tax directly affect the financing of LGUs. Given that the tax base is wide, and that the PIT revenue is devolved to regional and local units, PIT has become a very powerful and often used political tool. In order to gain popularity, politicians at the central level have often decreased the tax burden or altered the distribution (tax sharing) schedule, causing minor effects at the central level but producing serious consequences at lower levels of government. Since PIT is often perceived as "almighty" (aimed both at securing revenue for LGUs, and at interregional and interpersonal redistribution due to the progressive tax schedule) the PIT Law has been changed or amended on average more than once a year (Bajo & Primorac, 2015b). This makes the financing environment for LGUs unstable, which directly affects other aspects of their operations, especially investments (Fig. 3.3).

LGU revenue increased significantly after 2001, following the start of the fiscal decentralisation and the increase in the LGUs' share of PIT. The revenue structure is dominated by tax and non-tax revenue, and

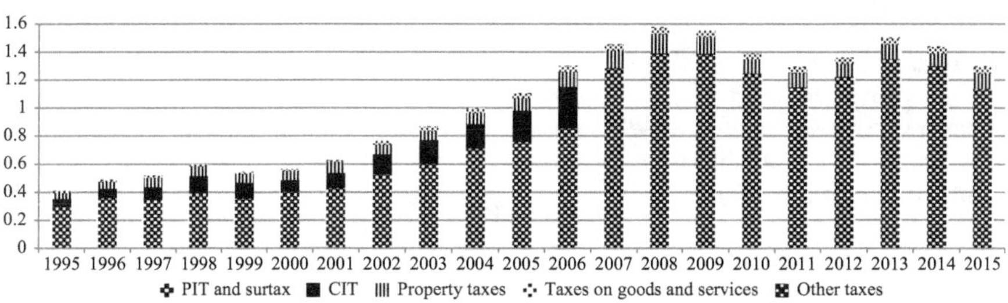

Fig. 3.3 Tax revenue of LGUs from 1995 to 2015 (in EUR billion). Source: Authors' calculation based on the data from the report on revenues and expenditures, receipts and expenses (Form PR-RAS) for the years 1995–2015

central government grants have been less significant. The second most important revenue components are local non-tax revenues consisting of fees, charges and "contributions" levied by councils and public utility companies. These have been mainly non-transparent and have not been properly associated with specific rights or services provided. A significant further revenue potential could be tapped by introducing property taxes.

Although it is a shared tax, the central government determines both the tax base and the tax rates for the PIT. The lack of influence over the determination of these elements of the PIT brings into question the real intensity of decentralisation and the extent to which PIT revenue can be seen as genuinely decentralised revenue rather than an opaque form of transfer. In practice it only creates an illusion of fiscal decentralisation, because LGUs do not have the power to alter any element of the tax in order to compete with other LGUs or adjust the fiscal costs and benefits to the preferences of their inhabitants. Moreover, it is not clear to what extent the revenue from own local taxes could be considered to be autonomous, since the central government determines the ceiling or the band in which LGUs can set the local tax rates, with the sole exception of the public land use tax (Table 3.4).

Overall, LGUs have limited autonomy in determining the rates of local taxes. This suggests that in addition to further decentralising the system,

Table 3.4 Autonomy in determining the tax rates

	Central government	Local units autonomously	Local units within limits
Shared taxes			
Personal income tax	•		
Real estate transfer tax	•		
County taxes	•		
Inheritance tax	•		
Tax on motor vehicles	•		
Tax on vessels	•		
Tax on gambling machines	•		
Municipal and city taxes			
Consumption tax			•
Tax on holiday houses			•
Tax on the use of public land		•	•
Tax on corporate title			•
Surtax (on personal income tax)			•

Source: Authors

the autonomy of LGUs should be gradually increased. This would enable LGUs to have a greater say in determining the rate of local taxes, in introducing new taxes, in determining the object of taxation and in determining the relevant tax base and other significant factors of local taxation.

Assignment of Functions

From 2001, the central government transferred the authority for financing health care, education, welfare and fire departments to those LGUs that had taken on the financing of decentralised functions. Most of the LGU expenditure relates to housing and communal amenities, general administrative services and education. Since 2001, the budgets for decentralised functions, particularly for health care, education and welfare, have increased considerably. The decentralisation process has also brought about an increase in current expenditures because most of the financing of current expenditure for education, firefighting and social welfare has been transferred to lower tiers of government. Fifty-three administrative units (20 counties, 32 cities and the City of Zagreb) have assumed the financing of decentralised functions and have received financial benefits through an additional share of PIT revenues and equalisation grants. The total budget of the 53 administrative units that assumed the financing of decentralised functions at that time accounted for about 70 per cent of the aggregate budget of all administrative units together.

Off-budget public utility companies provide most of the municipal services. Water, sewerage, irrigation, infrastructure, energy and sanitation are in principle considered to be mainly locally owned and managed. The central regulatory authorities in general set the service standards, whereas the tariffs are proposed by utility companies and decided upon by local councils, usually with an implicit subsidy component.

Local governments do finance certain functions (e.g. social care, secondary education) even though they have no legal obligation to do so. Other functions, such as health care, have been transferred to counties, which are not capable of financing those functions in full. A few LGUs assumed responsibility for financing certain public services, whereas the provision of public services in a number of LGUs is limited. Some cities (32 of 127) took over the function of primary education; while other decentralised

Table 3.5 Responsibilities according to government tiers

		Central gov.	Municipal.	Cities	Counties
1.	General public services	•	•	•	•
2.	Defence	•			
3.	Public order and security	•	•	•	
4.	Education	•	•	•	•
4.1.	Preschool		•	•	
4.2.	Elementary	•	•	•	•
4.3.	Secondary	•			•
4.4.	Tertiary	•			
5.	Health care	•			•
6.	Social security and welfare	•	•	•	•
7.	Housing and communal economy matters and services		•	•	
8.	Recreation, culture and religion		•	•	
9.	Agriculture, forestry, hunting, fishing	•			•
10.	Mining, industry, construction	•	•	•	•
11.	Traffic and communications	•	•	•	•
11.1.	Road transport	•	•	•	•
11.2.	Rail transport	•			
11.3.	Air transport	•			
12.	Other economic matters and services	•	•	•	•

Source: Ott and Bajo (2001)

functions largely remained under the jurisdiction of 20 counties. For the most part, only large and financially stable local units assumed decentralised functions for primary education and firefighting. Thus, the local units that cannot finance these services on their own ought to be mutually linked through cooperation agreements to finance these public services.

LGUs in Croatia have greater autonomy in providing services related to communal economic activity, preschool education and cultural, sporting and religious activities. Some tasks, however, by their nature ought to be centrally financed, including the provision of health services, energy supply and business development support. Although their formal responsibilities are laid down, LGUs have limited autonomy in financing such responsibilities because proceeds from tax sharing and central government grants are earmarked. Furthermore, a clear division of function between different government tiers does not exist, causing many functions to be dependent on multiple financing sources of finance from both central and local government levels (see Table 3.5).

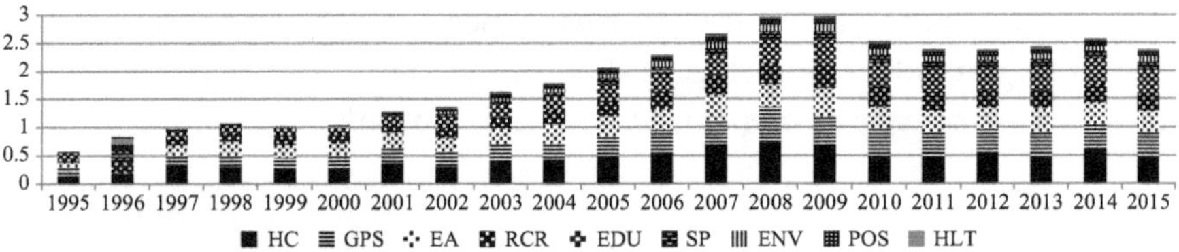

Fig. 3.4 Expenditure of local government units according to the functional classification from 1995 to 2015 (in EUR billion). Source: Authors' calculation based on the data from the report on revenues and expenditures, receipts and expenses (Form PR-RAS) for the years 1995–2015. Note: GPS—general public services, DEF—defence, POS—public order and safety, EA—economic affairs, ENV—environment, HC—housing and community, HLT—health, RCR—recreation, culture and religion, EDU—education, SP—social protection

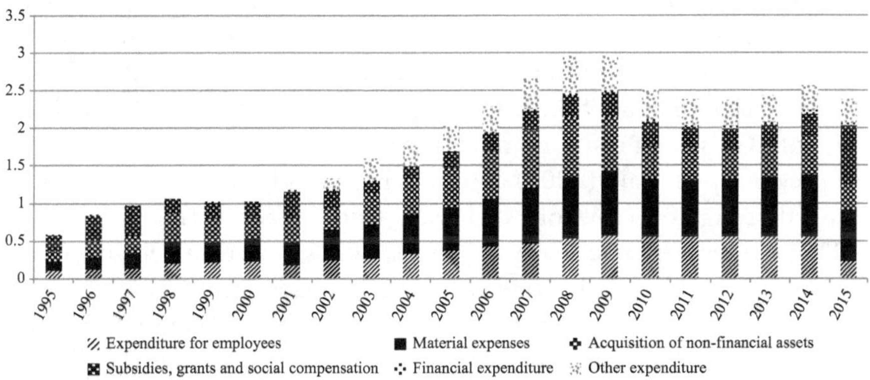

Fig. 3.5 Expenditure of local government units according to the economic classification from 1995 to 2015 (in EUR billion). Source: Authors' calculation based on the data from the report on revenues and expenditures, receipts and expenses (Form PR-RAS) for the years 1995–2015

The structure of the expenditure according to the functional classification reveals the relative intensity of performing various functions (see Figs. 3.4 and 3.5).

Over half of LGUs' expenditure relates to salaries and material expenses, whereas 16 per cent is set aside for investment; in comparison, before the crisis, a quarter of the budget was aimed at investment. Subsidies, mainly to large local utility companies, make up a relatively small part of subnational expenditure, except in the City of Zagreb. Although the national government pays teachers and doctors, expenditure for employees is the second largest category of local expenditures. For a detailed analysis of the structure of employment in LGUs, see Bajo (2009).

Borrowing

On the basis of the Budget Act,[3] the central government determines the constraints on borrowing by LGUs and their issuing of guarantees for the borrowing of their budgetary users through annual laws on the execution of the state budget. LGUs can borrow short-term and long-term with the prior approval of the government. Up to 2012 the government approved borrowing of LGUs up to 2.3 per cent of their total operating revenues (for all LGUs); in 2012, the limit moved to 2.5 per cent and in 2015 to 3 per cent. Besides the cumulative borrowing restrictions, the Budget Act also sets out individual borrowing rules which limit the total annual liability of LGUs to a maximum of 20 per cent of the revenues generated in the previous year. Bajo (2004) as well as Bajo and Primorac (2010b) provide a thorough overview of LGU borrowing in Croatia (Fig. 3.6).

Due to the restrictive borrowing rules, LGUs have relatively low levels of debt. However, this is often breached by extension of guarantees to local utility firms, and from 2008 to 2014 LGUs consistently borrowed over the prescribed limits, most significantly in 2014 when the City of Zagreb alone borrowed one billion kuna, boosting the growth of total local government debt considerably.

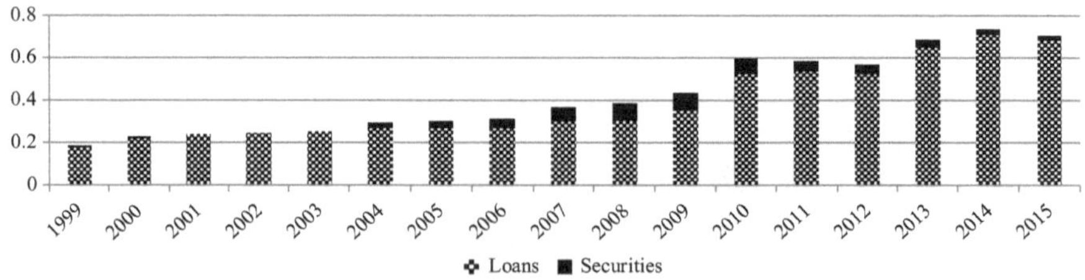

Fig. 3.6 The size and the structure of local government debt, 1999–2015 (in EUR billion). Source: Croatian National Bank (CNB)

Table 3.6 The size and the structure of active guarantees from 2008 to 2014 (in million euro)

	Cities	Zagreb	Municipalities	Counties	Total
2008	147	186	15	54	402
2009	111	208	24	63	406
2010	157	168	23	61	408
2011	122	144	25	57	348
2012	104	129	23	48	304
2013	103	102	21	62	288
2014	93	60	16	61	230

Source: Local government units' financial statements from 2008 to 2014

The direct debt (financial liabilities) of LGUs increased from less than €200 million in 1999 to around €700 million in 2015. While financial liabilities include all bills, securities and borrowings, the total debt is dominated by loans (more than 90 per cent) of which more than half are loans to cities comprise most of which relates to the debt of the City of Zagreb (Table 3.6).

Restrictive borrowing rules have led LGUs to borrow through the companies that they own to finance capital projects. Guarantees for such borrowings create contingent liabilities that require LGUs to repay a loan from their own revenue if the original borrower does not meet his obligations on time and in full. Such guarantees increased to more than €400 million by 2010, and then gradually fell to €230 million in 2014. The City of Zagreb has the largest number of active guarantees, having the same amount of guarantees as almost all other cities combined. However, the total cumulative risks of the financial operations of the local utility companies to local budgets are much higher than is evident from the number of active guarantees, because only part of the borrowing by local government enterprises is guaranteed (Bajo & Primorac, 2010a, 2014a, 2015a). The example of the City of Zagreb confirms that these contingent liabilities pose a great threat to the sustainability of local government financing (Bajo & Primorac, 2013b). Since a large number of local government enterprises benefit from generous subsidies, which sometimes account for over 90 per cent of total revenue, it is reasonable to question why these local public enterprises do not operate within the local budget (see Primorac, 2011).

EU Funds and Capital Investments

Following accession to the EU, Croatia benefits from new financial programmes that are directly linked to the EU budget through the multiannual financial perspective (currently the funds are budgeted for the period 2014–2020). These programmes are mostly directed to environmental protection, agriculture, transport infrastructure, promotion of entrepreneurship and the education system. The main emphasis however is on programmes related to the rural development of less developed regions. Since 2013, Croatia has been territorially divided into two statistical regions of Continental and Adricatic Croatia (under the Nomenclature of Territorial Units for Statistics—NUTS II) that are both eligible for withdrawing funds from the European structural and investment funds (ESIFs). With a budget of €454 billion for 2014–2020, the ESIFs are the EU's main financial instruments aimed at supporting activities that contribute to the implementation of EU policies. They include grants and other forms of aid for eligible selected projects.

EU member states can withdraw financial resources from the EU budget through five ESIFs: the European Regional Development Fund, the European Social Fund, the Cohesion Fund, the European Agricultural Fund for Rural Development and the European Maritime Fisheries Fund. In the current budgetary period, Croatia can draw €10.7 billion from these ESIFs to co-finance specific projects and programmes. These grants can be received directly by LGUs (counties, cities and municipalities) under the cross-border programmes, or indirectly by users of the national, county, city or municipality budgets which transfer the EU funds to them. Current EU grants are provided for financing operating expenditures (regular activities during an accounting period), whereas capital grants are used to finance non-financial fixed assets (Ott, Bronić, & Stanić, 2016).

Until 2014, EU grants were mostly used by counties, almost all of which secured EU financing and about half of the cities, whereas only a few municipalities took advantage of EU grants. The relatively high concentration of grants gives cause for concern because only a few LGUs have received the lion's share of total grants, while many LGUs have not received any grants. However, since 2011 the use of EU grants has shot

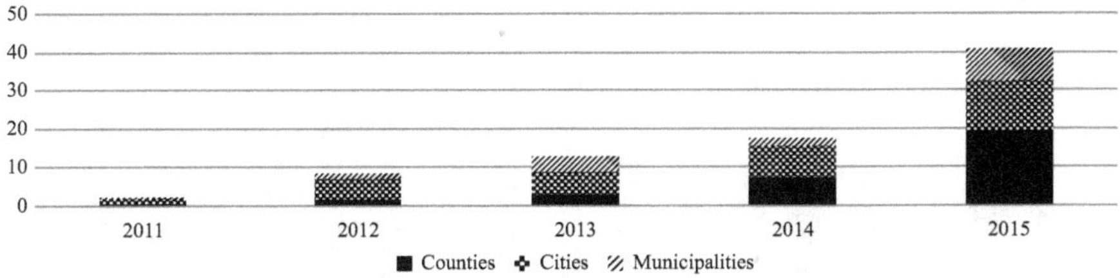

Fig. 3.7 EU grants from 2011 to 2015 (in EUR million). Source: Authors' calculation based on the data from the report on revenues and expenditures, receipts and expenses (Form PR-RAS) for the years 2011–2015

up, increasing almost 20 times in four years (from €2.3 million to €40.7 million) (Fig. 3.7).

Insufficient administrative capacities and poor co-financing potential explain the relatively weak absorption capacity of LGUs. To cope with the problem of co-financing, in 2015 the "Ministry of Regional Development and EU Funds" set up a special Fund to provide direct assistance for co-financing the implementation of EU projects at both local and regional levels. The Fund, which provides local users with the financial resources for co-financing, is financed from 1.5 per cent of the PIT revenues collected in LGUs (except those located in the supported areas). The amount of the aid from the Fund is related to the level of development of the beneficiary LGU, measured by an index of development.

Nevertheless, further efforts to increase the absorption capacities of LGUs are of utmost importance, especially since LGUs should use EU funds to be the main drivers of capital investments in Croatia. Currently, the operating expenditures of LGUs account for three quarters of the total expenditures, while the remaining quarter refers to the expenditure for acquisition of non-financial assets. After 2009, expenditures for acquiring non-financial assets were reduced due to the decline in revenue caused by the financial crisis, indicating prudent financial management by LGUs. Investments were largely put on hold to ensure the financing of core competences of LGUs. Although the financial position of LGUs has stabilised in recent years, the level of capital investment has still not reached its pre-crisis level (Fig. 3.8).

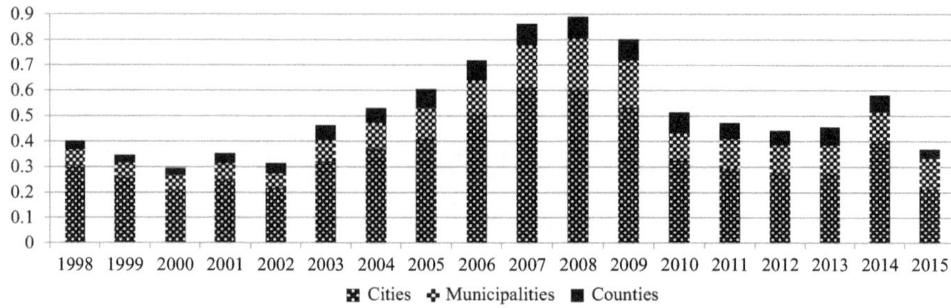

Fig. 3.8 Expenditure for acquisition of non-financial assets from 1998 to 2015 (in EUR billion). Source: Authors' calculation based on the data from the report on revenues and expenditures, receipts and expenses (Form PR-RAS) for the years 1998–2015

Criteria to access prospective EU funds through the National Development Fund for regional development investments have not yet been defined. The absence of transparent central government investment master plans at sector and regional levels[4] may negatively impinge on allocated efficiency and growth. This may also hinder Croatia from making full use of EU funds.

Besides dealing with these shortcomings, further strengthening of absorption capacities should become a priority for preparing and executing investment projects, especially taking into account the expected large inflow of finances from the EU funds. Currently, these capacities are weak due to excessive fragmentation, which prevents many small LGUs from increasing their financial resources.

Fiscal Equalisation

In accordance with the transfer of functional responsibilities from the central to lower levels of government, the central government also devolves revenue to finance those functions. Differences in the fiscal capacities and expenditure needs of administrative units of the same level of government have created horizontal fiscal inequalities. The objective of fiscal equalisation is to provide comparable levels of public services with comparable tax burdens in all LGUs.

The legal framework governing the process of horizontal fiscal equalisation is neither clear nor precise. Fiscal equalisation is only generally defined by the Constitution,[5] whose Article 137 states that local and regional governments have the right to their own revenues of which they can freely dispose in the performance of tasks within their scope. Revenues of local and regional governments must be proportional to their responsibilities provided by the Constitution and the law, and the *state is obliged to help the financially weaker LGUs in accordance with the law.*

Excessive fragmentation paired with poor regional development policies has created significant fiscal inequalities. Although an arsenal of fiscal instruments has been developed to cope with these problems, they failed to secure comparable levels of public goods and services with comparable tax burdens in all LGUs. This is mainly because the fiscal equalisation system relies on instruments that are simultaneously used to implement other policies with different and often even conflicting objectives. The fiscal equalisation system is based on PIT revenue sharing and the allocation of current grants from the central government budget. However, the utilisation of these instruments is based on criteria that have been set up under the regional development policy.

Although it is not quite clear what measures and instruments have been applied in the regional development policy and what measures have been implemented for fiscal equalisation; both policies have mostly relied on granting preferential financial treatment to certain groups of LGUs according to various criteria. Such preferential treatment has been conferred on the City of Zagreb, LGUs in areas of special national concern and in hilly and mountainous areas, and on islands through agreements on joint financing of island infrastructure.

Since they were mostly geographic in nature, the criteria for determining areas of special national concern and hilly and mountainous areas have not been very efficient (Bajo & Bronić, 2007; Primorac, 2015). These criteria have therefore gradually been abandoned and substituted by a development index measuring the extent to which the level of development of supported areas lags behind the national average and whose development should be further encouraged. The status of supported area is granted to LGUs with a development index below 75 per cent of the national average.

The development index is based on the unemployment rate, per capita income, budget revenues per capita, population trends and rates of education. The Ministry of Regional Development and EU Funds assesses the level of development of LGUs every three years, and sets out indicators for the development index, the formula for calculating its value, the weight of each indicator in the development index. The decision on the classification of LGUs is based on the value of the calculated development index. Although it is useful for supporting economically underdeveloped areas, the development index is not an appropriate criterion for implementing fiscal equalisation policy (Primorac, 2014) since it cannot ensure comparable levels of public services or comparable tax burdens in all LGUs.

The redistribution mechanism in Croatia is based on sharing the revenue from PIT and the allocation of current grants from the government budget. The PIT revenue allocation scheme has been altered a number of times (see, e.g. Bajo & Primorac, 2013a, 2014b). Before the reform of 2018, which transformed the fiscal equalisation system, the financing of LGUs was organised as follows. In addition to the basic shares belonging to different levels of government, LGUs that had acquired decentralised functions were entitled to a further share of the PIT (1.9 per cent for elementary education, 1.3 per cent for secondary education, 0.8 per cent for social welfare, 1.0 per cent for health and 1.0 per cent for firefighting). Those LGUs that took on decentralised functions, but did not generate sufficient funds to meet a minimum financial level from their additional share of the PIT were allocated additional funds from the equalisation fund for decentralised functions. This fund was financed by 16 per cent of the PIT according to the revenue sharing schedule, but LGUs having preferential treatment did not contribute to this fund. Moreover, those LGUs were entitled to higher shares of the PIT. Similarly, all LGUs except those in the supported areas contributed 1.5 per cent of the PIT collected in their area to the fund for co-financing local and regional EU project implementation. The distribution of the PIT revenue is presented in Table 3.7.

The preferential status of LGUs on islands with agreements on joint financing of island infrastructure was reflected in their release from the obligation to finance the equalisation fund for decentralised functions.

Table 3.7 The PIT sharing scheme as of 1 January 2015 (in per cent)

Group	City or municipality	County	Decentralised functions	Equalisation grants for dec. functions	Grants for EU projects	Capital projects
Supported	88	12				
Zagreb	76.5		6	16	1.5	
Islands	60	16.5	6		1.5	16
Other	60	16.5	6	16	1.5	

Source: The Law on the Financing of Local and Regional Self-Government Units. Cells in grey indicate that the function in question is not subject to an income tax sharing arrangement at the indicated government level

Those LGUs financed their capital projects from the equalisation fund, financed by other LGUs. The preferential treatment in the PIT sharing system was most prominent in case of LGUs in supported areas, which retained 88 per cent of the PIT revenue, while their counties retained the remaining 12 per cent.

The PIT sharing system has multiple roles in local government financing. It is used as an instrument to reduce economic inequalities and to finance capital projects and decentralised functions. However, such multiple roles are undesirable and should be relaxed. It is particularly questionable whether this instrument can be effective in reducing fiscal inequalities. Given that certain groups of LGUs were granted a preferential status in the tax sharing system and an increased share of PIT revenues, it might be possible to use this instrument for fiscal equalisation. However, the criteria for preferential treatment should be based on the calculation of fiscal capacities, the needs of LGUs and the calculation of fiscal inequalities, which was not the case before 2018.

As already mentioned earlier in this chapter, fiscal equalisation has also relied on the allocation of several types of current grants distributed according to various criteria. A part of these grants was initially aimed at mitigating inequalities at the county level (Bronić, 2010). Several other types of current grants have been used for correcting or neutralising the adverse implications of fiscal measures which were introduced as ad hoc interventions without any prior fiscal impact analyses.

For example, LGUs in supported areas were entitled to higher shares in the PIT revenue. At the same time, their inhabitants benefited from increased amounts of non-taxable personal allowance, decreasing the tax base and the capacity of those LGUs to raise PIT revenue. To avoid cancelling those measures, the government undertook to finance the return of the PIT revenue in those areas from the central government budget in the form of grants.

Despite the perception that the system of intergovernmental grants and fiscal equalisation in general was developed in detail and properly organised, it was in fact unclear, non-transparent and inefficient and required a comprehensive review and reform (Primorac, 2015). Moreover, the system has been malfunctioning due to political reasons (Bajo & Primorac, 2017). Primorac (2014) proposed a possible reform path and demonstrated that equalising differences in capacity to collect revenue from the PIT and surtax would alleviates most of the inequalities in the fiscal capacities of LGUs much better than the existing system and at the same cost. In line with this proposal, a new fiscal equalisation system based on simple, sound and transparent criteria was introduced in 2018. It is expected that the new system will increase efficiency and fairness, as well as the credibility of fiscal equalisation in Croatia.

Conclusion

Despite the administrative and political decentralisation that began in 1991, Croatia is still a fiscally centralised state. Since the establishment of a legislative framework for fiscal decentralisation in 2001, the degree of decentralisation of revenues, expenses and taxes has increased. Nevertheless, the local government sector currently makes up only around 12 per cent of the general government budget.

In financing, LGUs mainly rely on part of the revenue from the personal income tax, which is shared according to a predetermined schedule. Additional revenue could be generated by introducing a property tax. The variability of the tax base that LGUs rely on has brought about a decrease in tax revenues since the financial crisis.

Due to restrictive borrowing limits, local governments have relatively low debt. However, local government borrowing limits are often bypassed through the public utility companies owned by the LGUs. Since 2005, LGUs have kept auxiliary records of guarantees, and should better plan the amount of their guarantee reserves in case the guarantees are called on. The financial operations of LGUs and their utility companies are interlinked. Nevertheless, the utility companies are usually considered as separate entities, and LGUs are not obliged to prepare consolidated financial reports.

Since Croatia became an EU member state, the focus of decentralisation policies has gradually shifted towards ensuring balanced regional development and fiscal equalisation. This dual focus has been the most confusing part of fiscal decentralisation in Croatia. Although it has been unclear which measures were implemented under regional development policy, and which measures were implemented under fiscal equalisation, both policies relied on granting special status to certain groups of LGUs. Unclear criteria for applying fiscal decentralisation that are neither simple nor transparent have created room for political manipulation and discretionary decision-making in favour of special interest groups.

Such political influence does not just affect the equalisation system, but the whole local government financing system can be altered for political reasons. The central government has gradually increased the share of LGUs in the PIT. However, this was not followed by an increase in LGU autonomy in determining the main elements of taxation. In this way, LGUs have become increasingly dependent on the tax, which is wholly designed at central government level. Besides creating a false sense of fiscal decentralisation, this gives central government the power to shuffle the parameters of the PIT, thus making it more or less burdensome to certain groups of taxpayers and dependent on political circumstances without harming the central government budget. Unfortunately, PIT sharing has become an instrument for satisfying multiple goals, including reducing economic inequalities, and financing favoured capital projects and decentralised functions. This is not a desirable state of affairs. Tax sharing should only be used to ease vertical fiscal imbalances due to the lack of local government revenue to finance the transferred decentralised functions. A single general tax sharing scheme should be established, possibly including a real estate transfer tax.

As a result of a lack of consistent long-term policies, the allocation of central government grants is complex, unclear and subject to sporadic alteration. Determining the index of development prescribed by the Regional Development Act was a great help in recognising and supporting the economically underdeveloped areas. However, the development index could not at the same time serve as a criterion for implementing fiscal equalisation policy. While the fiscal equalisation system may be usefully aligned with the objectives of regional development, it should not be identified with those objectives.

Due to the numerous dilemmas discussed in this chapter, fiscal decentralisation policies should be established with clear goals and proposals for their solution. Introducing a better system of territorial organisation and a better framework for functional and fiscal decentralisation are urgent issues for Croatia, for both fiscal reasons and to improve the capacities of all levels of government to absorb EU structural funds.

Notes

1. Law on the City of Zagreb, Official Gazette, No. 62/2001, 125/2008, 36/2009.
2. Law on the Financing of Local and Regional Self-Government Units, Official Gazette, No. 117/1993, 33/2000, 73/2000, 59/2001, 107/2001, 117/2001, 150/2002, 147/2003, 132/2006, 26/2007—the Decision of the Croatian Constitutional Court, 73/2008, 25/2012 and 147/2014.
3. Budget Act, Official Gazette, No. 87/2008, 136/2012.
4. To help selection of subnational government investment projects, on the basis of *open competition* and *technical criteria* (e.g. cost-benefit, social rate of return).
5. Constitution of the Republic of Croatia, Official Gazette, No. 56/90, 135/97, 8/98, 113/00, 124/00, 28/01, 41/01, 55/01, 76/10, 85/10, 05/14.

References

Bajo, A. (1999). Zašto i kako mjeriti fiskalni kapacitet lokalnih jedinica? *Financijska praksa, 23*(3), 277–308.

Bajo, A. (2004). Zaduživanje lokalnih jedinica u Hrvatskoj: Mogućnosti i ograničenja. *Financijska teorija i praksa, 28*(2), 203–218.

Bajo, A. (2009). The structure of employment in local government units. *Newsletter—An Occasional Publication of the Institute of Public Finance, 11*(43). Retrieved from http://www.ijf.hr/eng/newsletter/43.pdf

Bajo, A., & Bronić, M. (2004). Fiskalna decentralisacija u Hrvatskoj: Problemi fiskalnog izravnanja. *Financijska teorija i praksa, 28*(4), 445–467.

Bajo, A., & Bronić, M. (2007). Procjene učinkovitosti modela fiskalnog izravnanja u Hrvatskoj. *Financijska teorija i praksa, 31*(1), 1–24.

Bajo, A., & Primorac, M. (2010a). The financial operations of local utility companies in Croatia. *Newsletter—An Occasional Publication of the Institute of Public Finance, 12*(52). Retrieved from http://www.ijf.hr/eng/newsletter/52.pdf

Bajo, A., & Primorac, M. (2010b). Local government borrowing practice in Croatia. *Financial Theory and Practice, 34*(4), 379–406.

Bajo, A., & Primorac, M. (2013a). Package of legislative amendments for a better Croatian regional policy. *Press Release, 61*. https://doi.org/10.3326/pr.2013.61

Bajo, A., & Primorac, M. (2013b). Zagreb holding: Time for restructuring. *Newsletter—An Occasional Publication of the Institute of Public Finance, 15*(73). https://doi.org/10.3326/nle.2013.73

Bajo, A., & Primorac, M. (2014a). The debt and fiscal risks of local and regional self-government units in Croatia. *Newsletter—An Occasional Publication of the Institute of Public Finance, 16*(93). https://doi.org/10.3326/nle.2014.93

Bajo, A., & Primorac, M. (2014b). New tax revenue distribution between central government and units of local and regional self-government in Croatia. Press Release, 72. https://doi.org/10.3326/pr.2014.72.

Bajo, A., & Primorac, M. (2015a). Audit of local government-owned companies. *Press Release, 74*. https://doi.org/10.3326/pr.2013.74

Bajo, A., & Primorac, M. (2015b). Fifteenth amendments to the local government unit financing act. *Press Release, 84*. https://doi.org/10.3326/pr.2015.84

Bajo, A., & Primorac, M. (2017). Political economy of fiscal equalisation: The case of Croatia. *Lex Localis—Journal of Local Self-Government, 15*(2), 155–173.

Blažić, H. (2004). Fiskalna decentralisacija u Hrvatskoj: Usporedna analiza s Europskom unijom i zemljama u tranziciji. In N. K. Aksentijević et al. (Eds.), *Ekonomska decentralizacija i lokalna samouprava* (pp. 249–267). Rijeka: University of Rijeka; Cleveland: Cleveland State University.

Bronić, M. (2010). Evaluating the current equalisation grant to counties in Croatia. *Financial Theory and Practice, 34*(1), 25–52.

Central Bureau of Statistics—CBS. (2013). *Statistical Yearbook 2012—Correction*. Retrieved from https://www.dzs.hr/Hrv_Eng/ljetopis/2012/correction1.pdf

Jurlina-Alibegović, D. (Ed.). (2010). *Analitičke podloge za učinkovitu decentralizaciju u Hrvatskoj*. Project Study. Zagreb: Institute of Economics.

Ott, K., & Bajo, A. (2001). Lokalne financije i lokalni proračuni. *Financijska teorija i praksa, 23*(3), 311–449.

Ott, K., Bronić, M., & Stanić, B. (2016). EU grants to Croatian counties, cities and municipalities, 2011–14. *Newsletter—An Occasional Publication of the Institute of Public Finance, 16*(105). https://doi.org/10.3326/nle.2016.105

Primorac, M. (2011). Local government and utility firms' debts. *Financial Theory and Practice, 35*(4), 443–464.

Primorac, M. (2014). The restructuring of the fiscal equalisation system in Croatia. *Zbornik radova Ekonomskog fakulteta u Rijeci: časopis za ekonomsku teoriju i praksu, 32*(2), 213–232.

Primorac, M. (2015). The effectiveness of fiscal equalisation in Croatia. *Economic Research-Ekonomska Istraživanja, 28*(1), 299–311. https://doi.org/10.1080/1331677X.2015.1043780

Part II

Crisis, Policy Reversals, and Local Government Debt

4

Serbia: Local Government Financing and Non-transparency of Fiscal Data

Sanja Kmezić and Katarina Đulić

Introduction

This chapter studies the process of decentralisation in Serbia in the period 1990–2016, with a particular focus on fiscal decentralisation. In recent Serbian history, this period can be characterised as tectonic from both political-ideological and socio-economic perspectives. During this time-frame, there were two radical social shifts—in 1990 and in 2000. The first was a collapse from socialism to state implosion with the dismemberment of the Socialist Federal Republic of Yugoslavia (henceforth "former Yugoslavia"), ethnic wars, and the collapse of the economic system. The second shift was a transition from the authoritarian nationalistic regime and remnants of the planned economy to the democratisation of society

S. Kmezić (✉)
University of Graz, Graz, Austria

K. Đulić
Faculty of Economics, Finance and Administration, FEFA, Belgrade, Serbia
e-mail: kdjulic@fefa.edu.rs

W. Bartlett et al. (eds.), *Fiscal Decentralisation, Local Government and Policy Reversals in Southeastern Europe*, https://doi.org/10.1007/978-3-319-96092-0_4

and market-oriented economy. This latter transformation was supported by the process of decentralisation, one of the key policy avenues used to achieve societal change. In fact, in the 2000s Serbia formally opted for decentralisation in its strategic policy documents and, thus, the purpose of this chapter is to examine the state of decentralisation in each phase and its outlook at the end of the period.

We cover three major aspects of the decentralisation process—territorial-administrative, political and, in particular, fiscal decentralisation. At the beginning of the transition period, in the early 2000s, local authorities received new mandates for providing public goods and services to citizens, as well as a new role in implementing economic policy, which required additional funds and sources of revenue. However, there were frequent regulatory changes in local public finance, leading to instability and unpredictability of local revenues and eventually to an overall decrease in municipal budgets, jeopardising the delivery of the newly decentralised public services. This is why the decentralisation of functions and finance is at the heart of this study.

To fully understand all aspects of these processes, we analysed the legal framework and regulatory changes that occurred over the past 26 years, with a focus on the content and dynamics of change of key regulations. In addition, we carried out a fiscal analysis to measure the budgetary effects of the regulatory changes, to gauge the overall cumulative effect, and to determine the state of fiscal decentralisation at the end of the period. The latter task was rather challenging since we experienced serious difficulties in obtaining municipal budgetary data. The issue proved to be more complex since the lack of access and transparency has not only been an external problem blocking critical expert analysis, but also an internal problem preventing institutional supervision and control of the entire system of public finance (Fiscal Council of the Republic of Serbia, 2017). We believe that non-transparency of fiscal data is such a flaw in the system that it is the special focus of this chapter.

The chapter has two main parts. The first part covers the unfolding of the decentralisation processes over the period of transition. We first present the territorial and administrative organisation of the country and the changes that took place between 1990 and 2016. Second, we present the system of election of local councils and mayors, and the changes in the political decentralisation. Then we focus on intergovernmental fiscal relations. This section follows the evolution of fiscal decentralisation in Serbia and is structured around three distinct phases. We examine the phases through the lenses of the division of powers and finance between central and local governments. The first phase features fiscal centralisation during the 1990s. The second phase covers the wave of decentralisation, which started with the democratisation of the society in 2000 and lasted until the outbreak of the financial crisis in 2008. The third phase is characterised by pseudo-decentralisation and the return to centralisation, which is on-going. The second part is dedicated to non-transparency of data on fiscal revenues and expenditures, which is the root of the systemic problems of the Serbian public finance and intergovernmental fiscal system. This is the main problem we encountered during our study of local public finance. The concluding section presents an analysis of the state of decentralisation in Serbia 26 years after the collapse of the former Yugoslavia.

Territorial-Administrative Organisation of the Country

The first phase of decentralisation took place during the 1990s and brought tectonic changes to the territory of the former Yugoslavia. The disintegration of Yugoslavia through wars and armed conflicts led to the birth of new, independent states. Serbia and Montenegro remained in a union—first, in the Federal Republic of Yugoslavia until 2003, and then in the State Union of Serbia and Montenegro until 2006, when Montenegro declared its independence after a referendum.

At the start of that turbulent period, the (then Socialist) Republic of Serbia adopted the 1990 Constitution,[1] which abolished the autonomy of the provinces of Vojvodina and Kosovo. This was a consequence of President Milošević's political decision to completely concentrate power at the central level of the Republic. After the 1998–1999 war over the status of Kosovo, the provisional status of this province was defined by the United Nations Security Council's Resolution 1244.[2] When Serbia became an independent state in 2006, it adopted a new Constitution,[3] which re-established the two autonomous provinces, defining them once again as autonomous provinces. Kosovo's status is currently regulated in line with the UN resolution, as well as with the Advisory Opinion of the International Court of Justice (ICJ) on the unilateral declaration of independence of Kosovo.[4]

Essentially, Serbian territorial organisation has an asymmetric form of decentralisation. The greater part of the territory of the country has only two levels of government, central and local tiers, while the other part also has an intermediate, provincial level of government. Yet, the 2009 Law on Regional Development[5] created five *statistical* regions to introduce the Nomenclature of Units for Territorial Statistics (NUTS). These are statistical units necessary for planning and implementing regional policy and for the programming of future EU cohesion funds (Avlijaš & Bartlett, 2011). The statistical regions are Vojvodina, Belgrade, Šumadija and Western Serbia, Southern and Eastern Serbia, and Kosovo and Metohija.

According to the 2006 Decree on Administrative Counties,[6] there are 29 counties (out of which five are in Kosovo). The counties do not represent a level of government or a form of real decentralisation of power and public functions. Instead, they are a form of de-concentration of the central government and are regional branches of the national government's ministries and other state administration organisations and authorities.

The local level of government, which is the subject matter of our analysis, includes cities and municipalities as basic forms of local self-government. According to the 2007 Law on Territorial Organisation of the Republic of Serbia,[7] there are 174 local government units (or LGU) in Serbia, out of which 29 are in Kosovo. In our analysis, we focus on 145 Serbian LGUs—119 municipalities, 25 cities, and the city of Belgrade, which has a special legal status.

The Law on Regional Development has introduced a classification of LGUs based on their level of development[8]:

1. The first group includes the most developed LGUs, with a level of development above the national average GDP per capita. Out of the 145 LGUs, 20 fall in this group.

2. The second group includes municipalities with a level of development between 80 per cent and 100 per cent of the national average. There are 34 LGUs in this group.
3. The third group consists of municipalities with a development level between 60 per cent and 80 per cent of average GDP per capita. This is the largest group with 47 LGUs.
4. The fourth group includes municipalities with a development level below 60 per cent of GDP per capita, while those with a development level below 50 per cent of GDP per capita average are considered *devastated*. This group of least developed LGUs contains 44 municipalities, of which 19 are defined as devastated.

From the aspect of municipal finance, this classification is important because the amount of non-categorical intergovernmental grants per LGU is calculated using the methodology that takes into account its level of development.

Due to political instability, further territorial reorganisation became a highly sensitive issue, so administrative decentralisation and the redefinition of LGUs did not follow the developments in the area of functional and fiscal decentralisation. For political reasons, policymakers could not take the system of territorial-administrative decentralisation into account when decentralising functions and finance to the municipal level, and so it is questionable whether the decentralisation of provision of public goods and services to the local level was optimal and whether it reflected natural economic boundaries or economies of scale.

Political Decentralisation

During the 1990s, Serbian local governments were deprived of their key financial and development instruments—revenues and assets—and municipal political governance was strictly controlled by the authoritarian regime that was in place at the time. Serbian mayors were elected indirectly, through local councils, while the election of local council members was based on a proportional system. In the second half of the 1990s, both the resistance of citizens and the political opposition at the local level grew significantly, provoking the central government to exercise greater pressure and impose further financial restrictions on municipalities (Kmezić, Kaluđerović, Jocović, & Đulić, 2016; Levitas, 2004). After the overturn of the regime in October 2000, the new government initiated a process of democratisation and the strengthening of local communities. On the one hand, the government introduced a series of legislative changes aimed at a significant increase in municipal revenues. On the other hand, the key boost to the empowerment of citizens was the introduction of the direct election of mayors in 2002 through a new Law on Local Self-Government,[9] which aimed to enhance political accountability and responsibility at the local level. Despite its advantages, this law was repealed as early as 2006 by the new Constitution,[10] which recognises only the local council (municipal assembly) as the main governing body of local government. The Constitution did not explicitly mention mayors, but rather left this matter to be regulated by future local government legislation. Already in 2007, the new Law on Local Self-Government[11] abolished the direct election of mayors and re-established the old system of the 1990s. The indirect election of mayors by municipal councils remains in place to this day. When it comes to the election of members of local councils, the system has not changed over the entire period. The latest legislative solution from the 2007 Law on Local Elections[12] still envisages the proportional system, that is, local representatives are elected from the lists proposed by political parties/coalitions or groups of citizens.

The system of direct election of mayors in Serbia proved to have many advantages in comparison to the indirect system. First, when citizens directly elect mayors, these officials not only have much greater legitimacy, but also express greater political accountability, personal responsibility, and freedom in decision-making. Second, the directly elected mayors are more resistant to pressures from central government coalitions and partisan politics. When the municipal assembly elects the mayors, that is, indirectly, their position to rule depends on the local governing coalition, which most frequently reflects political coalitions at the central level. Recent political history in Serbia has clearly shown that whenever the national government would change, the municipal ruling coalition would also change due to partisan pressures. Namely, in this system, a mayor's freedom of decision-making is substantially reduced and always dependent on the local council's partisan support (Kmezić, Kaluđerović, et al., 2016).

The described events in the domain of political decentralisation stand in sharp contrast to the positive trends in decentralisation of public functions and finance that were in full swing in the same period of the early 2000s. While the regulatory framework was directed towards establishing greater fiscal capacity and autonomy of local governments, the reversal of the trend in the local election of mayors indicated that the central government had no strategic commitment to decentralisation. It also revealed that there was no true desire for democratisation and citizens' political empowerment. Rather, it showed that local democracy was perceived solely through the prism of current partisan interests.

Intergovernmental Fiscal Relationships between 1990 and 2016

In the following sections, we analyse fiscal relationships between central and local governments and the system of municipal financing in Serbia during the transition period. This period of 26 years has seen seismic changes in the political and socio-economic history of Serbia. Three distinct phases can be identified: (1) the period 1990–2000 had a highly centralised authoritarian management of public affairs and provision of public services; (2) the period 2000–2008 was characterised by a rapid decentralisation of public functions and revenues within the context of general democratisation of the society and strong economic growth; and (3) the period 2009–2016 has been dominated by re-centralisation, particularly in the domain of public revenues, primarily the result of the global economic crisis that hit Serbia from 2009 onwards. In an effort to analyse local government budgets over this period, we faced serious difficulties in collecting data on municipal revenues and expenditures. Our quest for fiscal data and implications of non-transparency are deconstructed in a special section of this chapter, following our analysis of the process of fiscal decentralisation.

Phase 1: The First Wave of Fiscal Centralisation (1990–2000)

The former Yugoslavia experienced an economic crisis that culminated towards the end of the 1980s. The need for reform coincided with the tectonic global political changes and the trend of transition from planned to market-oriented economies. The first attempts at radical transition reform started in 1989 and included the reform of the public finance and fiscal system. The then federal government adopted a tax reform programme in 1990, which set the grounds for a new tax (fiscal) system. However, this federal programme was never implemented due to serious political instability in Yugoslavia (Stojanović, 2002).

At that time, the system of public finance was quite decentralised in the whole federation, including the fiscal system in Serbia, one of its republics. In the general atmosphere of political instability, the authoritarian regime of Slobodan Milošević started to concentrate power at the central (republican) level by adopting the new Constitution of the Republic of Serbia in 1990.[13] The Constitution changed the internal territorial and administrative organisation of the Republic, abolishing the existence of the two autonomous provinces and decreasing responsibilities and resources of local governments. The role of municipalities was reduced to the provision of the most basic administrative and utility services.[14] The Republic of Serbia centralised all social sector services, keeping the possibility to delegate some of these powers to the local level, together with the necessary, financial resources (Stojanović, 2005).

On the basis and principles of the never implemented federal fiscal reform programme, the Republic of Serbia introduced a new tax system in 1992, in order to conform it to the systems in market-oriented economies (Stojanović, 2002). One of the key changes in the new budgetary-fiscal framework was the establishment of the reformed intergovernmental fiscal governance. The main goal of this reform was to found a transparent, neutral, and fair tax system. Fiscal relationships between the newly established federation (the Federal Republic of Yugoslavia) and the Republic of Serbia were structured on a shared-revenue basis. On the other hand, the system within the Republic included both the revenues shared between the Republic and the local government as well as the local (municipal) own-source revenues. Shared revenues included revenues from the sales tax, the personal income tax, the property tax, and the revenues from various fees and charges. Own-source revenues, although administered by local governments, were always introduced by legislation adopted at the republican level. The 1992 law regulating public revenues and expenditures[15] defined the following levies as local own-source revenues: (1) local communal fees, (2) the construction land use charge, (3) the construction land development charge, (4) self-contribution, and (5) other revenues collected by local governments.[16] This system established in 1992 is the foundation of today's local government finance.

A new set of tax amendments was passed as early as in January 1994, as part of the new economic reform programme aimed at addressing the problems caused by the 1992–1993 hyperinflation and the international economic embargo (Stojanović, 2002). Responding to a huge budgetary deficit, the Government of Serbia started introducing a series of ad hoc fiscal levies. Although these levies were meant to be temporary, the prolonged budgetary difficulties transformed them into recurrent fiscal revenues. By the year 2000, the Serbian public finance system included more than 235 different impositions (Popović, 2000). This ad hoc fiscal mannerism, as an instrument in economic crisis management, would again become the accepted default model of governance in the post-2009 crisis period, which will be discussed in the sections to follow.

Apart from constantly introducing new fiscal levies, between 1992 and 2000, the Government of Serbia was also continuously changing the whole tax system by amending fiscal legislation and regulations. In fact, government decrees became the main instrument for conducting fiscal policy. At the end of this period, the tax system was distorted to the extent that it entirely departed from the original 1992 concept. For instance, one of the main ideas that was abandoned was the introduction of the less avoidable form of the consumption tax—the value-added tax (VAT) (Popović, 1999), a source of revenue that would wait for its full implementation for more than a decade. Thus, instead of achieving the promised stable, transparent, neutral, and fair fiscal framework, the country ended up with a totally perverted system.

During the 1990s, the lack of intergovernmental fiscal predictability and transparency became Milošević's means for fighting political opponents who were gaining power at the local level. Since local governments were predominantly financed from the shared sales tax, they were becoming increasingly fiscally dependent, as the amount to be transferred to municipalities was at the discretion of the central government. The decision on the amount was passed annually without clear criteria. The central government also transferred other supplementary funds (grants) to certain municipalities for the purpose of fiscal equalisation, again without clear and transparent criteria (Stojanović, 2005), which gave the government an instrument for supporting its local political and partisan allies.[17]

Not only was the government limiting financial resources to municipalities where the opposition was in power, but it also restricted municipal management of public property. Namely, in order to further curb local government resources, the regime passed legislation in 1995 that centralised the public property management system. According to this law,[18] if municipalities wanted to manage or dispose of a piece of "public" property on their territories, they needed to obtain the central government's permission.

Milošević's centralised intergovernmental fiscal policy served two major purposes at the same time—it was an instrument for responding to harsh economic conditions of the 1990s and a powerful tool for controlling political opponents at the local level. The fall of his regime and the democratic changes in 2000 also led to changes in the fiscal discourse. Concretely, local communities and opposition leaders at the municipal level were a major political force behind the overturn of Milošević. Hence, their contribution to democratisation created a legitimate claim of financially deprived local communities for a shift of the pendulum towards fiscal decentralisation.

Phase 2: The Wave of Fiscal Decentralisation (2000–2008)

The year 2000 was a turning point in Serbia, which led to an overall discontinuity with the previous authoritarian regime. The overturn of

Milošević triggered socio-economic transition processes including democratisation, public administration reform, privatisation, and other important systemic changes. Besides local political actors, the international donor community also had a key role in initiating and formulating the transition agenda. The main pillars of the public administration and public finance reforms were local government reform and fiscal decentralisation (Kmezić, Đulić, Jocović, & Kaluđerović, 2016). The wave of decentralisation lasted until the first spillover effects of the global economic crisis in Serbia in 2009.

Between 2000 and 2008, the Government of Serbia adopted strategic public administration documents, a new Constitution, and a series of laws and regulations aimed at implementing the decentralisation agenda to strengthen the role of cities and municipalities in performing public services. In particular, the Government of Serbia adopted the Public Administration Reform Strategy in 2004, which proclaimed decentralisation as one of the overarching goals. The new Serbian Constitution was adopted in 2006, reinstating the autonomous provinces. The parallel fiscal reform was grounded in the principles set back in 1992. The rationale behind this was to create a modern public finance system compatible with market-oriented economies (Stojanovic & Timofeev, 2005). Even before the new Constitution was adopted, the Autonomous Province of Vojvodina regained its fiscal autonomy and started again to participate in revenue-sharing as of 2002.[19]

During the period 2000–2008, the role of local governments evolved significantly, and the municipal finance system was redesigned. The paragraphs to follow will first focus on decentralisation of the delivery of public services and new municipal mandates and then on the architecture of the new municipal finance system.

The Functions of Local Governments Between 2000 and 2008

The purview of municipal functions was expanded as early as in 2002 with the adoption of the Law on Local Self-Government.[20] In addition to performing a set of basic local government services, which previously included utility and communal services, planning and development, local road and utility infrastructure investment and management, and municipal administrative services, cities and municipalities got an important role in performing functions in the social sector. Namely, local governments gained full competence over providing preschool education, the responsibility for covering capital maintenance and utility costs of elementary and high schools, as well as the responsibility for managing primary healthcare institutions. Furthermore, local governments got the right to provide additional social protection to the citizens on their territories.

Another major change occurred with a new set of amendments to this law in 2007.[21] First, the amendments confirmed two important competences introduced the year before (a) by the Constitution—the right of municipalities to manage their own property[22]—and (b) by the Law on Local Government Finance[23]—the right to set the rates and criteria for determining the amount of their own-source revenues. Second, the 2007 law defined some new local government functions: the right to develop and implement local economic development policies and projects, the mandate to provide substantial social protection and assistance to vulnerable populations, new competences in the area of human rights protection, as well as the responsibility to finance local culture. The 2002 and 2007 sets of competences and the new role of local governments required substantial resources, which assumed simultaneous changes and an increase in municipal funding.

Local Government Fiscal Revenues Between 2000 and 2008

In early 2001, immediately after the change of government in Serbia, the Parliament adopted the first legal amendments to the Law on Public Revenue and Public Expenditure[24] and the Law on Local Self-Government,[25] in order to strengthen local communities that had been financially weakened during the previous regime. Municipalities got an increased share in the collected property tax (from 25 per cent to 100 per cent), an increased rate for the real estate transfer tax (from 3 per cent to 5 per cent), the right to impose the payroll tax (up to 3.5 per cent), and an increased share in the sojourn fee (from 80 per cent to

100 per cent). Another financial boost for municipalities was introduced with the new Law on Local Self-Government in 2002,[26] when municipalities got 100 per cent of the share from most of the types of the personal income tax. Further, the share of municipalities in the revenues generated from the sales tax was increased to 8 per cent for municipalities, 10 per cent for cities, and 15 per cent for the capital city. The law also confirmed that the whole amount of revenues (100 per cent) collected from the property tax, the inheritance and gift tax, the real estate transfer tax, and the payroll tax belonged to local governments. Finally, the law prescribed that local governments are entitled to a share in certain charges coming from the use of common goods and natural resources on their territories.

In 2004, two systemic changes occurred—first, the abolition of the locally administered payroll tax and, second, the introduction of the VAT that replaced the sales tax.[27] These amendments had a serious negative effect on municipal budgets since the payroll and sales taxes were principal sources of local revenues. The central government increased the municipal share in the personal income tax from 5 per cent to 30 per cent, and later to 40 per cent, as well as additional grants, in order to compensate for financial losses. However, the compensatory grants proved to be only a transitory solution since they were not sufficient to close the financial gap at the local level. It became clear that such a major change as the introduction of the VAT required a redesign of the entire system of local government finance.

Similar to its engagement in other transition efforts in the country, the international donor community provided ample financial and technical support to fiscal decentralisation and local government reform in Serbia. The donor organisations, in particular the Council of Europe and USAID, provided advice and assistance to the Serbian association of local authorities to create a new system of municipal financing and draft the Law on Local Government Finance,[28] which was adopted in 2006.

The main goal of the law was to build a sound and consolidated system that would enable objective, transparent, and predictable local revenues. The law introduced two novelties: (a) decentralisation of the whole administration of the property tax, including determining the tax base and rate and managing the collection, and (b) a new model of intergovernmental grants for achieving horizontal and vertical balance. Municipal revenues are divided into three major categories:

1. own-source revenues, which include the property tax, administrative and communal fees, the charges on construction land use and development, and other local levies;
2. shared revenues, where the central government transfers to the local level 100 per cent of the collected real estate transfer tax, the inheritance and gift tax, and certain types of the personal income tax; 40 per cent of the collected wage tax based on an employee's residence; as well as different shares of the collected charges for using common goods and natural resources;
3. intergovernmental grants, which can be non-earmarked (non-categorical) and earmarked. Namely, 1.7 per cent of the country's GDP is transferred as non-earmarked grants to municipalities for horizontal and vertical equalisation. The right to horizontal equalisation is granted to a municipality that realises revenues from shared taxes below 90 per cent of the Serbian average (excluding large cities). The general transfer, which serves for vertical equalisation, is calculated based on the number of citizens and the area of the municipality, the number of structures and the number of classes in primary and secondary schools, and the number of structures and children in preschools in a municipality. Earmarked grants are ad hoc funds transferred to municipalities for specific functions and purposes.

The effects of the second phase of fiscal decentralisation on local government budgets were visible already at the very beginning of the period. For instance, as we can see in Table 4.1, local government revenues grew by more than 220 per cent from 2000 until 2004. Furthermore, the revenues of the capital city of Belgrade increased more than ten times between 2000 and 2006.

The 2006 law showed even more remarkable effects on local government finance in the budgetary years 2007 and 2008. First, it managed to substantially diminish fiscal inequalities between the richest and the poorest local governments. In addition, the revenues from property taxation and intergovernmental grants started to grow significantly.

Table 4.1 Total revenue of LGUs and their share in GDP, in CSD[a] million

Year	Nominal value of total revenues of LGUs	Real value of total revenues of LGUs (2004 prices)	Index (base year 2000)	GDP	Total local revenues (% of GDP)
2000	13,341	36,743	–	355,168	3.8
2001	30,434	44,371	120.8	708,442	4.3
2002	55,319	67,662	184.1	919,230	6.0
2003	68,196	74,674	203.2	1,088,000	6.3
2004[a]	81,421	81,421	221.6	1,284,100	6.3

Source: Stipanović (2006, p. 9)
[a]For 2004, Stipanović used the data on planned revenue

All of the described regulatory changes, which culminated with the adoption of the 2006 law, drastically strengthened local government budgets during the entire observed period. The law seemed to have fulfilled its aims to create objective, transparent, and predictable local revenues and additionally increase municipal budgets. However, the spillover effects of the 2008 financial crisis forestalled the growth of local government budgets and stopped further decentralisation.

Phase 3: Pseudo-Decentralisation and Renewal of Fiscal Centralisation (2009–2016)

As early as the first half of 2009, the Serbian central government faced serious fiscal difficulties provoked by the financial crisis. In order to fill the gaps on the revenue side of the national budget, the Serbian Ministry of Finance drastically reduced intergovernmental transfers to local governments by suspending the grant formula prescribed by the law.[29] Although initially the measure was expected to be only temporary, it became the first step of the new trend—the phase of re-centralisation and pseudo-decentralisation. This phase is characterised by:

1. Frequent ad hoc transfers of new functions (expenditure) to the local level without the allocation of the necessary funding;
2. Continuous ad hoc abolishment of and decrease in municipal revenue or change of methodology of calculation of municipal revenue;
3. Vertical imbalance between local revenue and expenditure (Kmezić, Kaluđerović, et al., 2016).

These measures created a policy of discretionary, non-transparent, unstable, and unpredictable local government financing.

Delegation of Functions Between 2009 and 2016

The fundamental problem with the delegation of functions in the period 2009–2016 was a complete lack of policy analysis, which would determine the optimal way of providing public goods and services to citizens, and thus, the optimal level of decentralisation. Not only have policymakers not provided economic argumentation and rationale for the adequate division of tasks between the central and local levels, but they also have failed to conduct any financial analysis that would assess the costs of service delivery and the necessary resources. For instance, local governments became responsible for providing primary healthcare to citizens on their territories. Apart from substantial municipal expenditures, this particular transfer also entailed additional hidden costs like the debt of healthcare centres and public pharmacies. At the same time, the central government neither changed the grant formula to account for primary healthcare expenditures nor did it appropriate new sources of revenue for local governments.

Moreover, such a flawed approach to the intergovernmental division of functions was further exacerbated by the fact that local authorities were completely excluded from the policy dialogue. Namely, the central government authorities responsible for policy- and legislation-making regularly failed to ensure any meaningful participation of municipalities in these processes. Furthermore, the central government often resorted to using inadequate legal instruments for the delegation of new mandates/expenditures like government decrees, decisions, rulebooks, and so on. Governing by bylaws instead of laws allowed the central government to behave opportunistically and to quickly respond to the immediate needs of the central budget, treating, in these processes, the local governments as parastatal bodies rather than as integral parts of the government. On the other side, such an "adhocracy" created an unstable, unpredictable, and non-transparent environment for local governance, negatively affecting municipal budgets and local resources. By amending *decrees*, the central government changed the methodology for calculating salaries for public employees in preschool education, cultural institutions, and local administration, which significantly exceeded the planned expenditures in the local budgets. Further, until recently, the base for the calculation and payment of salaries of all public sector employees had been regulated by the most non-transparent legal instrument—a government *decision*—an act that is not published in the Official Gazette. Also, many aspects of preschool education and the accompanying costs are regulated by *rulebooks*, and thus, are beyond the sphere of influence of local governments. Finally, salaries and other benefits of employees in educational and cultural institutions were subject to *collective bargaining* between the central government and unions only, but some costs ended up as the financial responsibility of local governments. This manner of transferring new expenditures to the local level is contrary to the Constitution, the Law on Local Self-Government, and the Law on Local Government Finance, which prescribe that new functions and expenditures can be delegated only by law, while the resources must be provided in the central government's budget.[30] Not only was there a lack of vertical intergovernmental consultation, but the policymaking process also lacked horizontal coordination between the ministries that delegate functions and the Ministry of Finance, which allocates resources. A lack of strategic planning and monitoring of decentralisation resulted in institutional inefficiency and legal uncertainty and, generally, showed a deep misunderstanding of the concept of fiscal decentralisation. Figure 4.1 illustrates the multitude of changes that led to an increase of expenditures at the local level during the timeline of the phase 2009–2016,

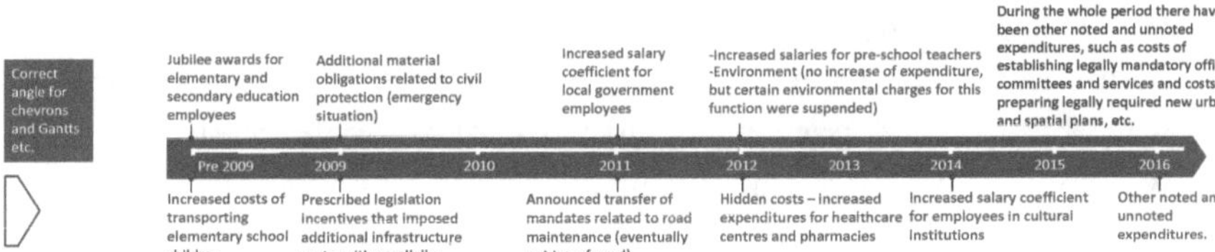

Fig. 4.1 Chronological overview of the increase in local government expenditures due to new mandates delegated by the central government between 2009 and 2016

which we call the wave of re-centralisation and pseudo-decentralisation. In addition to the fact that adequate resources did not accompany new expenditures, the existing sources of revenues were also abolished, suspended, or reduced in the observed period, which we will describe in the following paragraphs.

Local Government Finance Between 2009 and 2016

The phase of fiscal decentralisation formally ended in 2009, when the Serbian government, pressured by the increasing budgetary deficit, reduced non-earmarked grants to local governments and suspended the grant provisions of the Law on Local Government Finance. The central government adopted this measure in April, that is, in the middle of the budgetary year with an immediate effect and without any previous consultation with or warning to local authorities. Such an action would become the default model of governing in the years to follow. The government was altering the system incessantly, changing almost every source of revenue in every single group of local revenues. The changes on the revenue side were so frequent that it is a challenge to even track them all. There were at least 15 changes that we identified:

1. It started with the mentioned suspension of the formula for the calculation of non-earmarked transfers, which reduced the amount of grants from 1.7 per cent of the GDP to approximately 1 per cent of the GDP. This change, introduced in April 2009, lasted until mid-2011 and incurred a loss of RSD 50 billion to municipal budgets (Spirić & Bućić, 2012).
2. In 2011, the central government made a pseudo-decentralistic move by increasing the municipal share in the revenues collected from the wage tax from 40 per cent to 80 per cent.[31] However, this measure was soon annulled by new centralistic solutions when the government decreased the wage tax base and rate (from 12 per cent to 10 per cent).[32]
3. In the same year, the central government changed the methodology for the calculation of non-earmarked transfers, leading to greater non-transparency and unpredictability.[33]

4. In 2012, the central government amended this methodology again, further degrading the transparency of the formula.[34]
5. Under the pretext of improving the business climate at the local level, the central government abolished a number of local communal fees, as well as shared charges for using common goods and natural resources, resulting in a total local loss of RSD 5.5 billion. The hypocrisy of the government's measures towards improving the investment climate is showed by the fact that it simultaneously increased taxes and other levies financing the national budget (Kmezić, Kaluđerović, et al., 2016).
6. In 2013, the central government implemented the already-mentioned changes in the wage tax calculation, leading to additional losses at the local level.[35] Namely, instead of receiving the expected RSD 40 billion, local governments ended up with half of the planned amount (Spirić & Bućić, 2012).
7. The Law on the Property Tax was amended in 2013 with the aim of boosting the impoverished local budgets by allowing municipalities to tax legal entities by using the fair market value of the property to determine the tax base.[36] These amendments, however, failed to provide the expected amount of revenues.
8. The amendments to the Law on the Personal Income Tax reclassified the real estate rental income tax from local to central budgetary revenue.[37] This created an additional loss of RSD 3 billion in local budgets (Kmezić, Kaluđerović, et al., 2016).
9. In 2013, the Ministry of Finance introduced changes in the methodology for the calculation of administrative fees. Although the rationale behind this rulebook was to introduce transparency in the system of administrative fees, its provisions have never been implemented in practice.[38]
10. The persistently growing budgetary deficit at the national level was the reason for the reduction in non-earmarked transfers by RSD 3.7 billion in December 2013 for the following budgetary year.[39]
11. The same reduction happened again in December 2014 for the following budgetary year.[40]
12. In 2014, the obsolete construction land use charge was finally abolished with the justification that this fiscal relict was replaced with

modern property taxation of legal entities.[41] Yet, as mentioned above, the new levy failed to compensate for the losses of the old high-yielding revenue. The gross effect of the loss was estimated to be RSD 14 billion (Kmezić, Kaluđerović, et al., 2016).

13. The 2014 amendments to the Law on Planning and Construction introduced changes to another construction land-related revenue. The municipally administered construction land development charge was reformed and renamed "contribution".[42] Whether this change will incur gains or losses for local budgets remains to be seen.
14. In 2015, the Ministry of Finance adopted a new change to the methodology for the calculation of non-earmarked transfers.[43]
15. In October 2016, the Parliament adopted the amendments to the Law on Local Government Finance in order to reduce the shares of local governments in revenues collected from the wage tax.[44] The share of cities was reduced from 80 per cent to 77 per cent, the share of municipalities was reduced from 80 per cent to 74 per cent, while the share of the capital city of Belgrade was reduced from 70 per cent to 66 per cent. The latest amendments were expected to generate annual fiscal savings for the central government of RSD 4.8 billion annually as of 2017 (or 0.1 per cent of the GDP per year from 2017) (IMF, 2016).

To sum up, after listing all these changes, it is redundant to say that local governments have faced complete legal uncertainty and financial unpredictability. Figure 4.2 shows the timeline of the described changes on the revenue side (with the exception of the last changes).

In addition to its "adhocratic" nature, the major problem of Serbian intergovernmental fiscal governance is that it has not been embedded in any financial planning, that is, in any ex ante or ex post analysis. The implications of such an approach are that institutions cannot understand the real problems and local government needs and address them specifically, nor can they assess the effects and consequences of the implemented policy measures. The following chapter examines the issue of non-transparency of fiscal data and the inadequacy of databases, which prevent financial planning and policy analyses.

Correct angle for chevrons and Gantts etc.

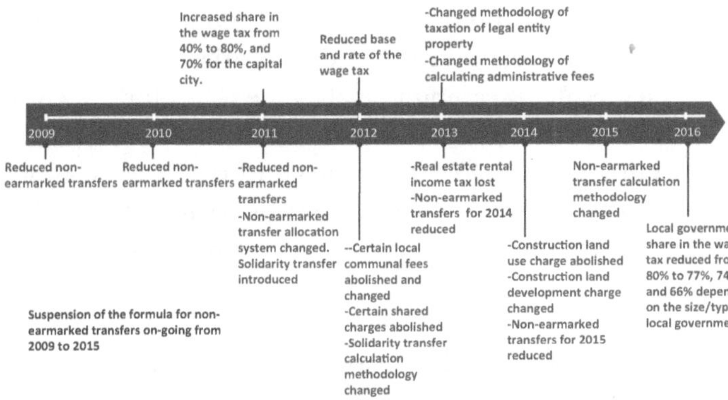

Fig. 4.2 Chronological overview of changes in local government revenues due to changes in central government regulations between 2009 and 2016

The Non-transparency of Fiscal Data and Its Implications

In this section, we discuss the problem of non-transparency of local public finance, including detailed data on municipal budgetary revenues and expenditures. As previously demonstrated, the lack of adequate data prevents a precise and comprehensive scrutiny of the fiscal effects of the intense regulatory changes, which have marked intergovernmental fiscal governance in Serbia. Namely, not only is the data non-transparent, but the existing databases are also not accurate, complete, well-managed, or integrated. In order to clarify the state of the databases with municipal fiscal data, we present here what types of information are, or might be, accessible to the public:

The Ministry of Finance of the Republic of Serbia issues monthly bulletins of public finance. This publication presents the aggregate data on total local government revenues and expenditures. In the category of revenues, there are total aggregate data on (a) the total current revenues (class seven), (b) the total proceeds from the sale of non-financial assets (class eight), and (c) the total proceeds from borrowing and the sale of financial assets (class nine). In the category of expenditures, there are total aggregate data on (a) the current expenditures (class four), (b) the expenses for non-financial assets (class five), and (c) the expenses for principal repayment and the acquisition of non-financial assets (class six). There are data on certain very broad categories of revenues; however, the sums are aggregate, meaning that they are totals for the entire local government population in Serbia. For instance, there is a total for the (locally collected) property tax for the entire country, but it is impossible to see how much is administered by each local government unit. The total sums for other individual sources of revenue are not available, so one cannot see, for instance, the collected amounts for other municipal tax or non-tax revenue sources (e.g. The December 2016 Bulletin of the Ministry of Finance of the Republic of Serbia). On the expenditure side, the data are available for certain categories of expenditures (based on the so-called economic classification of expenditures), but they are also the total sums for the entire local government population in the country. For instance, one can see the total local expenses for the municipal civil servants, for subsidies, or for social benefits paid from local budgets, but again, not per each municipality. Based on the type of data provided in the bulletins of the Ministry of Finance, we can calculate basic indicators, which are most frequently used in the literature (Bloechliger, 2013; Buser, 2011; Calamai, 2009; Cantarero & Gonzalez, 2009; Ezcurra & Pascual, 2008; Iimi, 2005; Rodriguez-Pose, 2009; Rodriguez-Pose & Bwire, 2004; Sagbas, Sen, & Kar, 2005; Thiessen, 2003; Woller & Phillips, 1998) to determine the level of fiscal decentralisation in a country—the share of total local government revenue or expenditure in total (consolidated) general government revenue or expenditure and in the GDP. The bulletin also provides information on revenues and expenditures per type of local government unit. So, the share of the city of Belgrade is 31.8 per cent, the share of cities is 32.7 per cent, and the share of municipalities is 35.5 per cent of all local revenues. On the expenditure side, the share of the city of Belgrade is 31.9 per cent, the share of cities is 32.1 per cent, and the share of municipalities is 36.0 per cent (The December 2016 Bulletin of the Ministry of Finance of the Republic of Serbia).

The Statistical Office of the Republic of Serbia annually issues the publication on municipalities and regions (e.g. The 2015 Report on Municipalities and Regions in the Republic of Serbia). This yearbook presents information on the totals and the already-mentioned broad, aggregate categories of revenues and expenditures for the entire population of all 145 Serbian local government units (municipalities, cities, and the city of Belgrade). Unlike the bulletin of the Ministry of Finance, this yearbook presents the said categories for each individual local government unit. However, there is no information on specific revenue and expenditure budgetary items. For instance, while one can see the total current revenues and expenditures for the City of Kragujevac or the Municipality of Bujanovac, one cannot see how much money these local governments collected from specific sources of revenues or spent on specific expenditure items. Such in-depth data would be valuable information for any meaningful and thorough fiscal analysis.

Local governments seem to be the only ones who manage and can issue the detailed data on all specific budgetary revenue and expenditure items. In their budgetary reports, which are or should be available to the public, one can see the precise data on each group of revenues—(a) own-source revenues, (b) shared revenues, (c) grants/transfers, and (d) other revenues—as well as on each individual source of revenue within these groups. In the same manner, municipalities manage and categorise the data on specific expenditure items based on the so-called economic and functional classifications of expenses. As already mentioned, while the functional classification presents expenditures in accordance with the United Nations Statistical Department's list of functions (e.g. administration, education, healthcare, security and public safety, and environmental protection), the economic classification gives us an insight into certain broader groups of economic expenses, such as the ones for municipal civil servants, subsidies, donations and grants, and social benefits. In order to analyse expenditure trends within certain functions, the data classified based on both economic and functional classification should be available and transparent (e.g. to analyse the salary expenditure trends for a municipal administration or to explore capital investment trends in education). However, the practical problem with municipal data is the fact that local governments use different software packages for database management and issue the data in different digital forms or, very often, exclusively in hard copy. These facts significantly complicate technical integration, cleaning, and comparison of municipal fiscal data.

More disturbingly, even though the data exist, local governments often ignore their legal obligation to disclose them. Moreover, they often fail to respond to official requests for access to this public information. Our personal experience in efforts to obtain budgetary data from local governments demonstrates this point. In an attempt to conduct a study on local government finance on a stratified random sample, we submitted multiple enquiries to 13 sampled local governments. Only two responded—the capital city of Belgrade and one of the most transparent and efficient local governments in Serbia, the Municipality of Paraćin. Yet, Belgrade provided the revenue data in hard copy and PDF files with non-cleaned and non-comprehensive expenditure data. On the other hand, Paraćin has been the only Serbian local government that provided us with complete fiscal data in an electronic form.

The Treasury Administration is an authority under the auspices of the Ministry of Finance that should be responsible for collecting and managing detailed municipal budgetary revenue and expenditure data for the entire population of 145 local government units. Our experience with the Ministry of Finance and its Treasury Administration reflects the Kafkaesque nature of the bureaucratic procedure for accessing public financial information in Serbia. In our attempt to obtain the necessary data for scientific research, we submitted official requests for access to public information to both institutions. The Ministry of Finance redirected us to the Treasury Administration, stating that it did not possess the requested information.[45] In a response to our first request to access the detailed fiscal data for all 145 local government units for the period 2006–2014, the Treasury Administration denied to issue this public information stating that "the data requested cover extensive materials, requiring a disproportionately large effort by the authority in question, which would substantially compromise its regular functioning in terms of performing tasks related to state administration."[46] We then submitted a second request for the same type of data and time period, reducing the number of municipalities to the sample of 13. However, the Treasury Administration denied this demand, too, providing a new justification—that it did not possess these data—redirecting us (back) to the Ministry of Finance.[47] The ultimate absurdity was that both institutions instructed us to file a complaint with the Commissioner for Information of Public

Importance. Upon receiving our complaint, the Commissioner's office explained that it did not have adequate inspection and enforcement mechanisms in cases when public authorities claim that they do not possess the requested public information. This vicious cycle of our roaming through meanders of the bureaucratic maze offers evidence that Serbian public authorities are not willing to ensure transparency of financial and budgetary data. After all our efforts, we are still not clear on (a) whether the authority—the Treasury Administration—responsible for tracking and recording municipal budgetary data does or does not possess this information; (b) in the case that it does, what kind of data it has (e.g. how complete and accurate the database is, what type of database format it uses, which budgetary years are covered, etc.); and (c) what are the real reasons behind non-transparency. In relation to this last point, we have to emphasise that claims from unofficial sources that these public institutions possess the relevant information have been confirmed by representatives of the association of municipalities and the Fiscal Council. This selective approach to transparency is demonstrated by the fact that the administration's data were used as a source in a number of publications analysing own-source revenues, shared revenues, and transfers, as well as expenditures based on the economic classification, including the analyses published by the Fiscal Council.

Not only do taxpayers, academic researchers, and other interested groups face the problem of non-transparent fiscal data, but institutions involved in the legislative and public policymaking processes also deal with the same challenges. To illustrate, the Ministry of Finance established an expert working group for drafting new legislation on local government financing in the fall of 2015, gathering different stakeholders. The members of the working group, including the representatives of the Serbian association of local authorities (gathering all 145 local government units), were supposed to run financial simulations, test different policy options, prepare fiscal impact projections in order to come up with optimal solutions, and draft the text of the law. Despite the delegated mandates, the working group was denied access to detailed fiscal data needed to perform any serious fiscal analysis. Instead of providing the working group with the necessary information, the representatives of the Ministry of Finance came up with a draft law without an accompanying analysis to substantiate the proposed solutions. Representatives of other institutions in the group were thus prevented from providing any meaningful input and objected the draft law by issuing a negative opinion. Nonetheless, the Ministry of Finance continued with the legislative procedure and initiated the phase of public hearing. The mayors of a large majority of cities and municipalities put aside their partisan differences and jointly voiced their opposition through the association of local governments, succeeding to stop the legislative procedure.[48] A year later, the mayors and the Ministry of Finance reached a consensus on the text of the legislation. However, the final solutions were the consequence of political agreement and not a result of any evidence-based fiscal analysis.

This apparently unreasonable and illogical behaviour of the Ministry of Finance is ultimately illustrated with its opinion issued in October 2016, to the Ministry of Public Administration and Local Self-Government (MPALSG), regarding the open government initiative. Namely, the MPALSG launched the project Partnership for Open Administration. One of the aims of this project was to establish an obligation for partner institutions to provide open and transparent data in digital form. The immediate response of the Ministry of Finance was negative. First, it insisted on excluding itself from the obligation to share the national budget and the final report on budget execution in an open, electronic form suitable for digital manipulation of the data necessary for any technical analysis. In its opinion, the Ministry of Finance justified its decision by stating that "publicising the data in any form other than pdf can endanger the accuracy of the publicised data". Moreover, the Ministry of Finance claimed that publicising the data in an open, electronic form suitable for digital manipulation of data "could lead to wrong conclusions and analyses due to the poor knowledge of public finance and the budgetary process of the Republic of Serbia" that interested parties might possess. Finally, as a response to the MPALSG's proposal to create an online application for monitoring the spending of public financial resources and, thus, ensuring the public supervision of stewardship, the Ministry of Finance took a quite negative position. It compromised the good intention of the whole initiative by stating that it requires entirely new legal ground. Namely, ignoring its own legal obligation to disclose the fiscal data to the public, the Ministry of Finance claimed that the proposed public monitoring of the stewardship could only be performed via the Anti-Corruption Agency. In order to share the fiscal data with this agency, the ministry allegedly needed new legal ground, which at that moment did not exist. The climax of this absurdity is the fact that the Ministry of Finance first insisted on "exempting certain types of data from public access" rather than proactively facilitating and enabling the process of digital openness and transparency.[49] This attitude and offered justifications of the Ministry of Finance indicate the fundamental mistrust between this public institution and a part of the government on the one hand, and its constituency, taxpayers, expert public, and other public authorities, on the other hand. The presented official correspondence shows that the default assumption of the Ministry of Finance is that citizens want to discredit the government by searching for potential misuses of public funds, overlooking the fact that this is a legitimate right of the public. In fact, the Ministry of Finance attempts to discredit taxpayers and the expert public by questioning their capability to understand the sophisticated matter of public finance. In this way, the ministry actually discredits itself by preventing an open dialogue, expert analysis, and constructive criticism of its constituency. This persistent non-transparent behaviour ultimately leads to the real and grounded mistrust of the public towards the government.

The presented examples show that the public policymaking cycle in the area of intergovernmental fiscal governance has serious drawbacks, which ultimately lead to suboptimal local government financing. The fact that databases are non-existent, inadequate, non-transparent, or unused affects each public policymaking phase. First, the lack of adequate data input undermines policy design and formulation, which require an ex ante analysis. Further, the Ministry of Finance's attitude towards fiscal data transparency prevents partner institutions and relevant stakeholders to participate and contribute meaningfully to the policymaking. Second, this non-transparency also directly affects policy implementation, as relevant institutions are not equipped with the adequate input needed for monitoring. This is exactly why the stakeholders, in the phase of policy evaluation, cannot assess the quality and the results of the adopted policies, that is, conduct an ex post analysis. Finally, such non-transparency causes a lack of oversight and control of intergovernmental fiscal governance/the public finance system by other public authorities, the expert and academic community, and taxpayers.

This behaviour of the Ministry of Finance and the government appears to be not only incompetent, but also non-democratic. Namely, the ministry undermines legal institutional processes at both the horizontal and vertical levels by downgrading the other relevant ministries (MPALSG, the Ministry of Education, the Ministry of Health, etc.), the Commissioner/Office for Information of Public Importance, its own bodies such as the Intergovernmental Finance Commission and the working group, as well as local governments and their association. Thus, the lack of adequate participation of institutions, which have a legal mandate and obligation to contribute to the process, calls into question the legitimacy of public policymaking. Moreover, such a non-democratic attitude towards the constituency, which cannot control the system, raises the question of public stewardship diligence, generates doubts about corruption, and leads to mistrust.

To sum up, the lack of adequate and accurate databases on municipal spending needs and expenditures on one hand, and the necessary financial resources and revenues on the other, causes serious vertical imbalances in local budgets and results in suboptimal local government financing. Non-disclosure of data is against the provisions of the Council of Europe's Charter of Local Self-Government and its accompanying recommendations,[50] as well as against the specific pieces of the "Six-pack" and "Two-pack" EU fiscal legislation.[51]

Conclusions

Our analysis shows that Serbia's commitment to decentralisation after 2000 has been questionable. First, after formally opting for decentralisation, the country adopted a series of policies and regulations to implement it. However, in 2006, while fiscal decentralisation was at its formal peak, Serbia had a major setback in political decentralisation by abandoning the direct election of mayors—an election system that started showing good results during the short four-year span during which it was in effect. Second, territorial decentralisation remained suboptimal because any substantial redefinition of local administrative boundaries could have opened a Pandora's box of further political or ethnic tensions. Third, as soon as the first signs of the financial crisis appeared, the central government changed its tune and reversed the political discourse towards centralisation.

Earlier public finance literature identifies two major cycles of intergovernmental fiscal relations in former Yugoslavia: (1) a phase of centralisation between 1946 and 1967, and (2) a phase of decentralisation from 1968 until 1990 (Bogoev, 1964; Raičević, 1977). We have identified three more cycles in the post-1990 period in Serbia: (1) a wave of fiscal centralisation during the 1990s, (2) a wave of fiscal decentralisation between 2000 and 2008, and (3) a phase of pseudo-decentralisation and the renewal of fiscal centralisation from 2009 until today. We conclude that centralisation and decentralisation have been used as key policy avenues for implementing major societal changes. Namely, centralisation was an instrument of choice in times of political or economic hardships. It has been used either to consolidate and stabilise the system or to concentrate power and take control over the state and its finances. On the other hand, decentralisation was also a strategic orientation in times of economic prosperity and liberalisation of society. Also, the cycles seem to have become shorter in recent times.

Our study further shows that the entire intergovernmental fiscal governance has been marked by profound institutional problems. Above all, the policy process lacks the necessary features of an effective policymaking cycle—planning and control. A major problem is a lack of analysis or, at least, adequate ex ante and ex post financial analyses needed for strategic planning, evidence-based policies, monitoring, and control over the public finance system. Moreover, the meta-problem behind such a policy approach is non-transparency and inadequacy of fiscal data. Based on what we have found, databases on budgetary revenues and expenditures are either non-transparent or do not exist; and the limited number of databases that do exist are inadequate, incomplete, or not used.

The absence of analysis coupled with the lack of institutional coordination has led to an ad hoc and disconnected approach to decentralisation of functions and finance. The discrepancy between delegating mandates and transferring adequate financial resources has created a vertical imbalance between municipal budgetary expenditures and revenues. Furthermore, the "adhocracy" and the divorce of functional and financial decentralisation has undermined financial planning and management at the local level. Local governments have been faced with substantial volatility of budgetary revenues and expenditures and, thus, with frequent liquidity problems. New functions and tasks, not accompanied with adequate funding, put enormous pressure on municipalities to maintain or increase the level of recurrent expenses (operating costs), usually accumulating arrears and debts. Together with the reduced creditworthiness and borrowing capacity, budgetary imbalances have forced local governments to consider capital investments in a rather restrictive way. Consequently, cities and municipalities are unable to focus on any kind of long-term financial planning, their provision of local public goods and services to citizens is compromised, and local economic development is jeopardised due to drastically reduced capital budgets.

In Fig. 4.3, we use the level of capital investment as a proxy for the capacity and effectiveness of local governments in implementing local economic development policies. The figure shows trends from 2006 to 2014.

As mentioned earlier, local governments are classified into four categories based on their level of development. The six trend lines in

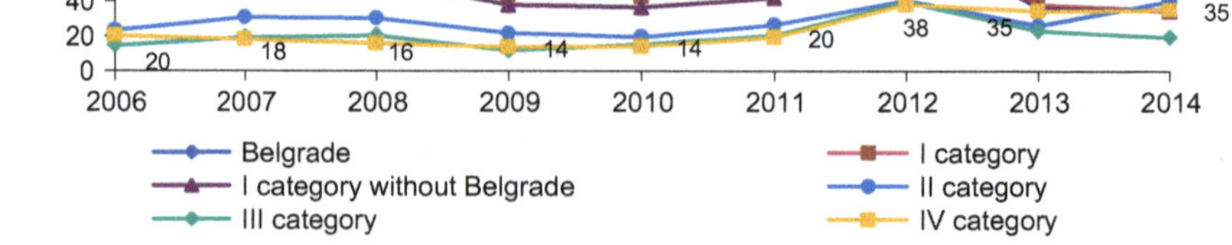

Fig. 4.3 Average of total capital expenditures (2006–2014)

Fig. 4.3 represent the aggregate capital investment for each category from category I, which is the richest, to category IV, which is the poorest, as well as for the capital city of Belgrade and category I without Belgrade. The capital city is the largest LGU, representing about one-third of total local revenues and expenditures and approximately the same share of the country's economic activity (employment) (Kmezić, Kaluđerović, et al., 2016). If we take 2006 as the base, which is also the year in which the Law on Local Government Finance was adopted, we can see that capital investment fell from EUR 112 per capita to EUR 47 per capita in 2014, which is a 58 per cent reduction. Encouraged by positive regulatory changes and an increase in budgetary revenues, Belgrade undertook a major investment project (the Bridge on Ada) up to 2011. However, due to a change in policy discourse, a series of centralising measures, and a dramatic fall in revenues, Belgrade cut capital investment as soon as the project was completed. As one can see in Fig. 4.3, the fall in 2014 was even more drastic (75 per cent) when investment activity is compared to its peak in 2011 (Kmezić, Kaluđerović, et al., 2016).

Furthermore, the fall in investment activity was registered in the whole category I, as well as in the four main cities in Serbia—Belgrade, Novi Sad, Kragujevac, and Nis—which represent around 50 per cent of total local government revenues and expenditures and two-thirds of total local public debt (Fiscal Council of the Republic of Serbia, 2017). In other words, the major cities and towns in Serbia that are supposed to be the drivers of local economic development have experienced an extreme decrease of investments. A rise in investment activity has taken place only in the poorer categories of municipalities. However, the level of investment in these municipalities was extremely low at the beginning of this period (see Fig. 4.3), and although the relative increase might seem significant, the absolute value of investment remains insufficient to resolve the problems of unbalanced regional development.

Finally, to determine the effect of the fiscal decentralisation process in Serbia we use standard measures of decentralisation: (a) the share of total local government revenues in consolidated general government revenues; (b) the share of total local government expenditures in consolidated general government expenditures; (c) the share of total local government

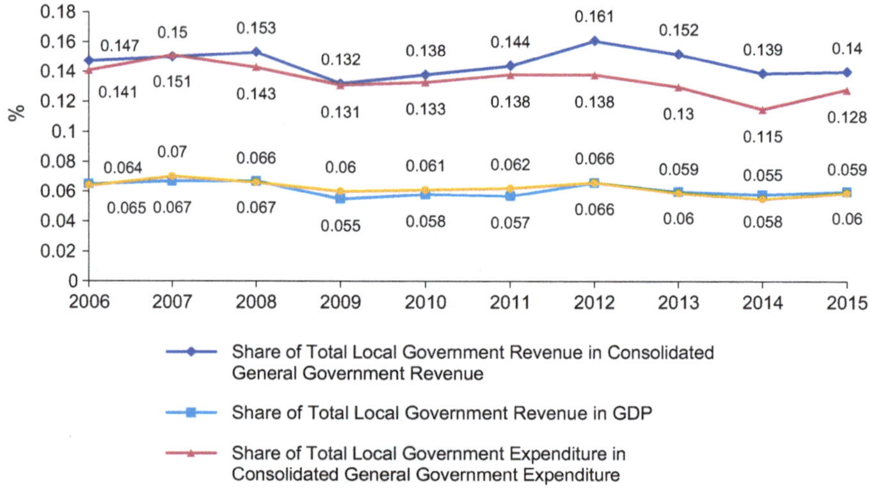

Fig. 4.4 Level of decentralisation (2006–2015)

revenues in GDP; and (d) the share of total local government expenditures in GDP. In Fig. 4.4, we represent these four parameters as trend lines.

The data on the level of decentralisation clearly show that the effect of the policies implemented in the period observed in this study has been centralising. When compared to 2006 and 2011, the share of total government revenue in consolidated general government revenue fell from 14.7 per cent and 16.1 per cent, respectively, to 14 per cent. The same is true for expenditure decentralisation, where the share of total government expenditure in consolidated general government expenditure was 12.8 per cent in 2015, while it reached 15.1 per cent in 2007, the first year of the implementation of the Law on Local Government Finance. When we compare the level of fiscal decentralisation using GDP as a benchmark, the trend is the same. The shares of both total local government revenues and expenditures in GDP were around 7.0 per cent at the peak of fiscal decentralisation. In 2015, the shares were 5.9 per cent and 6.0 per cent, respectively. Not only are these shares lower relative to the years when fiscal decentralisation was at its peak, but they are also lower than the same values at the very beginning of the decentralisation phase—in the period 2002–2005.[52] To sum up, the analysis presented in this chapter shows that Serbia is back on the centralising course again, which represents an annulment of all the decentralisation policies implemented in the period of transition and democratisation (2000–2016). Our observations suggest that a revival of decentralisation will most likely happen only when the Serbian economy is back on a sustained path of recovery.

Notes

1. The Constitution of the Republic of Serbia (Official Gazette of the Republic of Serbia No. 1/1990).
2. United Nations Security Council (UNSC) Resolution 1244 from 10 June 1999.
3. The Constitution of the Republic of Serbia (Official Gazette of the Republic of Serbia No. 98/2006).
4. International Court of Justice (ICJ), Advisory Opinion on the unilateral declaration of independence of Kosovo, 22 July 2010.
5. Article 5 of the Law on Regional Development (Official Gazette of the Republic of Serbia No. 51/2009, 30/2010, and 89/2015).
6. The Decree on Administrative Counties (Official Gazette of the Republic of Serbia No. 15/2006).
7. The Law on Territorial Organisation of the Republic of Serbia (Official Gazette of the Republic of Serbia No. 129//2007 and 18/2016).
8. See Articles 11 and 12a of the Law on Regional Development (Official Gazette of the Republic of Serbia No. 51/2009, 30/2010, and 89/2015), as well as the Decree on Establishing a Uniform List of Regions and Local Governments According to Their Development Levels for 2011 (Official Gazette of the Republic of Serbia No. 51/2010, 69/2011, 107/2012, 62/2013, and 104/2014) and the Decree on Setting the Methodology for Calculating the Levels of Development of Regions and Local Government Units (Official Gazette of the Republic of Serbia No. 62/2015).
9. The Law on Local Self-Government (Official Gazette of the Republic of Serbia No. 9/2002, 33/2004, and 135/2004).
10. The Constitution of the Republic of Serbia (Official Gazette of the Republic of Serbia No. 98/2006).

11. The Law on Local Self-Government (Official Gazette of the Republic of Serbia No. 129/2007).
12. The Law on Local Elections (Official Gazette of the Republic of Serbia No. 129/2007, 34/2010, and 54/2011).
13. The Constitution of the Republic of Serbia (Official Gazette of the Republic of Serbia No. 1/1990).
14. The Law on Territorial Organisation of the Republic of Serbia and Local Self-Government (Official Gazette of the Republic of Serbia No. 47/91, 79/92, 82/92, and 47/94).
15. The Law on Public Revenues and Public Expenditures (Official Gazette of the Republic of Serbia No. 76/91…135/04).
16. The Law on Public Revenues and Public Expenditures (Official Gazette of the Republic of Serbia No. 76/91…135/04).
17. Non-transparency was obvious in the example of sharing revenues from the sales tax with municipalities as the government changed the relevant law every year, starting from 1994, to factor in political changes at the local level (The annual laws on sharing the collected wage tax and sales tax with municipalities and cities, Official Gazette of the Republic of Serbia No. 44/94, 75/94, 53/95, 60/97, 44/98, 54/99, 22/01, and 15/02). A similar practice was evident in the allocation of intergovernmental transfers.
18. The Law on Assets Owned by the Republic of Serbia (Official Gazette of the Republic of Serbia No. 53/95, 3/96, 54/96, and 32/97).
19. The Law on Establishing Competences of the Autonomous Province (Official Gazette of the Republic of Serbia No. 6/02).
20. The Law on Local Self-Government (Official Gazette of the Republic of Serbia No. 9/2002, 33/2004, and 135/2004).
21. The Law on Local Self-Government (Official Gazette of the Republic of Serbia No. 129/2007).
22. The Constitution of the Republic of Serbia (Official Gazette of the Republic of Serbia No. 98/2006).
23. The Law on Local Government Finance (Official Gazette of the Republic of Serbia No. 62/2006, 47/2011, 93/2012, and 83/2016).
24. The Law Amending the Law on Public Revenues and Public Expenditures (Official Gazette of the Republic of Serbia No. 76/91, 18/ 93, 22/93, 37/93, 67/93, 45/94, 42/98, 54/99, 22/2001, and 33/2004).
25. The Law Amending the Law on Local Self-Government (Official Gazette of the Republic of Serbia No. 49/99 and 27/2001).

26. The Law on Local Self-Government (Official Gazette of the Republic of Serbia No. 9/2002, 33/2004, and 135/2004).
27. The Law on the Value Added Tax (Official Gazette of the Republic of Serbia No. 84/2004, 86/2004, 61/2005, 61/2007, 93/2012, 108/2013, 68/2014, and 142/2014).
28. The Law on Local Government Finance (Official Gazette of the Republic of Serbia No. 62/2006, 47/2011, 93/2012, and 83/2016).
29. The Law on Local Government Finance (Official Gazette of the Republic of Serbia No. 62/2006, 47/2011, 93/2012, and 83/2016).
30. Articles 177-178 of the Constitution of the Republic of Serbia (Official Gazette of the Republic of Serbia No. 98/2006); Article 21 of the Law on Local Self-Government (Official Gazette of the Republic of Serbia No. 9/2002, 33/2004, and 135/2004); and articles 3 and 44-46 of the Law on Local Government Finance (Official Gazette of the Republic of Serbia No. 62/2006, 47/2011, 93/2012, and 83/2016).
31. The Law on Local Government Finance (Official Gazette of the Republic of Serbia No. 62/2006, 47/2011, 93/2012, and 83/2016).
32. The Law on Amendments and Addenda to the Law on the Personal Income Tax (Official Gazette of the Republic of Serbia No. 47/2013).
33. The Law on Local Government Finance (Official Gazette of the Republic of Serbia No. 62/2006, 47/2011, 93/2012, and 83/2016).
34. The Law on Local Government Finance (Official Gazette of the Republic of Serbia No. 62/2006, 47/2011, 93/2012, and 83/2016).
35. The Law on Amendments and Addenda to the Law on the Personal Income Tax (Official Gazette of the Republic of Serbia No. 47/2013) and the Law on the Personal Income Tax (Official Gazette of the Republic of Serbia No. 24/2001…57/2014).
36. The Law on Property Taxes (Official Gazette of the Republic of Serbia No. 26/2001…68/2014).
37. The Law on the Personal Income Tax (Official Gazette of the Republic of Serbia No. 24/2001…57/2014).
38. The Rulebook on the Methodology and Criteria for Determining Costs of Providing Public Services (Official Gazette of the Republic of Serbia No. 14/2013, 25/2013, and 99/2013).
39. The Instruction for the Preparation of the Decision on the Local Government Budget for 2014 (and Projections for 2015 and 2016).
40. The Instruction for the Preparation of the Decision on the Local Government Budget for 2015 (and Projections for 2016 and 2017).

41. The Law on Planning and Construction (Official Gazette of the Republic of Serbia No. 72/2009, 81/2009, 64/2010, 121/2012, 132/2014, and 145/2014).
42. The Law on Planning and Construction (Official Gazette of the Republic of Serbia No. 72/2009, 81/2009, 64/2010, 121/2012, 132/2014, and 145/2014).
43. The Decree on Setting the Methodology for Calculating the Levels of Development of Regions and Local Government Units (Official Gazette of the Republic of Serbia No. 62/2015).
44. The Law on Local Government Finance (Official Gazette of the Republic of Serbia No. 62/2006, 47/2011, 93/2012, and 83/2016).
45. The Decision of the Ministry of Finance of the Republic of Serbia, No. 4-00-45/2015, 30 April 2015.
46. The Decision of the Treasury Administration of the Ministry of Finance of the Republic of Serbia No. 401-00-315/2015-001-007, 2 April 2015. The request was denied due to the fact that the volume of the data requested was too large. The justification was based on Article 13 of the Law on Free Access to Information of Public Importance (Official Gazette of the Republic of Serbia No. 120/2004…36/2010).
47. The Decision of the Treasury Administration of the Ministry of Finance of the Republic of Serbia No. 401-00-438/2015-001-007, 7 May 2015.
48. For instance, see the positions of the Standing Conference of Towns and Municipalities from 4 December 2015: http://www.skgo.org/reports/details/1722 and from 10 December 2015: http://www.skgo.org/files/fck/File/2015/Ministarstvo%20finansija,%20dopis.PDF
49. The Position of the Ministry of Finance of the Republic of Serbia, signed by the minister, Dr Dušan Vujović; 08 No.: 021-02-114/2016, 28 October 2016. For details, see: http://www.istinomer.rs/multimedia/pdfs/189549243807044.pdf
50. The Republic of Serbia adopted the European Charter of Local Self-Government (CETS No. 122, Strasbourg, 15 October 1985) and its financial provision, and incorporated it in its national legislation. The accompanying recommendations are the Council of Europe Recommendation of the Committee of Ministers to Member States on Financial and Budgetary Management at Local and Regional Levels (Recommendation Rec (2004) adopted by the Committee of Ministers on 8 January 2004) and the Council of Europe Recommendation of the Committee of Ministers to Member States on the Financial Resources of Local and Regional Authorities (Recommendation Rec (2005) adopted by the Committee of Ministers on 19 January 2005).

51. The failure to publish fiscal and budgetary data is contrary to the provisions of the Council Directive 2011/85/EU of 8 November 2011 on requirements for budgetary frameworks of the Member States, Regulation No. 1173/2011 of the European Parliament and the Council of 16 November 2011 on the effective enforcement of budgetary surveillance in the euro area, and Regulation (EU) No. 473/2013 of the European Parliament and the Council of 21 May 2013 on common provisions for monitoring and assessing draft budgetary plans and ensuring the correction of excessive deficits of the Member States in the euro area.
52. See Table 4.1 of this chapter.

References

Avlijaš, S., & Bartlett, W. (2011). *The political economy of decentralisation and regional policy in Serbia: Choices and outcomes*. LSEE Papers on Decentralisation and Regional Policy.

Bloechliger, H. (2013). *Decentralization and economic growth part 1: How fiscal federalism affects long-term economic growth*. OECD Working Papers on Fiscal Federalism No. 14. Paris: OECD.

Bogoev, K. (1964). *Lokalne finansije Jugoslavije*. Beograd: Savez ekonomista Jugoslavije.

Buser, W. (2011). The impact of fiscal decentralization on economic performance in high-income OECD nations: An institutional approach. *Public Choice, 149*(1–2), 31–48.

Calamai, L. (2009). The link between devolution and regional disparities: Evidence from the Italian regions. *Environment and Planning A, 41*(5), 1129–1151.

Cantarero, D., & Gonzalez, P. P. (2009). Fiscal decentralization and economic growth: Evidence from Spanish regions. Public Budgeting & Finance, 29 Winter, 24-44.

Ezcurra, R., & Pascual, P. (2008). Fiscal decentralization and regional disparities: Evidence from several European Union countries. *Environment and Planning A, 40*(5), 1185–1201.

Fiscal Council of the Republic of Serbia / Fiskalni savet Republike Srbije. (2017). *Lokalne javne finansije: Problemi, rizici i preporuke*, 48 and 52. Beograd: Fiskalni savet Republike Srbije.

Iimi, A. (2005). Decentralization and economic growth revisited: An empirical note. *Journal of Urban Economics, 57*(3), 449–461.

International Monetary Fund. (2016). *IMF country report no. 16/386—Sixth review under the stand-by arrangement and modification of the arrangement review schedule for the Republic of Serbia*. Washington, DC: IMF.

Kmezić, S., Đulić, K., Jocović, M., & Kaluđerović, J. (2016). *Fiscal decentralisation and local government financing in Serbia and Montenegro*. Maribor: Institute for Local Self-Government and Public Procurement—Lex Localis.

Kmezić, S., Kaluđerović, J., Jocović, M., & Đulić, K. (2016). Fiscal decentralisation and local government financing in Montenegro from 2002 to 2015. *Lex Localis—Journal of Local Self-Government, 14*(3), 431–450.

Levitas, A. (2004). Reforma sistema finansiranja lokalne samouprave u Srbiji. In A. Levitas & G. Peteri (Eds.), *Reforma sistema finansiranja lokalne samouprave*. Beograd: PALGO.

Popović, D. (1999). Jesenji poreski paket Vlade Srbije. *MAP br. 10/99*, 35–39. Beograd: Institut ekonomskih nauka.

Popović, D. (2000, November 8). *Reform of the fiscal system in Serbia*. Paper presented at Reform of the Fiscal System, Media Centre, Belgrade.

Raičević, B. (1977). *Osobenosti razvoja fiskalnog sistema u uslovima federativnog uređenja Jugoslavije*. Beograd: Ekonomski institut.

Rodriguez-Pose, A. (2009). Fiscal decentralization and economic growth in central and Eastern Europe. *Growth and Change, 40*(3), 387–417.

Rodriguez-Pose, A., & Bwire, A. (2004). The economic (in)efficiency of devolution. *Environment and Planning A, 36*, 1907–1928.

Sagbas, I., Sen, H., & Kar, M. (2005). Fiscal decentralisation, the size of the public sector, and economic growth in Turkey. *Environment and Planning C: Government and Policy, 23*(1), 3–19.

Spirić, D., & Bućić, A. (2012, October). Ka stabilnom i održivom sistemu finansiranja lokalne samouprave u Republici Srbiji. *Polis Magazine, 1*, 9–14.

Stipanović, B. (2006). Local government finance system and fiscal equalization in the Republic of Serbia. The Fiscal Decentralization Initiative for Central and Eastern Europe. Retrieved from http://pdf.usaid.gov/pdf_docs/pnadk279.pdf

Stojanović, S. R. (2002). *Zajednica prihoda u poreskom sistemu Srbije*. Beograd: Želnid.

Stojanović, S. R. (2005). *Fiskalni federalizam*. Beograd: Institut za uporedno pravo, Centar za antiratnu akciju.

Stojanovic, S. R., & Timofeev, A. (2005). Country report: An assessment of fiscal decentralization reform in Serbia. In UNDP (Ed.), *Fiscal decentralization in transition economies: Case studies from the Balkans and Caucasus*. Bratislava: UNDP.

The 2015 report on municipalities and regions in the Republic of Serbia. Retrieved from http://pod2.stat.gov.rs/ObjavljenePublikacije/G2015/pdf/G20152017.pdf

The December 2016 bulletin of the Ministry of Finance of the Republic of Serbia. Retrieved from http://www.mfin.gov.rs/UserFiles/File/bilten%20javne%20finansije/2017/Bilten%20148%20SRB%200203.pdf

Thiessen, U. (2003). Fiscal decentralisation and economic growth in high-income OECD countries. *Fiscal Studies, 24*(3), 237–274.

Woller, G. M., & Phillips, K. (1998). Fiscal decentralisation and LDC economic growth: An empirical investigation. *Journal of Development Studies, 34*(4), 139–148.

5

Montenegro: Volatile Municipal Revenues

Jadranka Kaluđerović and Mijat Jocović

Introduction

Montenegro, located on the Adriatic Sea coast of the Balkan Peninsula has a population of just 620,000. The country's modern capital is Podgorica, while Cetinje is its old royal capital. Montenegro's independence was declared and ratified by its parliament on 3 June 2006 following a referendum earlier that year. The country's parliament is a unicameral legislative body, with 81 members elected for four-year terms, the last parliamentary elections having been held in

J. Kaluđerović (✉)
Faculty for International Economics, Finance and Business, University Donja Gorica (UDG), Podgorica, Montenegro

Institute for Strategic Studies and Prognoses (ISSP), Podgorica, Montenegro
e-mail: jkaludjerovic@t-com.me

M. Jocović
Faculty of Economics, University of Montenegro, Podgorica, Montenegro
e-mail: mijatj@ac.me

W. Bartlett et al. (eds.), *Fiscal Decentralisation, Local Government and Policy Reversals in Southeastern Europe*, https://doi.org/10.1007/978-3-319-96092-0_5

October 2016. The Government of Montenegro, as the executive branch of state authority, is headed by the prime minister and currently has 18 ministries, among them the Ministry of Public Administration, while the local government system consists of 23 units.

During the last decade of the twentieth century, Montenegro experienced the disintegration of Yugoslavia, conflict, sanctions, and political changes, all of which worsened an already very weak economic situation, and by 1999, economic activity was 61 per cent lower than it had been in 1989 (Vukotić, 2003). This economic and state crisis required immediate action, so important economic and institutional reforms were initiated as early as 1998, when Montenegro was still formally in a state union with Serbia. However, it was evident that the two countries had different economic systems as well as divergent plans for the future. The reforms carried out in Montenegro were based on deregulation, liberalisation, and privatisation, and were aimed at boosting private entrepreneurial initiatives. Monetary reform led to the privatisation of the banking system and the introduction of the euro as the official currency in 2002, while fiscal reform resulted in the introduction of a treasury system and the creation of a new tax and customs system. Prices were liberalised and business procedures were significantly simplified. These economic changes were implemented in parallel with institutional and administrative reforms, which changed the organisational structure of Montenegro's government, altered the status of some institutions, and abolished a number of ministries and agencies. The number of public servants was also reduced, although not significantly, leaving Montenegro's administrative system still with the largest number of civil servants in Europe. This contributed to the inefficiency of public administration, which, along with the intention to align Montenegro with the decentralisation tendencies seen in developed democracies, was a major reason for initiating administrative reform. Thus, in 2003, the first Public Administration Reform Strategy (2003–2009) was adopted, aimed at fulfilling two major goals of state administration reform: enhancing the efficiency of the administration system and integrating the administration system into a wider social system.

Decentralisation was one of the most important parts of the strategic administrative reforms that were initiated, and the strategy clearly identified a need to allocate and introduce new functions and change local government financial mechanisms accordingly. For this reason, in the same year that the strategy was adopted, the government adopted two major pieces of legislation relevant to local government—the Law on Local Self-Government[1] and the Law on Local Government Finance.[2] These laws established a well-designed framework for local government finance that both enabled municipalities to adequately fund the functions delegated to them and significantly increased local fiscal capacities and autonomy. However, it should be noted that Montenegrin municipalities have never performed financially demanding functions such as the provision of primary healthcare or pre-primary and primary education, which remained at the national level even after the decentralisation reforms. The new local administrative and financial system, along with an overall improvement in the country's economic performance, resulted in a 350 per cent increase in public revenue, from 77.5 million euros in 2004 to 347.8 million euros in 2008. Similarly, total local government expenditure experienced strong growth until 2008, when it reached a peak of 316.3 million euros. However, these positive trends were not long-lived, and the effects of the global economic crisis became evident in 2008. These negative trends coincided with two legislative changes introduced by the national government aimed at improving the business climate by decreasing the fiscal burden at the local level. As early as 2006, the central government adopted the Law on Local Communal Fees,[3] which was implemented from 2008 and which abolished fees for the three most profitable economic activities. The central government also adopted the Law on Spatial Planning and the Construction of Structures[4] in 2008, which was implemented from 2009 and which abolished the construction land use charge. Negative economic trends, along with the changes introduced through these laws, significantly decreased government revenue, by 20 per cent in 2009, an additional 11 per cent in 2010, and another 11 per cent in 2011. Consequently, municipal expenditure experienced a similar trend with a huge drop between 2008 and 2011.

The central government adopted amendments to the Law on Local Government Finance in 2010 due to liquidity problems. Although the changes introduced by these amendments were aimed at stabilising the financial situation in municipalities, they in fact reduced the number and share of own-source revenue. After several financially difficult years, local government revenue started to increase in 2012, a trend which has continued up until 2016.

However, one of the most significant changes observed since the beginning of the fiscal decentralisation process in Montenegro is related to changes to the structure of local government expenditure. While the "current expenditure" category remained very stable at 30 per cent over the whole observation period, the "capital expenditure" and "other expenditure" categories experienced significant fluctuations. For example, capital expenditure amounted to 45 per cent of total expenditure in 2008, while by 2015 it had dropped to 23 per cent. Moreover, the "other expenditure" category, including loans, credits and other debt servicing, was 18 per cent of the total in 2008, but by 2015 it had risen to 55 per cent. These data, together with data on the level of local government debt, which by the end of 2016 amounted to 175 million euros, indicate that local government resorted to borrowing in order to service the huge liabilities incurred during the period of economic boom. The fact that arrears and outstanding bills account for almost 70 per cent of the total debt shows that the investments were so large that they not only required additional borrowing, but also jeopardised current duties such as the payment of taxes and benefits for local government officials, as these make up around 40 per cent of the total arrears.

In 2016, more than a decade after the initiation of a decentralisation process aimed at increasing the autonomy and efficiency of local government in Montenegro, the financial situation was so difficult that the central government had to intervene. Thus, in 2015, the Montenegrin government adopted amendments to the Law on Real Estate Tax[5] and the Tax Debt Repayment Programme,[6] while also issuing credit guarantees to some municipalities. The effect of these measures will be seen in the future, but it may be concluded that the current problematic situation is the result of several causes. Among these, the most significant are the irresponsible maintenance of public finances at the local level, changes introduced at the national level that negatively affected local public revenue, and the global financial crisis.

Administrative and Territorial Organisation

Montenegro was the smallest out of the six republics of the Socialist Federal Republic of Yugoslavia. After the disintegration of the country at the beginning of the 1990s, it remained in union with Serbia. The new two-member federation was established in April 1992 under the name Federal Republic of Yugoslavia. In October of the same year, Montenegro adopted a new Constitution,[7] in which the country was defined as a democratic, social, and ecological state.

The new Constitution continued the practice of the previous 1974 Constitution of the Socialist Federative Republic of Yugoslavia[8] and referred to the principle of local self-government and to the citizens' right to manage local affairs through local administration. Also, it continued with the tradition of the one-tier level of administrative organisation, which had been present in Montenegro since 1957, when the second level of administration, the so-called srez, was abandoned. Territorial organisation of the country was defined by Article 8 of the 1992 Constitution, which stated that the territory of Montenegro is integral, inalienable, and territorially organised into municipalities.

As during this time the political, economic, and social systems in Montenegro and in Serbia became significantly different, the countries signed the Constitutional Charter of the State Community of Serbia and Montenegro[9] in 2003 by which the State Union of Serbia and Montenegro was created. According to the Charter, each member of the Union had the right to declare independence after a referendum. Montenegro used that right and organised a referendum in 2006. The majority of the voters voted for independence, and in May 2006 Montenegro declared independence. The new Constitution[10] of independent Montenegro was adopted in 2007.

The new 2007 Constitution covered the issue of local self-government organisation in more detail than the previous one and had an entire section with five articles (from 113 to 117) that was dedicated to the issue of its organisation and functioning. Similar to the 1992 Constitution, the new Constitution prescribed that the main form of self-government organisation is the municipality. However, in contrast to the previous

Constitution, the new one stated that other forms of local self-governance could also be established, which created a basis for the creation of city municipalities. There were no changes in the new Constitution related to the decision-making process and main institutions at the municipal level. A novelty was that the new Constitution stated that the municipality has the status of a legal entity; it has its statute and other acts, its property and budget that may be financed by its own municipal sources or state funds. One article defines municipal independence and states that the central government may only interfere with municipal governance if the president and/or parliament of the municipality do not perform their function for six months.

According to the 2007 Constitution, Podgorica is the Capital City, while Cetinje is the Old Royal Capital of the country. The functioning of these two municipalities was regulated by separate pieces of legislation, the Law on the Capital City[11] adopted in 2006 and the Law on the Old Royal Capital[12] adopted in 2008. According to the 2006 Law on the Capital City, the capital city is the administrative centre and an individual unit of local self-government. The main specificity of the Capital City in comparison with other local government units (LGUs) is the existence of city municipalities as sub-LGUs, the status of which is defined by the Law on the Capital City. Currently, Podgorica has two city municipalities, Tuzi and Golubovci. City municipalities have a parliament and a president, they are legal entities, and they have a budget in which the majority of the sources are transferred from the municipal budget, partly based on the revenues collected on the territory of the city municipality. The 2006 Law on the Old Royal Capital defines Cetinje as the historical and cultural centre of Montenegro. Its main specificities in comparison to the other municipalities are related to certain statutory and protocol issues such as the residence of the president of the country is located in the Old Royal Capital, the headquarters of some public and cultural institutions are located there, and the first regular meetings of the Parliament are always held there.

In terms of territorial organisation, the 2007 Constitution did not introduce any changes, and the municipality remained the main territorial unit in the country. From 1960, territorial organisation of Montenegro was defined in accordance with the Law on the Division of the People's

Republic of Montenegro.[13] This 1960 law decreased the number of municipalities from the previous 28 to 20. Since then, the number of municipalities was not changed until 1990 when the municipality of Andrijevica was established. Although significant changes in the state status and its organisation have occurred since 1960, the new Law on the Territorial Organisation of Montenegro,[14] which defined names, territories, and borders of municipalities, was adopted as late as 2011. The new law recognised 21 municipalities, including the Capital City and the Old Royal Capital. Through the amendments of the 2011 Law on the Territorial Organisation of Montenegro,[15] two new municipalities were established: Petnjica in 2013 and Gusinje in 2014. Thus, in 2016, Montenegrin territory consisted of 23 municipalities, including the Capital City Podgorica and the Old Royal Capital Cetinje (Table 5.1).

Table 5.1 Population by municipality in 2011

Municipality	Number of inhabitants	Share in total population (%)	Area in km^2
Andrijevica	5,071	0.82	283
Bar	42,048	6.78	598
Berane	33,970	5.48	717
Bijelo Polje	46,051	7.43	924
Budva	19,218	3.10	122
Cetinje	16,657	2.69	899
Danilovgrad	18,472	2.98	501
Herceg Novi	30,864	4.98	235
Kolašin	8,380	1.35	897
Kotor	22,601	3.65	335
Mojkovac	8,622	1.39	367
Nikšić	72,443	11.68	2,065
Plav	13,108	2.11	486
Pljevlja	30,786	4.97	854
Plužine	3,246	0.52	1,346
Podgorica	185,937	29.99	1,399
Rožaje	22,964	3.70	432
Šavnik	2,070	0.33	553
Tivat	14,031	2.26	46
Ulcinj	19,921	3.21	255
Žabljak	3,569	0.58	445
TOTAL	620,029		

Source: MONSTAT (2011)

The average number of inhabitants per municipality, including the Old Royal Capital and the Capital City, is 27,000. The largest municipality is the Capital City Podgorica, in which 30 per cent of the country's total population lives. The number of inhabitants in the other municipalities ranges from 2,070 in Šavnik to 72,443 in Nikšić. There are also significant differences in the land area covered by municipalities, ranging from 46 km^2 for Tivat to 2,064 km^2 for Nikšić. These differences, alongside geographical location, significantly impact the level of economic activity in these municipalities, and consequently affect the municipalities' ability to manage local budgets.

Local government and its development are also subject to the Law on Regional Development[16] adopted in 2011 with the goal of enabling equal development of local government in the country. The law defines three regions—Coastal, Central, and Northern—and allocates each municipality to one of these regions. The law also defines the methodology and criteria for defining the level of competitiveness and development of municipalities, figures that are used as the basis for supporting interventions (development index), and indictors for monitoring and evaluation (competitiveness index), according to the policy framework defined in the Strategy for Regional Development 2014–2020. The level of development is calculated based on several indicators on the municipal level: unemployment, income per capita, budget revenues per capita, population growth, and level of education of the population. According to the development index, municipalities are divided into six groups, and those that have a development index below 75 per cent of the average index in the country are considered to be less developed municipalities. According to the latest data for the 2010–2012 period, the highest number of the less developed municipalities is in the Northern region, 10 out of 11 municipalities. On the other side, out of the seven municipalities that are in the group with the highest level of development, all except one are from the Coastal region. The level of competitiveness of municipalities is expressed by the index of competitiveness, which is calculated based on the following group of factors: business environment and business sector development, demographic, health and educational characteristics of the population, availability of basic infrastructure, public sector, investment and entrepreneurship development, and level of economic development.

According to the calculation for the period 2009 and 2011, the most competitive municipality is coastal Budva, while the least competitive is Andrijevica, located in the Northern part.

Political Decentralisation

Both the 1992 and 2007 Constitutions state that the local assembly and the presidency are the two main institutions of a municipality. The election of representatives in the local assemblies was implemented according to the Law on the Election of Councillors and Members of Parliament, which was changed several times during the observed period, with the changes mainly related to the residence condition for voters, electoral units, voting procedures, and so on.

The current procedure for the election of councillors for the municipal parliament, the parliament of the Capital City, and the Old Royal Capital is defined by the Law on the Election of Councillors and Members of Parliament, last amended in 2016.[17] For a local parliament, 30 councillors and 1 more per every 5,000 electors are delegated. However, the exact number of councillors is defined by a special decision adopted by the assembly not later than the day of the call for elections. A councillor is elected on the basis of the electoral lists of political parties, coalitions of political parties, or groups of citizens. Four-year mandates are divided proportionally to the number of the votes obtained at the local elections. A councillor cannot be recalled. In the division of mandates only those parties that have more than 3 per cent of the votes in the electoral unit may participate.

The right to choose and be chosen as councillor belongs to every citizen of Montenegro who is at least 18 years old, with business capacity and permanent residence in Montenegro for no less than two years, as well as permanent residence in a municipality or a city municipality as an electoral district for no less than six months prior to the polling day.

The Law on the Elections of Mayors, adopted in 2003,[18] presented a specific legal act that for the first time specifically defined the election of the mayor as well as the characteristics of a mayor's mandate. The 2003 law introduced the practice of direct mayoral election, which presented a positive step in the development of citizens' rights. However, with the changes to the Law on Self-Government in 2009, the election of the mayor was again placed into the hands of the local parliament. Since then, the mayor is elected by the majority of delegates in the local parliament.

The Genesis of Fiscal Decentralisation

Considering the changes that happened since the beginning of the 1990s in the administrative, territorial, political as well as fiscal decentralisation processes in Montenegro, we can observe three distinct phases:

1. First phase (1992–2003)—A period of high centralisation due to the change of the state legal status and unfavourable political, social, and economic situation in the country.
2. Second phase (2003–2008)—A period of administrative, political, and fiscal decentralisation characterised by a stable legislative environment and an increase in local government revenue.
3. Third phase (2008–2016)—A period characterised by several centralising changes to the legislative framework and a decrease in public revenue.

Our analysis is primarily focused on functional and financial decentralisation and its impact on local government budgets, as during the observed period, changes in the administrative and territorial organisation were minor and they have all already been explained.

During the first phase, the functioning of the local governments was defined in accordance with the 1991 amendments to the Constitution from 1974 and 1992 Constitution. By this act the previous "communal system" was abandoned,[19] and a system of local self-government was introduced with a division of administrative and political power between the central and local governments. However, in the 1992 Constitution, the local self-government issue was very modestly covered. Only two articles referred to the functioning of local self-government. Article 66 defined the right for self-government organisation that may take place in municipalities and the Capital City. Citizens in local governments decide directly through their elected representatives on different affairs of interest to local citizens. Also, the Constitution defined the local assembly and the presidency as the two main institutions of the municipality. The same article states that the Republic would support local administration. In the second article, Article 99, it was stated that ministries and administrative bodies perform state administration affairs, while some of these activities may be transferred to the local self-governments by law or a government act. In order to ratify the new state organisation and practices that were previously regulated by the federal laws, the adoption of the 1992 Constitution was soon after followed by the drafting and adoption of a set of legalisation that regulated the organisation of the state administration and the division of state affairs at different levels of government.[20] Although some of these documents may be seen as formal steps towards decentralisation, they were adopted at a time of high political instability and very difficult economic situation, which caused excessive centralisation in practice. Thus, the beginning of the 1990s was characterised by centralistic behaviour of the administration, with ministries holding the main power and local governments with a completely marginalised role.

A positive step towards decentralisation was made in 1995 when the 1991 Law on Self-Government was changed.[21] The new law introduced the right of citizens to initiate changes of legislation through citizens' initiatives, widened the functions of local governments, and defined the internal organisation of the local administration. With these changes, the power of the local administration was strengthened. However, significant decentralisation practices were again not observed in practice. One of the reasons was the existing system of municipal financing. At that period, the financing of local governments was still regulated by the (1993) Law on the Public Revenue System.[22] This was a very comprehensive piece of legislation, which, besides the financing of local governments, regulated the financing of the central government. According to this law, local governments in Montenegro were entitled to the following revenues: local communal fees, local administrative fees, charges on the exploitation of public interest goods, and the construction land use charge. Also, local revenue included revenue generated by local government bodies through their activities, as well as revenue generated by public institutions financed from local municipal budgets. Thus, municipalities were entitled to a small share of the general public funds that were limited by low trade and economic activity.

During this first phase of observation, the decentralisation process was part of the complex changes that were happening, such as the disintegration of Yugoslavia, the establishment of the country's new legal status, regional conflicts and the management of the post-conflict situation, as well as the political transition from a single-party system to a parliamentary democracy. The first multi-party elections were organised in 1990. Although various political parties participated in the elections, they were won by the successor to the Communist Party, which was in a position to use all the available state resources. Following this, that party gained a majority in all elections at central and local levels for the next seven years (Darmanović, 2016). Thus, the Montenegrin multi-party system was actually a system with one dominant political party, which made possible a stable relationship between the central and local authorities, with a dominant centre. These circumstances defined the nature of the decentralisation process, which was very limited, general, and administrative.

In 1997, the dominant political party split, which defined the future for political relations in the country. Although, the reformist, modern offshoot of the party won the 1998 elections, it was no longer as large, homogeneous, and powerful as the previously united party. Moreover, it was confronted with certain political issues at the federal level. For all these reasons, the dominant party needed the support of the opposition in the years to come. However, the political coalitions formed in that period proved very stable over the next decade. The new division of power and dynamics in the political arena contributed to the actualisation of the issue of decentralisation. At the end of the 1990s it become evident that the existing framework for the functioning and financing of local governments did not provide a satisfactory basis for decentralisation and that reforms were needed. Moreover, reforms were accelerated by the trend for decentralisation of public administration in the European Union and other western democracies, and they were supported and advocated for by the donor community present in the country.

The second phase, starting in 2003, was a phase of implementation of the decentralisation process in the country, involving the actual transfer of responsibilities and resources from the central to the local level. Implementation of decentralisation started after two election years (2001, 2002) in which the political system became even further polarised (Darmanović, 2016) and relations with Serbia were redefined, with the Union becoming looser. These processes created the need for the decentralisation process to cover all political, administrative, and financial aspects. The implementation of decentralisation started with the adoption of the first Public Administration Reform Strategy in Montenegro (2003–2009). The Strategy set two major goals: improvement in the administrative system efficiency and integration of the administration system into the wider social system. The adoption of the Strategy was followed by the implementation of the Law on Local Self-Government and the Law on Local Government Finance in the same year. The 2003 Law on Local Self-Government provided local government with over 40 original mandates, which have not changed since then. Some of the most important mandates are to perform and develop communal activities; to maintain and safeguard local and non-categorised roads; to regulate and provide passenger transportation in urban and suburban areas; to provide preconditions for entrepreneurial development; to protect the environment; to safeguard local public interest goods; to manage watercourses, the surrounding land and structures of local importance and cultural development; and to safeguard cultural heritage. Local government in Montenegro does not provide health, social or educational services, but legally it is allowed to contribute to the provision of these services in accordance with its financial liabilities.

The 2003 Law on Local Government Finance set out four sources of municipal revenue: own-source revenue, shared revenue, equalisation fund revenue, and the central budget. The law introduced the real estate tax, the personal income surtax, the local consumption tax, the firm name display tax, a tax on underdeveloped construction land, and a tax on lotteries and games of chance as own-source municipal revenue. The law also standardised the share of the personal income tax received by local government at 10 per cent for all municipalities except the Capital City and the Old Royal Capital. Also, one of the main innovations of the law was the establishment of the Equalisation Fund as a transparent and criteria-based mechanism for allocating inter-municipal grants.

Equalisation funds are secured from the personal income tax, while the funds are allocated based on the municipal capacity index, the municipal budgetary spending index, and the local communal infrastructure development index.

These legal changes came into force in 2004 and had an immediate impact on the structure of municipal revenues. Own-source revenues share increased in only one year from 30 per cent to 60 per cent, while the share of shared revenues dropped from 55 to 18 per cent. Moreover, during the following four-year period characterised by significant growth of economic activity, municipal revenues increased by 350 per cent mainly as a result of the increase of the own-source revenues from the land development charge, the personal income tax and surtax, as well as the share of revenue from the real estate transfer tax. Having legal preconditions as well as significant budgetary funds, the local governments exhibited a more proactive role in practising public management, that is, selling municipal assets, taking loans, and initiating big infrastructural or communal projects. Also, local governments used this opportunity to both increase salaries and increase the number of employees in local authorities.

Based on the facts presented here, it may be concluded that the 2003 Law on Local Government Finance served as a good foundation for the decentralisation of municipal finance. However, the growth in local revenue between 2004 and 2008 was mainly caused by increased economic activity and the sale of municipal assets, while it was only to a small extent a consequence of improved local government efficiency in public financial management, as will become evident when looking at the following years (Fig. 5.1).

The third phase in the process of decentralisation in Montenegro started in 2008 with the implementation of two legislative changes aimed at further boosting economic growth by creating more favourable conditions for business. The first change was related to the 2006 Law on Local Communal Fees and suspended local communal fees for the most profitable economic activities: telecommunications, electricity transfer, and exploitation of the seashore. The second was the 2008 Law on Spatial Planning and Construction of Structures, which suspended the

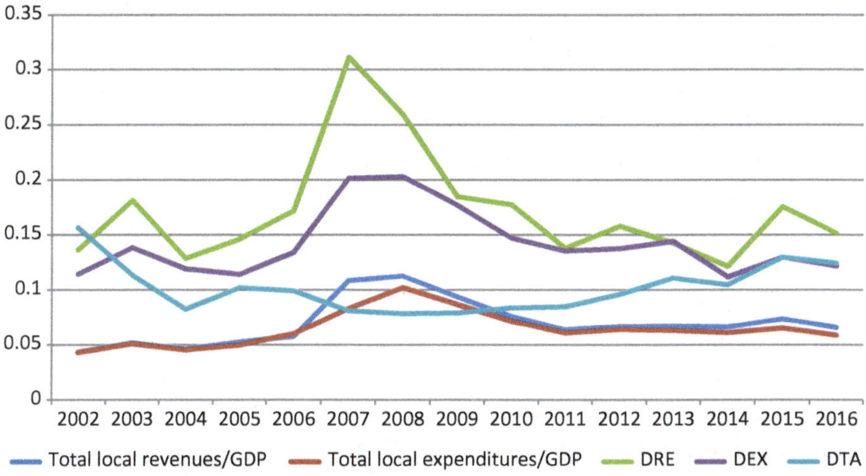

Fig. 5.1 Fiscal decentralisation in Montenegro from 2002 to 2016. Source: Authors' calculation based on Ministry of Finance data on local government revenue and expenditure 2002–2016. Note: DRE—the ratio of the total revenue of local and general government; DEX—the ratio of the total expenditure of local and general government; DTA—the ratio of the total tax revenues of local and general government; TLR/GDP—the ratio between total local revenues and gross domestic product (GDP); TLE/GDP—the ratio of total local expenditures and GDP. General government meaning consolidated public revenues/expenditures

construction land use charge, one of the main sources of municipal revenues, due to the new ownership relations and state-owned land management.

Unfortunately, the implementation of these changes coincided with the effects of the global financial crisis and a decrease in economic activity of about three p.p. Moreover, the drop especially hit those sectors that had previously contributed most to municipal revenue, such as industry, construction, real estate, and trade. Consequently, municipalities began to experience a drop in overall revenue and thus suffer liquidity problems. The central government, with its decision to eliminate the construction land use charge, was and still is seen as a major culprit for this turning point in the financial situation of local governments. However, a detailed analysis of the changes to local government budgets (Kmezić, Đulić, Jocović, & Kaluđerović, 2016; Kmezić,

Kaluđerović, Jocović, & Đulić, 2016) shows that in the year before this decision was implemented, revenue from the construction land use charge accounted for only around 5 per cent of total local government revenue. Thus, it may be concluded that abolishing the construction land use charge only contributed to the negative impact of the economic crisis on municipal budgets.

As the downward trend in municipal revenue continued over the following two years, the central government in 2010 introduced several changes to the Law on Local Government Finance in order to stabilise the local financial situation. One set of measures meant an increase of the personal income surtax and the percentage share of local government revenue coming from the personal income tax, the real estate transfer tax, and concession from natural resources. In addition, the equalisation fund criteria were also significantly amended, and the list of sources of revenue was broadened. Another set of measures was the elimination of certain local government revenue sources, such as the consumption tax, the firm or business display tax, and the games of chance and entertainment games tax. Despite the aim of those changes, they were centralising in nature, as they decreased the number and share of own-source municipal revenues.

The positive effects of these changes became obvious immediately through the increase of total municipal revenues, which then had stabilised as a result of improved economic activity and the tendency of municipalities to rely on better collection and administration of own-source revenue, such as the real estate tax, the municipal road use charge, and other own-source categories.

Decentralisation of Revenues

The Law on Local Government Finance defines local governments as having four sources of funding to finance their mandates: own-source revenues; revenues shared by law; the Equalisation Fund; and the central budget. Currently (in 2016), own-source revenues present the main source of municipal revenues with almost 70 per cent. Shared revenues make up 18 per cent of municipal revenue, while the Equalisation Fund makes up an average of 11 per cent. The conditional donations from the central government make up a steady 1 per cent. This is a completely different structure than the one from 2003, before the initiation of the decentralisation process, when shared revenues made up 55 per cent of total revenues, while own-source revenues or local revenues had accounted for around 30 per cent.

There are four categories of own-source revenues. The first and main category is taxes—the real estate tax and the surtax on the personal income tax. The second group of revenues are charges that include the municipal roads use charge, concession fees for the contracts signed and concluded by the LGUs, the environmental protection charge, and the construction land development charge. The third group of revenues is comprised of fees—local administrative and local communal fees. Finally, the fourth group consists of other revenues, which vary for each municipality and may include revenue from the sale and lease of municipal property, revenue from capital, revenue from concessions, and donations.

With the initiation of the decentralisation process in 2003, the nature of revenue from the real estate tax was changed from shared to own-source revenue. In 2003, real estate tax revenue amounted to 5.5 per cent of total municipal revenue, while in 2016 it was at the level of 20 per cent. Considering that the average real estate tax rate is 0.26 per cent, it seems that this rising trend was primarily a result of improved efficiency of tax collection rather than of the tax rate increase introduced in 2011 (Kmezić, Đulić, et al., 2016). Although tax collection has improved, the collection rate is still very low mainly due to inaccurate and outdated cadastre records. In addition, several other problems regarding the collection of this revenue have been noted by municipalities, including a lack of penalties for failure to submit a tax return or for filing incorrect tax returns and forced collection that is usually not implemented in practice. In order to resolve the solvency issues of LGUs and improve their financial situation, the central government adopted new amendments to the law, which came into force on 1 January 2016. These changes include an increase in the tax rate threshold from 0.1 to 0.25 per cent of the market value of real estate and a number of tax exemptions. Such exemptions cover, for example, structures and special parts of residential buildings owned by investors and defined as investments in progress, finished products inventory intended for resale, or secondary buildings that have a lease contract with a travel agency. The amendments also refer to sanctions for failure by various legal entities to submit data to municipalities. There is still no assessment or analysis on whether these changes have affected local government revenue and if so how.

The personal income tax surtax is also own-source revenue since 2003. Municipalities are allowed to impose a personal income surtax at a rate of up to 13 per cent in municipalities, while the Capital City and the Old Royal Capital may impose a rate of 15 per cent. All municipalities impose the highest rate allowed by the law. The share of revenue from the personal income surtax in total municipal revenues decreased since the start of the decentralisation process from 14 per cent in 2004 to 7 per cent in 2016 mainly due to a decrease in the personal income tax rate as part of the creation of a favourable business climate in the country.

In the second category of own-source revenues/charges, the land development charge is the most important, especially as it is the only local government revenue from construction land after the elimination of the land use charge in 2009. The charge may only be used by LGUs for the preparation and development of construction land in the area where a structure is being constructed. Municipalities agree with investors on the terms, manner, deadlines, and procedure according to which the charge is to be paid, but the central government must give prior consent for all of these elements. Municipalities often criticise this practice. As this category has not undergone any legal changes since 2003, it may be concluded that the fluctuations seen during the observation period are solely the result of changes in economic activity and the demand for land. This category accounted for less than 10 per cent of total revenue in 2003, while in 2016 the figure was 12 per cent, and at the economic peak in 2008 it was 27 per cent.

Local administrative and communal fees are two main fee revenue sources. The level of administrative fees for actions and documents is determined by the local fee tariff. However, the level of local fee may not be greater than the fees payable for similar documents and actions conducted before the state administration bodies, which limits the autonomy of the LGU to set the local fees. The revenues from the administrative fees did not change significantly during the observed period and amounted up to 1 per cent of total local government revenues. The Law on Local Communal Fees states that municipalities may determine the amount of their local communal fees depending on the type of activity, area, location, or zone in which the buildings or objects are located or in which services subject to the fee are performed. As LGUs are free to set all these elements, the implementation, administration, and collection of local municipal fees are significantly different among municipalities. As this enables competitiveness among municipalities, it also leads to the situation in which fees are significantly different despite the fact that real costs to which they refer are not. The most important change that this law has undergone was the suspension of local communal fees for the most profitable economic activities in 2006. This significantly contributed to a decrease in the share of communal fees in total revenues from 4.5 per cent in 2003 to 1 per cent in 2016, especially because the legal basis was found to compensate for the adverse effects this had on LGU budgets.

Two groups of shared revenues may be defined. The first consists of shared revenues from personal income taxes and revenues from real estate sales taxes, and the second group comprises shared revenues from concessions and other charges for the use of natural resources that are granted by the state, the annual charge for vehicle registration, and the so-called environmental charge paid when registering vehicles. In the Montenegrin shared revenues system, there is no revenue fully transferred to the local government.

The main category of shared revenue is the personal income tax. The personal income tax is collected by the central government and subsequently redirected to municipal budgets. Under the current legal solution, municipalities receive 12 per cent of revenue (16 per cent for the Capital City and 13 per cent for the Old Royal Capital) from the personal income tax levied within their territory. Personal income tax legislation has undergone several changes since the initiation of the decentralisation process. The Law on the Personal Income Tax[23] (adopted in 2001) has been amended twice: in 2004, when tax rates were reduced to 0 per cent, 15 per cent, 19 per cent, and 23 per cent, and in 2007, when a single 15 per cent tax rate was introduced, which was then reduced to 12 per cent in 2009 and 9 per cent in 2010. Due to the constant decrease of the tax rate, as well as a slowdown of economic activity, the proportion of total revenue made up by the personal income tax decreased by 16 p.p. in 12 years, from around 24 per cent in 2003 to 8 per cent in 2016. In order to stabilise the financial situation after the financial crisis, the government amended the Law on the Personal Income Tax in 2013 and introduced a crisis tax on the salaries that are above the country's average. Despite the fact that this was introduced as temporary, this measure is still implemented currently by the 11 per cent rate.

In the case of the real estate sales tax, a municipality should directly receive 80 per cent of revenue generated within its territory, while an additional 10 per cent is transferred to the municipality through the Equalisation Fund. Revenues from the real estate sales tax were at the level of 4 per cent of total revenues with some fluctuations during the years of the economic boom. In the case of concessions, a municipality should receive 70 per cent of revenues from concessions and other charges for the use of natural resources (with two exemptions amounting to 20 per cent in the case of port and marine use). Revenues from the concession have been at an average level of 2 per cent since 2003, but a slight increase has been observed during the last few years (in 2016 the level was at 4 per cent). However, the concession system in the country is facing a number of issues such as irregular payments and poor coordination between central and local authorities, which makes it very inefficient especially for local governments (Fig. 5.2).

The Equalisation Fund is used as a mechanism for equalising municipal finance. The Law on Local Government Finance defines the source of revenue, the right to use it, and the criteria applied in allocating Equalisation Fund resources. The Equalisation Fund's assets are secured from (a) the personal income tax at a rate of 11 per cent of total revenue; (b) the real estate tax at a rate of 10 per cent of total revenue; (c) concession charges from games of chance at a rate of 40 per cent of total revenue; and (d) the tax on the use of motor vehicles, vessels, and aircrafts at a rate of 100 per cent of total revenue. The right to use the fund's resources is conditional upon a municipality's per capita fiscal capacity in the three preceding fiscal years. Municipalities with an average per capita fiscal capacity lower than the average capacity of all municipalities for the same period are entitled to the fund's resources. Resources are awarded throughout the year in the form of monthly advances, as well as after the final allocation at the end of the year, with 60 per cent of revenue being

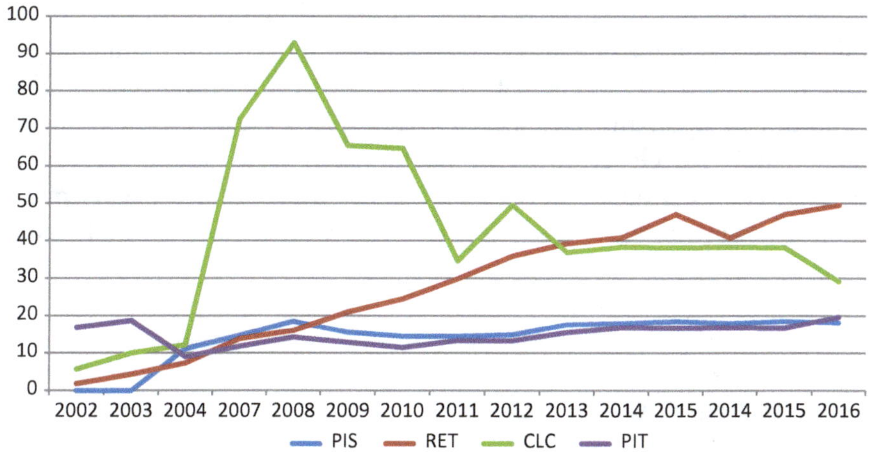

Fig. 5.2 Trend of selected local government revenue categories (in million EURO). Source: Authors' calculation based on Ministry of Finance data on local government revenue and expenditure 2002–2016. Note: PIS—personal income surtax, PIT—personal income tax, RET—real estate tax, CLC—construction land development charge

allocated based on fiscal capacity and the remaining 40 per cent based on budgetary needs. Fund resources are primarily intended to settle current local government expenditure or the current activities of municipalities.

The Equalisation Fund was defined as a mechanism for reducing the regional disparities in the previous strategic document related to the country's regional development. However, this is not the case with the new 2014–2020 Regional Development Strategy, which is based on the assumption that policymakers expect that LGUs, which are the beneficiaries of the Equalisation Fund, will develop and strengthen their fiscal capacity. Bearing in mind the current financial situation of municipalities, this may be considered a very optimistic scenario.

Between 2004 and 2015, the proportion of total municipal revenue made up by Equalisation Fund resources increased from 3 to 10 per cent. The majority (around 70 per cent) of those funds was directed towards local government in the least developed northern region. These resources amounted to an average of 69.58 per cent of the total fund resources in the reporting period. In 2015, the total value of revenue from the fund was 26 million euros.

Local governments may also get conditional grants from the central budget for the implementation of investment projects. The grant amount may not exceed 50 per cent of the total value of the investment and is conditioned upon the existence of a municipal multi-year investment plan. Also, the Government of Montenegro is to adopt the grants decisions at the proposal of the Ministry of Finance. This category made up 1 per cent of total municipal revenues during the whole observed period and was not under the influence of the economic trends or the fiscal decentralisation process.

Assignment of Functions

The current Law on Local Government defines 40 different principal functions of local governments. The main principal functions are related to communal and utility activities and include performing and developing of communal activities the maintenance of local and non-categorised roads, passenger transportation in urban and suburban areas, the setting/monitoring of conditions for the construction of buildings, supervision of the use of construction land, and watercourse management. Besides these, LGU's own functions also include providing preconditions for entrepreneurial development, environmental protection, safeguarding local public interest goods, cultural development, and safeguarding cultural heritage. Additional tasks of an LGU are related to maintaining local government assets, defining the level of own-source revenues, organising, maintaining, and controlling own-source revenue collection, defining public interest in the case of expropriation of real estate of public interest; record keeping, inspecting controls, providing legal aid to citizens, establishing public awards, as well as performing other functions of interest for local citizens. Besides this, LGU performs administrative functions that are related to the development and adoption of development plans, development strategic documents, spatial plans, the budget, and so on.

It is important to emphasise that the law does not define municipal legal obligations in the education and healthcare systems, but prescribes that local government should, in accordance with its abilities, contribute

Table 5.2 Distribution of functions according to the level of government

		Central govt.	Municipal
1.	General public services	•	•
2.	Defence	•	
3.	Public order and security	•	
4.	Education	•	
4.1.	Preschool		
4.2.	Elementary	•	
4.3.	Secondary	•	
4.4.	Tertiary	•	
5.	Healthcare	•	
6.	Social security and welfare	•	
7.	Housing and communal economy matters and services	•	•
8.	Recreation, culture, and religion		•
9.	Agriculture, forestry, hunting, fishing	•	
10.	Mining, industry, construction	•	•
11.	Traffic and communications	•	•
11.1.	Road transport	•	•
11.2.	Rail transport	•	
11.3.	Air transport	•	
12.	Other economic matters and services	•	•

Source: Authors' presentation based on the classification and presentation of Ott and Bajo (2001)

to creating the necessary conditions and improving healthcare, education, social and child protection services, employment opportunities, and other areas of local public interest. However, in practice, municipalities do not perform these additional functions (Table 5.2).

The Law on Local Self-Government defines LGU's principal functions in general, yet a number of other pieces of legislation prescribe those functions in detail. The most important example is the Law on Communal Activities, which is the most important regulation for understanding LGU functions, even more important than the Law on Local Self-Government. In addition, other legal acts add certain responsibilities to LGUs, such as the Law on Healthcare,[24] the Law on Rafting,[25] the Law on Alcohol and Alcoholic Beverages,[26] and the Law on Wine[27]. This practice makes the monitoring of municipal functions and efficiency very difficult. In addition, in the majority of cases, these acts define responsibilities of the municipalities without defining proper sources of financing for them

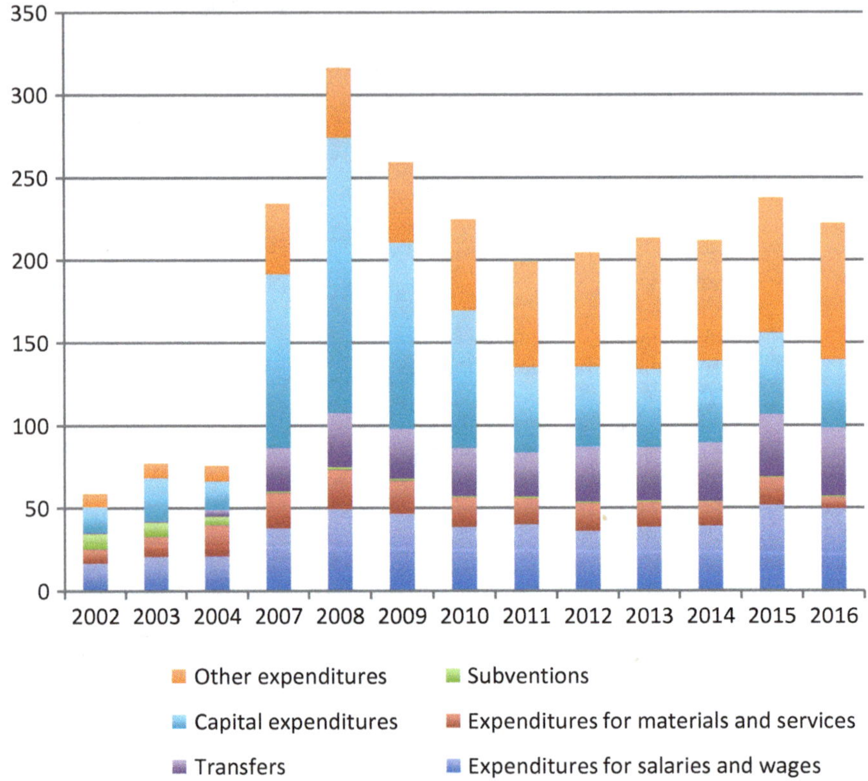

Fig. 5.3 Expenditures of local government units according to the economic classification from 2002 to 2016 (in million EURO). Source: Authors' calculation based on Ministry of Finance data on local government revenue and expenditure 2002–2016

and create an additional burden on the budget. That is why the improvement of links between functions of LGU and the financial means for their implementation is important for a more efficient performance of LGU.

The data on the LGU expenditures according to the functional classification are not available, and that is why we focus on the analysis of the expenditures according to the economic classification (Fig. 5.3).

Since the initiation of the decentralisation process in 2003, local government expenditure has experienced a trend similar to that seen for total revenue. Total expenditure grew from 58 million euros in 2002 to 220 million euros at the end of 2016, with a peak of 316.3 million euros in 2008. An analysis of the structure of expenditure shows significant changes over the years. While the "current expenditure" category remained very stable at 30 per cent over the whole observation period, the "capital expenditure" and "other expenditure" categories experienced significant fluctuations. The most important expenditure item in current expenditures is gross wages, making up around 60 per cent of current expenditures or 20 per cent of total expenditures of all local governments in 2016. In comparison with the pre-crisis period, this category recorded an increase of about ten p.p. Capital expenditure amounted to 45 per cent of total expenditure before the crisis, while by 2016 it had dropped to 20 per cent. However, the complete picture of the current financial situation of LGUs is seen through the "other expenditure" category, which includes loans, credits, and other types of debt servicing. Data show that this category made up 8 per cent of total expenditure in 2008, rising to 60 per cent by 2015. The main reason for this huge increase is repayment of debts, which increased by 20 p.p. during the observed period.

Thus, it seems LGUs not only used all rising revenues during the period of economic boom (2004–2008) for the increase of capital, and also current consumption, but also borrowed additional funds. Due to this, LGUs are facing big liquidity and financial problems, which require support from the central government. That is why we will now focus our analysis on issues of borrowing, outstanding bills, and arrears.

Local Public Debt: Borrowing, Outstanding Bills, and Arrears

The fiscal decentralisation process, or more precisely the second phase of the decentralisation process defined previously, coincided with an increase in economic activity in Montenegro brought about by significant foreign direct investment, domestic investment, increased consumption due to credit growth, and the revitalisation of several economic sectors—namely, tourism, and construction. In a very short period of time, these processes created a completely new situation for municipalities, which now had significantly greater authority to spend the consistently rising financial sources. Municipalities used their increased budgets to increase the number of employed persons, current expenditures, as well as capital investments. In this way, salary expenditures increased by over 50 per cent in the period 2004–2007; similarly, capital expenditures increased by over 500 per cent in the same period. In addition, municipalities began to borrow at the very start (2004) of the decentralisation process. Thus, data show that municipal debt amounted to 30 per cent of total expenditures in 2004 and 10 per cent in 2007. These trends indicate irresponsible behaviour by certain local authorities. But, it later became obvious that this was not primarily caused by a lack of management knowledge and skills in implementing activities that were valuable for and beneficial to the local community. Such behaviour was also motivated by a wish to improve the economic and political position of the ruling elites. For this reason, the actions of local authorities were mainly aimed at promoting local officials and increasing their salaries, employing people close to the ruling party/ies through very unclear employment procedures (Đurnić, 2017) and implementing investment projects involving people close to government officials.[28]

The question of local government borrowing in this period was defined by the 2003 Law on Local Government Finance. This law prescribes that municipalities may borrow by issuing securities or taking out a loan. In regard to credit indebtedness, the law differentiates between short-term borrowing (up to one year) that occurs because of short-term liquidity needs and long-term borrowing (more than one year). Long-term borrowing is possible only for financing capital investment expenditure or for purchasing capital assets in accordance with an approved multi-year investment plan. This law emphasises that "long-term borrowing may not be used for financing current expenditures". Furthermore, the law allows for municipalities to issue financial guarantees. According to the law, a municipality may borrow so long as the total principal and interest repayment, payment on the basis of a leasing contract, repayment of obligations from a previous period, and all other kinds of debt do not exceed 10 per cent of realised current revenue in the year preceding the year when the borrowing took place. In addition, the government must consent to the borrowing.

When this law was amended in 2010, an opportunity was missed to implement hard budgetary constraints and change the method of municipal borrowing, although it started to become evident that local governments were facing significant problems. The law is still in effect in 2017.

Although there were legal restrictions in terms of municipal borrowing, as well as a clear borrowing procedure, municipalities did not abide by these. The State Audit Institution reports for some LGUs clearly confirm this practice. It must be asked why this behaviour was tolerated by the central government. Part of the answer probably lies in the political relations between central and local government. In spite of this, the situation was not alarming until 2009. However, in 2009, the effects of the financial crisis started to be felt in Montenegro, leading to a significant drop in economic activity. Consequently, local revenue decreased greatly, and municipalities found themselves in a situation in which they could not perform their duties, with debt beginning to accumulate. In addition, as they were unable to pay off their debt, municipalities began to accumulate unpaid obligations. The following data clearly demonstrate the condition in local government finance in the years that followed.

In 2009, local government debt was 60 million euros, while by the end of 2016 it was slightly above 140 million euros. The figure rises further if we take into account funds borrowed by the central government from foreign creditors that are then transferred to municipalities according to a subcredit agreement with the state. In that case, the total debt of municipalities at the end of 2015 was 20 per cent higher, amounting to 175 million euros or 75 per cent of total local government expenditures (unconsolidated debt at the end of 2014 was 128 million euros, while consolidated debt amounted to 166 million euros).

The majority of the debt, around 80 per cent according to 2014 data, is owed to foreign financial institutions. As can be seen from the Fig. 5.4, the municipality with the largest debt by far, amounting to 60 million euros, is the coastal town of Budva, which experienced the most significant increase in revenue during the economic boom, thanks to revenue from construction land charges and real estate taxes. Two other municipalities

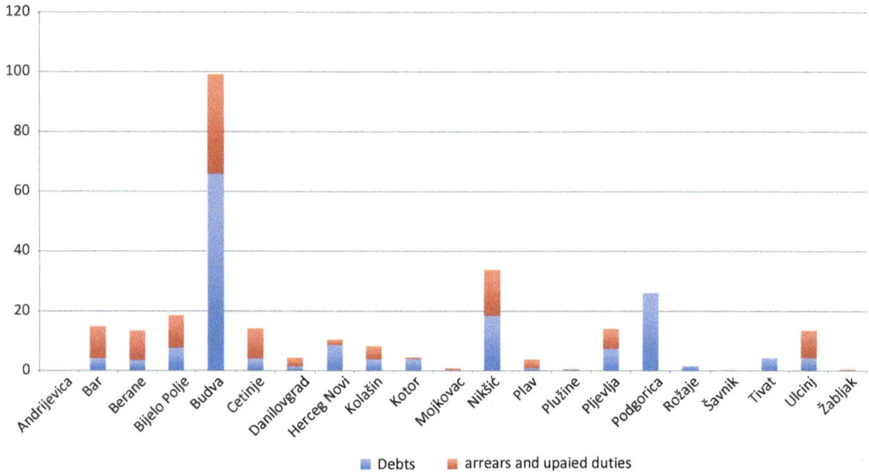

Fig. 5.4 Debts and arrears of LGUs in 2014 (in million EURO). Source: Authors' calculation based on Ministry of Finance data on local government revenue and expenditure 2009–2015

with a high level of debt, around 20 million euros, are Podgorica (the Capital City) and Nikšić, the country's second largest municipality.

In addition to the high level of debt, municipalities have huge unpaid obligations and arrears, amounting to 119.2 million euros at the end of 2014. The majority (54 per cent) of 2014 arrears was for current expenditure, mainly wages and salaries. An additional 19 per cent are unpaid duties for capital expenses, while another 19 per cent are credits and loans. Again, Budva is the municipality with the highest level of arrears, with 32 million euros at the end of 2014. Nikšić also had around 15 million euros of arrears, while a number of other municipalities, such as Bar, Berane, Bijelo Polje, Ulcinj, and Cetinje, had arrears of around ten million euros. However, Podgorica does not have any unpaid duties and arrears (Fig. 5.5).

The high level of debt and arrears for wages and salaries indicates significant and evident overstaffing and rise of salaries (Pradelli, Nitti, Wachira, Obradovic, & Madzarevic-Sujster, 2015), which were not so evident when analysed by the share of the wage and salary expenditures in total expenditures. This data indicates that taxes and duty on

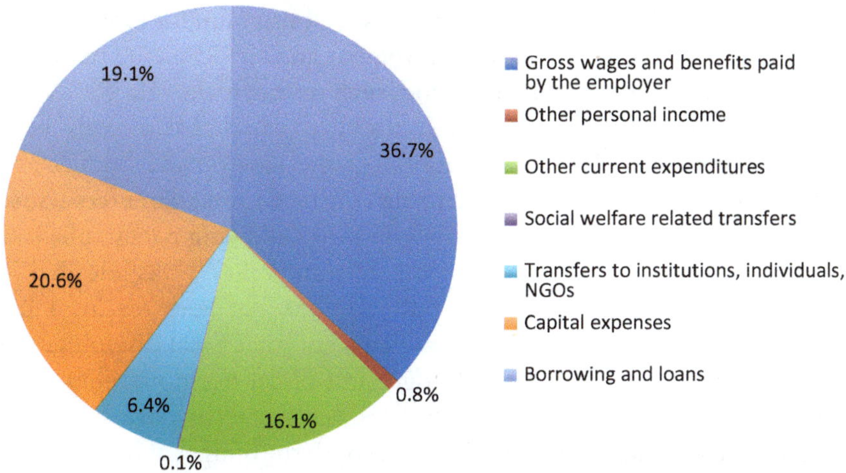

Fig. 5.5 The structure of arrears and unpaid debt in 2014. Source: Authors' calculation based on Ministry of Finance data on local government revenue and expenditure 2009–2015

salaries were not paid by local authorities and that this practice was tolerated by the central government and other national institutions. However, this issue was "officially" recognised by the central government a year before the financial problems escalated. For this reason, the Public Administration Reform Strategy for 2011–2016 envisioned an internal reorganisation, and a plan for this was adopted in 2013. However, the number of employees in both local administration and municipally owned companies increased rather than decreased, from 10,503 at the end of June 2013 to 11,780 at the end of September 2014.[29] This practice was mostly evident in southern municipalities such as Tivat and Budva, the municipalities with the highest foreign direct investment and with strong political connections to the central government.

The sum total of local government arrears and debt (bank liabilities) at the end of 2014 was 286 million euros or 8.2 per cent of the 2014 GDP. Although this accounts for a very small portion of total Montenegrin public debt, which amounts to almost 70 per cent of the GDP, it presents a financial distress to many municipalities.

This very problematic and unstable financial situation for local governments required significant state involvement and the implementation of several consolidation measures. One such measure is related to the changes to the Law on the Real Estate Tax, which has already been explained. Another three, the adoption of the Law on the Budget and Fiscal Accountability, debt-restructuring contracts, and guarantees issued by the central government, are outlined in the following paragraphs.

The Law on the Budget and Fiscal Accountability[30] was adopted in 2014 after it became evident that public finances at both the local and national level were facing serious problems and that fiscal discipline was very low. The 2014 Law on the Budget and Fiscal Accountability regulates budget planning and execution, fiscal accountability, loans, guarantees and other questions of importance for both the budget of Montenegro and the LGU budgets. In terms of municipalities, this law defines several issues, from the fiscal regulation concerning the level of the budget deficit of local government bodies to the procedure of adopting municipal budgets. As far as fiscal restrictions are concerned, the law prescribes that municipal budget deficit in one year cannot be greater than 10 per cent of the municipality's revenue in that same year. An exception to this rule is possible if a municipality wishes to finance capital expenditures. In this case, the municipality must submit a request to the Ministry of Finance by 31 March of the current year by which it seeks approval for exceeding the legally defined limit. If a municipality exceeds the budget deficit limit without the Ministry's approval, the minister is obligated to cease the transfer of funds from the central to the local budget in the amount equal to the amount by which the limit has been exceeded.

The Ministry of Finance oversees the procedure of budget adoption. Namely, the responsible municipal body is required to seek an opinion from the Ministry of Finance on the suggested level and structure of expenditures, earnings policy, capital expenditures, sources of financing, and levels of surplus and deficit prior to the adoption of a decision on the municipal budget. The Ministry of Finance opinion represents an integral part of the proposed decision on the municipal budget adopted by the local assembly. The law clearly prescribes that if the Ministry of Finance opinion is a negative one, the local assembly is not in a position to adopt the decision on the budget. In addition to the budget decision, municipalities must also submit a three-year plan of receipts and expenditures and an overview of long-term contractual obligations, expenditures, and investment programmes. When it comes to borrowing and the issuing of guarantees, this law tightens the conditions under which municipalities may borrow in the long-term. Namely, the law clearly states that municipalities may borrow in the long-term and issue guarantees only with previously obtained consent of the government. Such approval is granted at the advice of the Ministry.

In February 2015, the government issued a statement on restructuring debt related to taxes and contributions to wages and salaries, calculated as 89.7 million euros at the end of 2014. Of this total, 74.46 million euros relate to municipalities that use the Equalisation Fund, with repayment extended by 20 years, starting from 1 July 2015. For the southern municipalities of Bar and Budva, which have an above average fiscal capacity, the repayment of 14.6 million euros was extended by five years. In addition, the government signed agreements with the northern municipalities of Andrijevica and Žabljak to extend repayment of 1.18 million euros for the wages and salaries of employees of state-owned companies established by the municipality by 20 years. During 2015, the central government signed contracts to restructure arrears with 16 of Montenegro's 23 municipalities. According to recommendations from municipalities, monthly annuities are set at a lower level for the first few years of the repayment period. Municipalities that sign the contract are obligated to pay taxes and duties on wages and salaries regularly and issue a bill of exchange and a letter of authorisation to the Tax Authority. Municipalities must also prepare and adopt a plan for internal reorganisation aimed at reducing the number of employees in administration as well as setting up agencies and state-owned companies. The final obligation for municipalities is to seek approval from the Ministry of Finance for each new employee. An additional consolidation measure implemented during 2015 was the issuing of guarantees to municipalities with high debt and arrears. Up until the end of 2015, the government issued guarantees amounting to 42.89 million euros. After the restructuring and the implemented measures, the levels of debt and unpaid obligations of local governments were reduced, amounting to 175 million euros and 26 million euros, respectively, by the end of 2016.

Although the consolidation measures initiated in 2015 represent a good step forward, especially in terms of the debt-restructuring contracts, which set very clearly defined obligations for municipalities, it seems that there is a problem with implementation. It is evident from the government's 2016 reports on implementation that almost all municipalities have violated at least one requirement prescribed by the contract. Despite that, there are still yet to be any disciplinary procedures or court cases for these violations. This indicates that further effort, as well as political will, would be needed to fully implement the contracts and allow their goals to be achieved. However, restoring the sustainability of municipalities, such as Budva, Nikšić and Bijelo Polje, in very difficult financial situations would probably require difficult consolidation measures such as reprogramming bank liabilities and a significant decrease in expenditure, primarily by rationalising the number of employees, relying further on own-source revenues, and so on. In the long run, it may also require the rationalisation of some functions currently performed at the local level.

Conclusion

Montenegro is a small country with a simple one-tier local government system with 23 municipalities, the Capital City Podgorica and the Old Royal Capital Cetinje. The administrative and territorial organisation of the country has not changed significantly since the 1960s, despite the fact that state status changed several times over that period. Since the disintegration of Yugoslavia, the country functioned in a federation (from 1992 to 2003) and a union (from 2003 to 2006) with Serbia. In 2006, after a referendum, Montenegro declared its independence.

Legal competencies are divided between a local (municipal) parliament, which performs a law-making role at the local level, and a local administration, which consists of secretariats responsible for specific policy areas. The head of local administration is the President of the Municipality. Thirty councillors and one more per every 5,000 electors are delegated for the local parliament. A councillor is elected for a four-year mandate on the basis of electoral lists of political parties, coalitions of political parties, or groups of citizens and cannot be recalled.

In the division of mandates, only those parties that have more than 3 per cent of the votes in an electoral unit can participate. Although there was a legal decision that the president of a municipality is to be chosen in a direct election since 2003, the decision was abolished in 2009. Since that time, the local parliament chooses the president.

The analysis of the genesis of the fiscal decentralisation process from the beginning of the 1990s to today reveals three phases. The first phase covers the period from 1992 to 2003 and is characterised by the absence of real decentralisation despite the existence of basic legal conditions for its implementation. The reason for this absence is found in the socioeconomic situation during that period, during which there were conflicts in the region, sanctions, low economic activity, and a tense political situation. In such conditions, it is expected that questions surrounding decentralisation would be unimportant on the political agenda and that the role of municipalities in making and implementing decisions would be minimal. The second period took place from 2003 to 2008. In this second phase, Montenegro achieved political and economic stability, which allowed policy makers to turn their attention to processes that were neglected in the previous period, among which was the issue of decentralisation. In addition, the international donor community also supported the process of decentralisation. Thus, in 2003, Montenegro adopted the 2003–2009 Public Administration Reform Strategy, which defined decentralisation as a strategic goal. After this, Montenegro adopted the Law on Local Self-Government and the Law on Local Government Finance, which laid the legal foundation for the process of decentralisation. However, it should be emphasised that the process of decentralisation was, more than anything else, directed at fiscal decentralisation, as municipal functions were and still are restricted to the most basic. This phase of fiscal decentralisation is characterised by a stable legal framework and a constant increase of budget revenues. The third phase of fiscal decentralisation covers the period from 2008 to today, or rather until 2016. This phase began with the adoption of several legal amendments that had the goal of improving the business environment in Montenegro by abolishing local communal taxes for the most profitable economic activities as well as the construction land use charges. These changes decreased municipal revenue and were implemented at a time of lowered economic activity, which further decreased revenue. In order to stabilise the state of local finances, the government implemented legal amendments that increased shared revenue, on the one hand, and decreased the number of own-source revenues for municipalities, on the other. Regardless of the actual goal of these measures, they were essentially centralistic in nature.

The analysis of revenue decentralisation shows that from the beginning of the process until today (2016), the structure of revenues has been significantly changed in the favour of own-source revenue. Today, around 70 per cent of revenues of local governments are made up of own-source revenues and only somewhat less than 20 per cent of shared revenues. The most important own-source revenues are property revenues (which on their own make up around 20 per cent of total revenues), as well as revenues from the personal income surtax. In addition, local communal and administrative fees and charges, among which the most important is the construction land development charge, are major own-source revenues. The most valuable shared revenue is from the personal income tax, as well as from the real estate tax, while the most significant charges are the charges for the use of natural resources. Furthermore, the Equalisation Fund is a principal source of revenue, especially for less developed municipalities with limited fiscal capacity from the northern region.

Competencies are directed at administrative and communal activities, the maintenance of roads, the organisation of local traffic, and other similar activities. Municipalities do not perform financially demanding functions that have to do with education, healthcare, or social protection, although the legal possibility is there for them to contribute to these activities as well. However, such contribution rarely takes place in practice. A poor practice that should be much improved is the tendency for municipal competencies to be defined in great detail by a large number of specific laws, and not the Law on Local Self-Government. In a significant number of such cases, there is no connection between the defining of competencies and the sources of funding needed for their financing.

In the structure of expenditures, current expenditures dominate, among which salary expenditures make up around 20 per cent of the total. However, the category of capital expenditures experienced the greatest increase during the period of economic growth (2004–2008) due to the initiation of a significant number of investment projects. Namely, municipalities were spurred by economic growth and a constant increase in revenue, and they began a great number of capital projects, increased the number of employees, and increased employee salaries. The growth of expenditures was such that it required additional borrowing. Although there were clear legal regulations that defined the level of borrowing, these were not adhered to in practice.

When economic activity slowed in 2009 and current revenues notably decreased, municipalities were not in a position to pay their obligations. By the end of 2014, the consolidated debt of Montenegrin municipalities had reached 8.2 per cent of the GDP. Although this situation was further aggravated by exogenous factors, such as the economic situation and the acts of the central government, it is primarily and evidently the result of non-compliance with the law, a lack of fiscal capacity of municipalities, their inability to perform financial management, and their unwillingness to resolve certain issues that imposed a burden, primarily overstaffing. Such irresponsible behaviour was mainly motivated by a wish to fulfil local political and personal interests. The deterioration of local finance in some municipalities required the involvement of central government. The Ministry of Finance in 2014 adopted the Law on the Budget and Fiscal Accountability, and it signed debt-restructuring contracts with 16 municipalities with the aim of restructuring tax liabilities. Unfortunately, full implementation of these new legal acts was once again lacking. This is why the stabilisation of the financial situation in Montenegro at the local level would require some additional debt-restructuring programmes in the future, as well as some difficult consolidation measures. However, this will not be possible without full political commitment.

Overall, the decentralisation process in Montenegro only partly achieved its major goal, set in 2003, of improving the efficiency of the administrative system. This was not because of inappropriate assignment of functions, as functions were not changed substantially. Nor was it due to insufficient resources, as resources were available. It was partly due to factors beyond the control of the administration, such as imbalances in the levels of development of municipalities, economic crises, and urbanisation. It was also in very small part due to the measures and decisions of central government, as it tried to respond to all the problems that occurred, although with delay in some cases. However, it seems that it was mainly due to the fact that interests other than the public diverted government expenditure away from better and more efficient use of public revenue.

Notes

1. Law on Local Self-Government, Official Gazette of Republic of Montenegro, No., br. 42/03, 28/04, 75/05 and 13/06 and Official Gazette of Montenegro, No. 88/09, 38/12, 10/14 and 3/16.
2. Law on Local Government Finance, Official Gazette of Republic of Montenegro, No. 42/03 and 44/03, and Official Gazette of Montenegro, No. 5/08, 51/08, 74/10 and 1/15.
3. Law on Local Communal Fees, Official Gazette of Republic of Montenegro, No. 27/06.
4. Law on Spatial Planning and the Construction of Structures, Official Gazette of Republic of Montenegro, No. 51/08.
5. Law on Real Estate Tax, Official Gazette of Republic of Montenegro No. 65/01, Official Gazette of Montenegro No. 75/10 and 09/15.
6. Tax Debt Repayment Programme, Report from the Government Session held on 19 February 2015, Retrieved from http://www.gov.me/biblioteka/Informacije?AccessibilityFontSize=default&alphabet=cyr%3Fquery%3DUnesite+pojam%3A&sortDirection=Desc&pagerIndex=48
7. Constitution of the Republic of Montenegro, Official Gazette of Republic of Montenegro, No. 48/92.
8. Constitution of the Socialist Federative Republic of Yugoslavia, Official Gazette of Socialist Federative Republic of Yugoslavia, No. 09/74.
9. Constitutional Charter of the State Community of Serbia and Montenegro, Official Gazette of Serbia and Montenegro, No. 01/03.
10. Constitution of Montenegro, Official Gazette of Montenegro, No. 01/07.
11. Law on Capital City, Official Gazette of Montenegro, No. 65/05.
12. Law on the Old Royal capital, Official Gazette of Montenegro, No. 47/08.

13. Law on Division of People's Republic of Montenegro, Official Gazette of the People's Republic of Montenegro, No. 10/60.
14. Law on the Territorial Organisation of Montenegro, Official Gazette of Montenegro, No. 54/11 and 26/12.
15. Amendments to the Law on the Territorial Organisation of Montenegro, Official Gazette No. 27/13, 62/13 and 12/14.
16. Law on Regional Development, Official Gazette of Montenegro, No. 20/11.
17. Law on the Election of Councillors and Members of Parliament, Official Gazette of Republic of Montenegro, No. 4/98, 5/98, 17/98, 14/00,18/00, Official Gazette of Federal Republic of Yugoslavia, No. 73/00, 9/01, 41/02, 46/02, 45/04, 48/06, 56/06, Official Gazette of Montenegro, No. 46/11, 14/14, 47/14 and 12/16.
18. Law on the Elections of Mayors, Official Gazette of Republic of Montenegro, No. 11/03.
19. In the "communal system", municipalities did not have any political autonomy. Their role was only to implement decisions made at a higher level of government. However, their role in the economic and social life was not negligible. Municipalities provided infrastructure, transport, and other facilities and also had certain influence on business and investment decisions.
20. Law on the Organisation of the State Administration, Official Gazette of the Republic Montenegro, No. 56/93; Law on the Transfer of State Administration Affairs to Local Self-Governments, Official Gazette of the Republic, No. 30/92; Decree on the Organisation and Functioning of State Administration, Official Gazette of the Republic of Montenegro, No. 8/93 and 09/03; Decree of the Montenegrin Government on the Delegation of State Affairs to Local Self-Government, Official Gazette of the Republic of Montenegro, No. 28/92; Law on the Old Royal Capital, Official Gazette of the Republic of Montenegro, No. 56/93.
21. Law on the changes and amendments to the Law on Local Self-Government, Official Gazette of Montenegro, No. 16/95.
22. Law on Public Revenue Systems, Official Gazette of Republic of Montenegro, No. 30/93, 3/94, 42/94, 1/96, 13/96 and 45/98.
23. Law on Personal Income Tax, Official Gazette of Republic Montenegro, No. 065/01, 012/02, 037/04, 029/05, 078/06, 004/07, and Official Gazette of Montenegro, No. 086/09, 073/10, 040/11, 014/12,006/13, 062/13, 060/14,079/15 and 083/16.

24. Law on Healthcare, Official Gazette of Montenegro, No. 3/16.
25. Law on Rafting, Official Gazette of Montenegro, No. 53/11.
26. Law on Alcohol and Alcoholic Beverages, Official Gazette of Montenegro, No. 83/09.
27. Law on Wine, Official Gazette of Montenegro, No. 41/16.
28. Several local government officials were accused of involvement in this type of corruption.
29. Some of the latest data shows that there are around 4,000 employees in local government units and an additional 16,000 in local public companies and public institutions established or owned by municipalities.
30. The Law on the Budget and Fiscal Accountability, Official Gazette of Montenegro, No. 20/14.

References

Darmanović, S. (2016). Political system in Montenegro. In S. Darmanovic & V. Goati (Eds.), *Electoral and party system in Montenegro, A perspective of internal party democracy development* (pp. 11–47). Retrieved from https://www.academia.edu/27034687/Electoral_and_Party_System_in_Montenegro_-_A_Perspective_of_Internal_Party_Democracy/

Đurnić, A. (2017). *Between party patronage, nepotism and corruption: Local sector employment in Montenegro*. Retrieved from http://institut-alternativa.org/en/between-party-patronage-nepotism-and-corruption-local-sector-employment-in-montenegro/

Kmezić, S., Đulić, K., Jocović, M., & Kaluđerović, J. (2016). *Fiscal decentralisation and local government financing in Serbia and Montenegro*. Maribor: Institute for Local Self-Government and Public Procurement—Lex Localis.

Kmezić, S., Kaluđerović, J., Jocović, M., & Đulić, K. (2016). Fiscal decentralisation and local government financing in Montenegro from 2002 to 2015. *Lex Localis—Journal of Local Self-Government, 14*(3). https://doi.org/10.4335/14.3.431-450(2016)

MONSTAT. (2011). *Census data 2011* [Data file]. Retrieved from https://www.monstat.org/cg/page.php?id=533&pageid=322

Ott, K., & Bajo, A. (2001). Lokalne financije i lokalni proračuni. *Financijska teorija i praksa, 23*(3), 311–449.

Pradelli, J., Nitti, R., Wachira, D.W., Obradovic, N., & Madzarevic-Sujster, S. (2015). *Montenegro—Options to restore fiscal sustainability and improve spending efficiency at subnational level.* Washington, DC: World Bank Group. Retrieved from http://documents.worldbank.org/curated/en/306331468197341782/Montenegro-Options-to-restore-fiscal-sustainability-and-improve-spending-efficiency-at-subnational-level

Vukotić, V. (2003). Transition report for Montenegro. In A. Jovanovic & V. Vukotić (Eds.), *Transition report for Serbia and Montenegro*. Belgrade, Serbia: G17 Institute.

6

Bosnia and Herzegovina: Local Government Debt

Halko Basarić, Nina Branković, and Lejla Lazović-Pita

Introduction

The aim of this chapter is to analyse intergovernmental fiscal relations in an asymmetric confederative country: Bosnia and Herzegovina (BiH). We evaluate and assess the changes in the status of local government units (LGUs) in BiH over the last 20 years in terms of the assignment of expenditures and revenues. As BiH consists of two separate entities, as well as one self-governing unit, we aim to determine the position of LGUs in each of the two entities, since one is more fiscally decentralised than the

H. Basarić
Sarajevo, Bosnia and Herzegovina

N. Branković
University of Zagreb, Zagreb, Croatia

L. Lazović-Pita (✉)
Faculty of Economics, University of Sarajevo,
Sarajevo, Bosnia and Herzegovina
e-mail: lejla.lazovic@efsa.unsa.ba

W. Bartlett et al. (eds.), *Fiscal Decentralisation, Local Government and Policy Reversals in Southeastern Europe*, https://doi.org/10.1007/978-3-319-96092-0_6

other. A special focus will be placed upon aspects of the political economy of fiscal decentralisation in BiH, due to its unique constitutional organisation, which is reflected in the political and institutional dynamics that affect the speed of fiscal reforms in BiH.

The chapter is organised as follows: after the Introduction, we briefly analyse the constitutional and fiscal structure of BiH and fiscal reforms undertaken since 1995. Through a detailed analysis of fiscal reforms in BiH over the past 20 years, we have determined three phases that affected the position of LGUs' revenue sources: the first phase from 1995 to 2006, the second from 2006 up to the outbreak of the global financial crisis (GFC) in 2008, and the final, third, phase from 2008 up to the present day. Our analysis shows that the share of LGU revenues and expenditures to total revenues/expenditures/gross domestic product (GDP) has been increasing over the past decade, which might indicate the successful implementation of the ideas presented in the first generation of fiscal federalism (Oates, 1972). However, the case of BiH has one peculiarity in comparison to other fiscally decentralised countries. The usual question about assessing the level of fiscal decentralisation is related to identifying the motivation of a central government to give up powers and resources to local governments (Eaton, Kaiser, & Smoke, 2010). Hence, politically motivated strategies conducted at the central level influence the size and sequence of political, administrative, and fiscal decentralisation (Eaton et al., 2010, p. 10). However, in BiH, we can determine that the opposite process occurred with the centralisation of indirect taxes at the state level during the second phase, which, in turn, brought multiple benefits to all subnational levels of government, including LGUs. A significant increase in the amount of collected revenues from indirect taxes brought about easier and more transparent LGU budget planning on one side, but caused a higher dependence on indirect tax revenues on the other. So, when a short-term fall in revenues from indirect taxes during the first years of the GFC triggered fiscal stress at the LGU level in both entities, LGUs began to run budget deficits and to borrow more. Even though LGUs in both entities were not assigned greater expenditure responsibilities during the third phase, they were affected by the fall in tax revenues and the central government's fiscal consolidation and austerity plans.

This is especially highlighted by the fall in LGUs' capital investments and problems of increased local public debts. Furthermore, a status quo in the expenditure assignment at the level of LGUs might also be indicative of inefficient public spending (Antić, 2013). Large and growing local public debts are possibly the single most significant concern in terms of a sustainable provision of local public goods in the long run in BiH. The idea of maintaining hard budget constraints as one of five necessary conditions[1] defined in the second generation of fiscal federalism (Weingast, 2007) might seem appropriate now. We evaluate an option that the budget deficits that LGUs were running are not a consequence of structural vertical imbalances, but instead of spending decisions at the local level that increased the expenditure side of the budgets. These spending decisions have been brought in at the local level, which might indicate that local mayors are acting in their own-self-interest rather than in the interest of the community. This type of behaviour has also been recognised in the second generation of fiscal federalism (Weingast, 2007).

Territorial and Administrative Organisation of BiH since 1995

BiH became an independent state on 1 March 1992, but due to the war in BiH from 1992 to 1995, its constitutional and therefore fiscal structure could not be determined until the adoption of the new BiH Constitution (i.e. the Dayton Agreement[2]), which was signed in December 1995. Two structural elements of the constitutional fiscal federalism in BiH are as follows:

- The Constitution of BiH forms a federal structure, and although its text does not define decisively the type of country, it certainly shows a somewhat weaker structure for the Federation of BiH (FBiH)[3]; and
- From the economic point of view, the Constitution provides a solution of typical economic federalism, both in the full freedom of movement of goods, services, and capital within BiH. The authority is given to entities and institutions of BiH to constitute basic elements of an

economic system (monetary system, customs, export trade, international financial relations, etc.) and key instruments of economic policy. (all [sic])

(Begić, 2000, p. 23)

The Dayton Agreement as an official BiH Constitution indicated the organisation of the country as an asymmetric confederation consisting of two entities: FBiH and Republika Srpska (RS). Brčko District[4] (BD) was established through a final arbitration decision in March 1999 and is a self-governing administrative unit under the sovereignty of BiH. In both FBiH and RS, LGUs exist in the form of municipalities and cities, even though the Dayton Agreement does not define LGUs as a constitutional category (Mujakić, 2010, p. 1047). In FBiH, there is an intermediate level of government between the federal level and the municipalities—the Cantons. Hence, BiH is sometimes referred to as an asymmetric confederation, since the federal level (the FBiH entity) is below the state level (BiH). At the same time, FBiH is a fiscally decentralised entity (federal level, cantons, and municipalities and cities) whereas RS is a more centralised entity (RS itself, and its municipalities and cities). Each entity has its own Constitution, which must be fully compliant with the BiH Constitution (under Article 3.3). The current structure of BiH is shown in Fig. 6.1.

The idea for organisation of BiH in terms of a loosely fiscally decentralised country came from the previous organisation of Yugoslavia. In terms of significant hallmarks in the improvements of fiscal federalism in BiH, Antić (2014) identifies three phases which parallel those highlighted in this chapter. The first phase is characterised by the high level of asymmetry and extremely high degree of fiscal decentralisation. During this period, we cannot determine benefits of fiscal decentralisation at the level of LGUs in either entity since the entire country depended on significant post-war international aid for reconstruction and development. Hence, there is no national data available (for the period 1995–2003) to identify the position of LGUs since during most of the first phase all government levels were being established and operationalised. During this phase, two associations of local authorities were established in both entities (in 1998 in RS and in 2002 in FBiH) as LGU representatives.

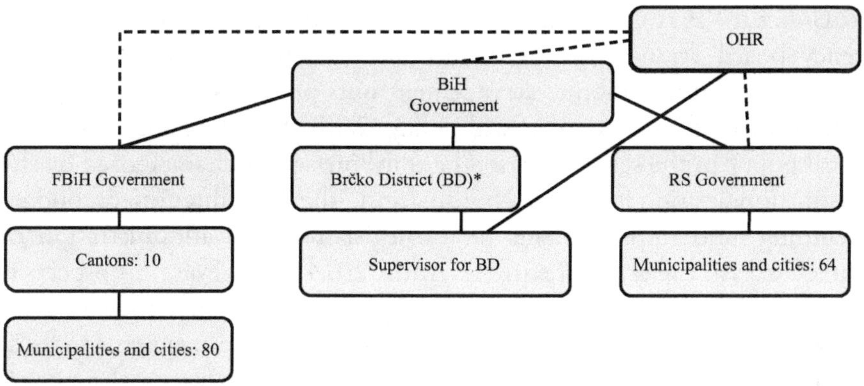

Fig. 6.1 Constitutional organisation of Bosnia and Herzegovina. Source: Kreso (2005, p. 256); Antić, (2013, p. 304). Note: Solid line indicates direct supervision; dashed line indicates indirect supervision. *Under Article 10 of the Dayton Agreement, OHR stands for "Office of the High Representative" which oversees the civilian implementation of the Dayton Agreement. The Principal Deputy High Representative serves as Brčko District Supervisor; since 1999, the number of municipalities in FB&H has decreased (from 84 to 79 due to new organisation of the City of Mostar). The City of Sarajevo in FB&H includes four municipalities in its structure, and the City of East Sarajevo in RS includes six municipalities. According to the data from RS Institute of Statistics (2016), there are 58 municipalities and 6 cities in RS

Their negotiating power increased steadily throughout three phases. In the first phase, LGUs were also assigned most local expenditures which changed insignificantly throughout three phases.

When we discuss the process of fiscal decentralisation in BiH and the possible success of fiscal federalism, we must bear in mind that state (BiH) government during most of first phase was very weak and that has caused most impediments to the speed and success of the entire decentralisation process in BiH. With the centralisation of indirect taxes in the second phase, the central government of BiH became functionally and institutionally more powerful, assignments for expenditures at the level of BiH increased, which all reflected in the integration of BiH's economic space and removal of barriers to movement of goods and services, capital, and people. Additionally, Antić (2014) highlights the significance of the integration of BiH's economic space as one of the necessary preconditions for a successful functioning of the second generation of fiscal federalism.

Under the BiH Constitution, monetary policy under an orthodox currency board arrangement is defined to be conducted at the level of BiH. This macroeconomic arrangement puts pressures and increases the significance of an adequate fiscal policy. With the improvements in the fiscal policy in the second phase, the third phase was characterised by the institutionalisation of fiscal coordination, the introduction of budget planning, and improvements in the legislation and administration of direct taxes at the levels of entities (Antić, 2014). However, this process is still unfinished, and this is reflected by the LGUs. Therefore, authors such as Antić (2013, 2014) have suggested further improvements to fiscal coordination in terms of an institutional framework for fiscal management, establishing relations between levels of government, and imposing obligatory rules for all governments. In terms of a political economy of fiscal federalism in BiH, Antić (2014) describes the relationship between entities as a form of competitive federalism with the aim of attracting foreign direct investment (FDI). She classifies some functions, such as inter-entity fiscal coordination, as a combination of cooperative and executive federalism (Antić, 2013, 2014).

In comparison to the pre-transition period, the current BiH territorial and administrative structure is characterised by a larger number of LGUs in the post-transition period (namely, there were 109 LGUs in 1989 (Savezni zavod za statistiku, 1989) in comparison to the current 143 LGUs). The growth in number of LGUs is—in the most part—a direct consequence of the peculiar post-war position of certain LGUs that were divided between the two entities. So, the "new" municipalities are organised along entity lines, with mostly weak administrative and fiscal capacities. This is contrary to any economic rationale, especially since the results of 2013 BiH Census indicate a significant fall in BiH's total population to its current 3.5 million inhabitants.[5] Currently, there are 2.2 million inhabitants living in FBiH, 1.2 million in RS, and 83,500 in BD (BHAS, 2016). The majority (52.3 per cent) of the BiH population lives in LGUs (municipalities and cities) that have between 10,000 and 50,000 inhabitants. Current laws on principles of local self-government in FBiH and RS[6] define criteria for organisation of cities in terms of population (minimum of 30,000 inhabitants in FBiH and 50,000 in RS) or other criteria (e.g. a municipality with less than 30,000 inhabitants that is a cantonal seat in FBiH can become a city or, in RS, a municipality with less than

50,000 inhabitants, but with a defined status of developed LGU can become a city). The LGUs in RS mostly retained their administrative and territorial organisation before and after the transition process. Most administrative and territorial changes occurred in FBiH with the introduction of Cantons, which took on some of the LGUs' traditional expenditure assignments. The reason lies in the fact that FBiH was constituted (in 1994) before the signing of the Dayton Agreement, and was, as such, incorporated into the current organisation of BiH. Early papers (Čaušević, 2001; Ivanić, 2000; Kreso, 2005) dealt with intergovernmental fiscal relations between higher levels of government, mostly omitting LGUs. Only international projects dealt with the position of LGUs (e.g. USAID, 2005) in terms of their position in the "new" revenue-sharing mechanism that was introduced with the implementation of value added tax (VAT) as of 2006.

Fiscal Decentralisation in BiH

The peculiar constitutional organisation of BiH causes several impediments to the implementation of tax policy conducted in BiH. Fiscal policy in BiH is divided, in terms of jurisdictions, between state and entity levels. Since 2006 indirect taxes (VAT, excise duties, customs, and road fees) are collected at the state level whereas direct taxes (personal income tax—PIT, corporate income tax—CIT, and property taxes) together with social security contributions (SSC) are regulated at entity levels (Lazović-Pita, 2015). During three phases of fiscal decentralisation, most changes occurred at the higher tiers of government, which affected LGUs and significantly improved their position in terms of the size of allocated revenues to LGUs.

The First Phase: Post-war Reconstruction, International Aid, and the Decentralisation of Revenues

As noted before, LGUs in both entities were not recognised in the Dayton Agreement (Mujakić, 2010) but were recognised in two entity constitutions and by the European Charter of Local Self-Government. As most of the first phase was characterised by international aid for reconstruction and development, budgets at all levels of government suffered from horizontal and vertical imbalances due to mismatch between the allocation of responsibilities and available funds. Hence, LGUs were heavily underfunded and the provision of public services was poor and dependent on international aid. However, this issue was identified as being in urgent need of rectification, and subsequently the Parliament of RS adopted the Law on Local Self-Government of the RS in 2004, which set out municipal competences in detail, and listed the sources of revenues, defining LGUs' authority to set local charges and stamp duties. The first law related to the position of LGUs in FBiH was enacted in 1995. This law was subjected to several amendments prior to a new law being introduced in 2006 (Mujakić, 2010). For example, the legal provisions from 1995 had to be amended to include a definition of a city as an LGU (in 1996), in terms of the status of the city of Sarajevo (as a capital) and city of Mostar (in 1997). Since FBiH has additional sub-central level of government—canton unlike RS, during this phase, RS was more proactive than FBiH in its legal set-up regarding the position of LGUs. In RS, the role and authority of a mayor in LGUs was legally defined in 2005, whereas in FBiH this occurred in 2006. The law redefined political power locally and increased the stakes in the outcome of local governmental performance, due to the fact the mayor became responsible for developing and submitting municipal/city budget drafts for adoption by the municipal council. Before 2004, mayors were elected from the members of the municipal councils in both entities, but following the 2004 elections, mayors, together with members of municipal councils in both entities, have been elected in local democratic elections organised every four years. The only exceptions today exist in the cities of Sarajevo, East Sarajevo and Mostar, where mayors are still elected by the municipal councils.

During this phase, LGUs were assigned responsibilities over local expenditures which mostly remained unchanged throughout three phases (Table 6.2). In terms of revenues, Lazović-Pita and Štambuk (2015) give a detailed overview of tax reforms in both BiH entities per tax type, throughout three phases. In the early years of transition and during the first phase, revenues in FBiH were divided between the FBiH governmental level and the cantons, as defined in the law adopted in 1996.[7]

Revenues that belonged to FBiH level were customs, excise duties, and other federal stamp duties. Cantonal revenues were revenues from retail sales tax (RST), CIT, and schedular income tax (wage tax) and cantonal stamp duties. In 1996, LGU revenues were determined by cantonal regulations. LGUs had authority over communal taxes, fines, and so on and regulation over property taxes. The most buoyant taxes, RST and wage tax, were legislated and collected at the FBiH level by the tax administration, but the distribution of those revenues was regulated by cantons. Since 2001, when the FBiH law was amended, revenues from certain groups of excise duties also began to be shared between FBiH level and cantonal level. From 2003, RST was distributed between cantons and LGUs on a derivate basis. As a result, this created a situation in which LGUs enjoy different positions in each of the ten cantons. The share of revenues assigned to LGUs in each canton varied significantly and was dependent on cantonal or entity laws for each tax type. For example, Canton Sarajevo financed its LGUs by means of grants and shared property taxes. In 2003, total LGU revenues in FBiH were €175.32 m, while in 2006 total revenues were €286.31 m, giving an average annual increase of 17.7 per cent.

Prior to 2006, RST was shared based on cantonal laws, and cantons assigned varying proportions of RST revenues to the LGUs in their jurisdiction. Revenues from RST among ten cantons were mostly shared so that 75–80 per cent of RST revenues belonged to the cantonal budget, and 20 per cent or 25 per cent to LGUs' budgets. The position of LGUs varied significantly in each canton—from Canton Sarajevo,[8] which shared only property tax with its LGUs and otherwise financed its LGUs by allocating unconditional grants—to Tuzla Canton which shared most of its revenues with LGUs. This can be said for revenues from all taxes—wage tax, property taxes, and so on except the revenues from CIT which were shared between FBiH and cantons. USAID (2005) provided a detailed summary of the revenue-sharing mechanism per tax type in FBiH in the first phase.

In RS, the redistribution of revenues from RST was organised so that at least 30 per cent of collected RST revenues in the LGUs were redistributed back to LGUs, while the City of Banja Luka was entitled to 35 per cent of collected RST revenues. The other most important shared tax revenues came from the schedular wage tax and other property taxes, whereas CIT revenues were fully retained within the budget of RS. The Law on the Budget System of RS from 2003 specified that LGUs were entitled to receive 25 per cent of the wage tax generated in their jurisdictions. Hence, all tax revenues in RS were shared, except for property taxes, which were legally paid at the entity level, although revenues from property taxes entirely belonged to LGUs. During this phase, the total amount of LGU revenues in 2003 was €152.47 m, while in 2006 total LGU revenues amounted to €249.79 m, giving an average annual increase of 17 per cent which is similar to that of FBiH.

The 2003 Law on the Budget System of RS[9] attempted to fiscally equalise LGUs. The Law divided municipalities into four categories, depending on the development index, and based on criteria adopted by the National Assembly of RS. According to the adopted criteria, developed municipalities received 30 per cent of RST revenues, semi-developed municipalities 40 per cent, underdeveloped 50 per cent and extremely underdeveloped 60 per cent of collected RST revenues in LGUs. Cities received 35 per cent of RST revenues. However, this system failed to equalise between the developed and underdeveloped LGUs, as assigning an additional percentage of RST revenues to underdeveloped LGUs with low fiscal capacities did not produce equalisation effects, and so the system was abolished.

During the first phase, the main characteristic in both entities was a very low level of autonomy of LGUs over revenues. The greatest proportion of revenues was transferred to LGUs in the form of unconditional grants. LGUs could not set their own tax base or rate for any major revenue source. Own sources, or non-tax revenues of LGUs, mainly came from different user fees and charges, various communal charges, income from renting, or building fees. In this phase, LGUs were not the focus of reform activities, as state-building was the priority for both the international community and local actors.

Long-term[10] data availability for LGUs in BiH is scarce, and currently relies on aggregated datasets from the International Monetary Fund (IMF) Government Finance Statistics (GFS). Aggregated data is useful for cross-country comparison, but inevitably leads to a loss of information and a lack of possibility for pinpointing clear distinctions between own revenues and shared revenues, especially at the level of LGUs.

Similarly, on the expenditure side we can only use IMF GFS classification of expenditures since functional classification of expenditures in BiH according to IMF GFS is available starting from 2013.

BiH collects significant amount of revenues, especially tax revenues measured as a percentage of GDP. The share of total consolidated government revenues[11] to GDP during the three phases was on average 43.3 per cent of GDP (2003–2016), and the share of tax revenues to GDP was on average 23.1 per cent. From Fig. 6.2, we can determine that LGU revenues in RS have an average share of 17.0 per cent of total revenues and an average share of 6.7 per cent of GDP (2003–2016). On the other side, due to another intergovernmental level—the cantons in FBiH—the share of LGU revenues to total revenues and GDP in FBiH is smaller, amounting on average to 10.2 per cent and 4 per cent respectively (2003–2016). The share of LGU revenues in both entities in absolute amounts is nearly identical on an annual basis. During this phase, the position of LGUs improved significantly in terms of the size of allocated revenues even though we have data available as of 2003. During this period, LGUs were not assigned greater expenditures nor were given the authority over any additional revenues.

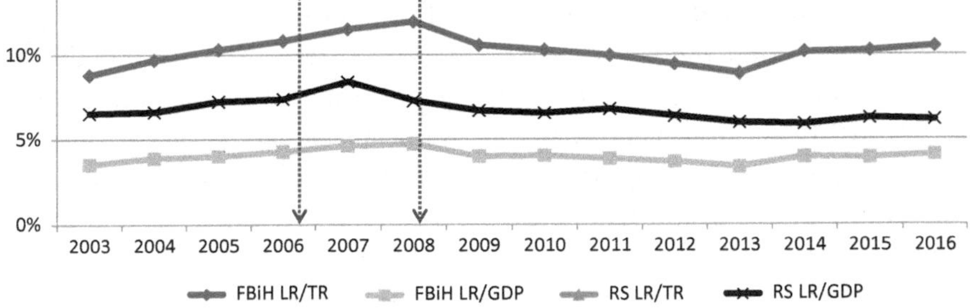

Fig. 6.2 The share of LGUs' revenues to total revenues and to GDP in RS and FBiH. Source: CBBiH, 2016,[12] own interpretation. Note: LR—local revenues; TR—total revenues

The Second Phase: Consolidation of Indirect Taxes in BiH and the Decentralisation of Revenues

In 2006, the Parliament of the Federation of Bosnia and Herzegovina adopted the Law on Principles of Local Self-Government in FBiH, which redefined the role of LGUs. Unlike in the case of RS, where the law was explicit in the determination of LGUs' responsibilities, in FBiH the law was general, and indicated that each canton has the authority to determine the responsibilities of LGUs within the canton itself. To date, most cantons have adopted LGU-related laws, even though some cantonal laws in this respect have still not been brought. The most significant change from the previous system has been the legally defined ability and formal regulation of LGUs regarding the borrowing and/or issuing of bonds. In terms of responsibilities of mayors in FBiH and RS, Mujakić (2010, 2012) provides a detailed analysis. His research shows that with the legal changes in both entities, mayors' relationships to municipal councils changed, and that mayors gained greater responsibilities. Surveys conducted among citizens have shown that the local level of government enjoys the highest degree of trust from citizens in comparison to other tiers of government (Analitika, 2014; Transparency International, 2014). The relationship between council and directly elected mayor brought new positive dynamics at local level, in the sense that accountability was strengthened through mayors' sole responsibility for quality of services at local level. The mayor could not be recalled by the municipal assembly any more, but only by the referendum of all registered voters in municipality. Mujakić (2010) also analysed the revenue position of the LGUs in FBiH and RS (without an analysis of expenditure assignment). His research indicated that LGUs in RS were—in terms of revenue allocation—in a better position, receiving a greater share of total revenues than LGUs in FBiH. However, measured by the Organisation for Economic Cooperation and Development (OECD) methodology and internationally comparable indicators, Antić (2013, p. 291) indicates that fiscal autonomy of local communities in BiH is "very low considering that the share of revenue on which they decide entirely (non-tax revenue) or partially (tax on property) is low".

We have already determined that the preconditions for implementation of the second phase began in the first phase. In 2003, the High Representative for Bosnia and Herzegovina proclaimed a unified Law on Customs and Excise Duties, which provided a basis for further developments in indirect taxation and the proclamation of the Decision on the Establishment of the Commission for Indirect Taxation Policy.[13] Since customs policy is the only constitutional provision regarding fiscal policy harmonisation in BiH, customs administrations were incorporated into an independent institution, the Indirect Tax Authority (ITA), which is the institution responsible for the collection of all indirect taxes in BiH (i.e. excise duties, VAT, customs, and road excise). The ITA became operational in 2005 when the VAT law was adopted. VAT was introduced in 2006, at a single rate of 17 per cent. With the centralisation of indirect taxes at the state level, the sources of financing for BiH institutions changed considerably (Fig. 6.3) since up to that point, entities contributed towards BiH budget (two thirds of the budget were financed from FBiH and a remaining third by RS).

Inter-entity and BD revenue-sharing mechanism is determined (mostly) on an annual basis by a decision from the ITA board of directors,[14] so room for improvement in this area still exists. Hence, the

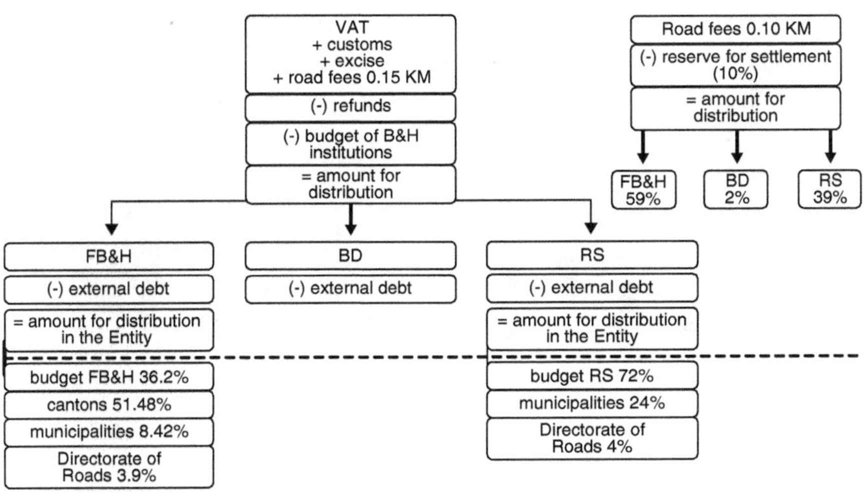

Fig. 6.3 Distribution of indirect tax revenues in BiH. Source: Antić (2013, p. 286)

percentage of indirect tax revenues belonging to each entity varied from 2006, and, at present 63.83 per cent belongs to FBiH, 32.62 per cent to RS, and 3.55 per cent to BD (ITA, 2016). Figure 6.3 shows the current division of indirect tax revenues between BiH and the entities, whereas inter-entity distribution of indirect tax revenues is regulated by two independent laws (one for each entity). These laws also define redistribution of other sources of revenue, namely direct taxes. This entire revenue-sharing mechanism is relevant for evaluation of the overall process of fiscal decentralisation in BiH since it shows that the political economy behind the decentralisation process and the operationalisation of fiscal federalism in BiH is determined by setting clear rules of intergovernmental fiscal relations at higher tiers of government and not at the level of LGUs. This means that as indirect tax system was clearly established, LGUs in both entities were in a better position in comparison to prior times especially in terms of budget planning as well as the size of revenues belonging to LGUs (Figs. 6.4 and 6.5).

In FBiH, based on the Law on Allocation of Public Revenues from 2006, the vertical division of revenues from indirect taxes is defined as in Fig. 6.3, so 8.42 per cent is being allocated to municipality/city level. The horizontal allocation is based on several weightings that capture the expenditure needs of jurisdictions and their fiscal capacities (Table 6.1).

In addition to this, the formula contained weighting for the special spending needs of Canton Sarajevo, which is to a factor of two and three

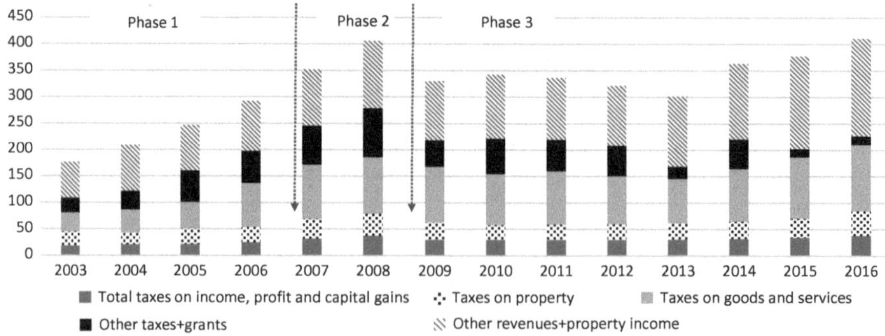

Fig. 6.4 FBiH LGUs' structure of revenues 2003–2016, in millions of EUR. Source: Central Bank of Bosnia and Herzegovina (2017), own calculation

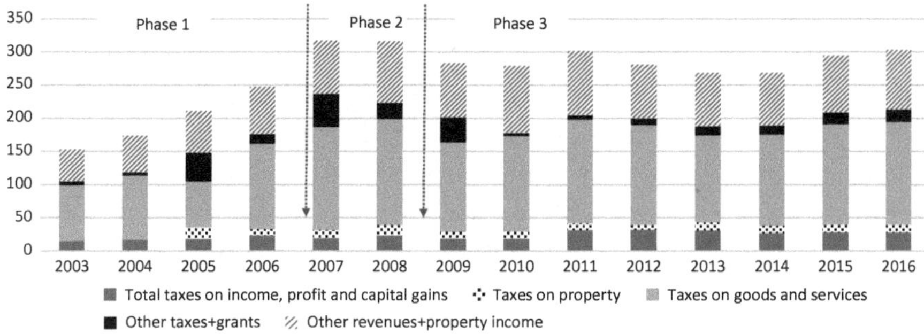

Fig. 6.5 RS LGUs' structure of revenues 2003–2016, in millions of EUR. Source: CBBH (2017), own calculation

Table 6.1 Criteria for revenue sharing of indirect taxes in FBiH

Weights	Area	Population	Elementary school children	Secondary school children	Development index
Cantons	0.06	0.57	0.24	0.13	
Municipalities	0.05	0.68	0.20		0.07

Source: Own calculation

other cantons with the smallest revenue from RST in the derivation-based system, which were also given a special weighting (1.1, 1.5, and 1.8). A newer formula also incorporated a weighting factor of 1.2 for LGUs with over 60,000 inhabitants, and 1.5 for LGUs, which cover the costs of their elementary schools.[15] The Index of Development measured the fiscal capacity factors of the LGUs. It was calculated as the average of the collected revenues from RST and Wage Tax for respective LGUs for 2005. Weightings for fiscal capacity were in the range of between 1.8 for LGUs with below 20 per cent of the FBiH average collection of taxes and 1.2 for LGUs with below 80 per cent of the average. At least 28.5 per cent of Wage Tax (replaced by PIT in 2009) revenues collected within the jurisdiction of LGUs was also assigned to LGUs in FBiH. The new system had a phase-in period of six years (2006–2011), over which time the new municipal share was increased. Exceptions were LGUs in Canton Sarajevo which continued to receive unconditional grants from the cantonal government until 2014. The allocation of CIT and property tax revenues remained the same as in the first phase.

One of the greatest disputes in the implementation of the 2006 Law on Allocation of Public Revenues was the unreliable data on population. BiH was not able to carry out a census of its population until 2013. The census prior to this was undertaken in 1991, the last pre-war year. The question of a new census was highly politicised, and continues to be a debatable issue, although official results have been published. For some LGUs, the 2013 Census results revealed a significant underestimation of population, which had direct implications on the calculations of LGUs' share in horizontal distribution of, primarily, indirect tax revenues. Other municipalities/cities saw increases in their revenues from indirect taxes. However, there has been no significant change in the indirect tax revenue sharing in either entity since 2006 or in the third phase. In FBiH, it is expected that the new law on allocation of revenues will consider the results from 2013 Census, which will certainly reflect on small LGUs.

The Law on the Budget System of RS was amended in 2006, so that indirect tax revenues could be distributed vertically and horizontally. Initially, the vertical share from indirect tax revenues was as follows:

- 73.5 per cent, RS government
- 23.0 per cent, LGU level
- 3.5 per cent, Road Fund

The criteria for horizontal distribution of indirect tax revenues between cities and municipalities in 2006 were as follows:

- 75 per cent based on population
- 5 per cent based on area
- 15 per cent based on secondary school pupils
- 5 per cent based on elementary school pupils

Additionally, in 2006 special weighting for horizontal distribution of indirect tax revenues was assigned to the City of Banja Luka and several smaller LGUs. The phase-in period of the new system was six years. The RS government amended the law in the same year, increasing the vertical share for LGUs to 24 per cent and decreasing its own share to 72.5 per cent of indirect tax revenues (Fig. 6.3), which remained to date. More importantly, the government of the RS extended the phase-in period to ten years, and changed the criteria for horizontal distribution:

- 75 per cent based on population
- 15 per cent based on area
- 10 per cent based on secondary school pupils

As before, Wage Tax was shared 75 per cent for the Entity budget, and 25 per cent for LGUs' budgets. CIT revenues were retained at the entity level, and other revenues, such as different concessions for natural resources, were also shared with LGUs. The allocation of CIT and property tax revenues remained the same as during the first phase. With the introduction of a new revenue-sharing system, the provision from the Law on the Budget System of RS from 2003 on equalisation between municipalities ceased to exist, and weights attached in the previous amendment to some underdeveloped municipalities were also removed.

Throughout this phase, LGUs in both entities received a higher share of indirect tax revenues because of the new revenue-sharing mechanism. There was a significant increase in revenues from property taxes and wage tax as an expected result of overall stronger economic growth in both entities. During this phase, LGUs were not given the authority over any additional revenues.

The Third Phase: The Outbreak of GFC and Rising Public Debt

After initial growth of revenues from indirect taxes (2006–2008), the global crisis affected the budgets and triggered fiscal stress across all levels of government. During the third phase, LGUs were affected by the fall in tax revenues and the central government's fiscal consolidation and austerity plans, which was reflected in the running of budget deficits by LGUs, and their beginning to borrow more.

Regarding this phase, in terms of tax reforms, both entities went through PIT reforms in 2009, switching from schedular to synthetic PIT, with a flat tax rate of 10 per cent applied in FBiH. Furthermore, with the changes of PIT from schedular to synthetic, in FBiH, cantons had to harmonise tax laws under their jurisdiction. In RS, PIT reform included introduction of a flat PIT rate at 8 per cent, but in 2011 this was increased to 10 per cent. Throughout this phase, RS's PIT law was changed and amended numerous times, affecting the share of PIT to total revenues (and the PIT share belonging to LGUs). Simultaneously, CIT went through several legislative changes, but in the third phase the CIT rate was set at 10 per cent in both entities. We cannot say that during this phase the tax reforms were deliberately aimed at centralisation of revenues since they were planned prior to the outbreak of the GFC. The centralisation of revenues brought greater fiscal discipline, simplified the tax procedures, increased simplification of the tax system, and the elimination of myriad (cantonal) tax codes which, in turn, brought benefits to LGUs in terms of greater revenues (Figs. 6.4 and 6.5).

Since 2008 and the outbreak of GFC, the redistribution of indirect taxes in both entities has remained virtually unchanged. The only (minor) alteration appeared in 2014, when LGUs in Canton Sarajevo were directly included in revenue sharing of indirect taxes from the entity level, replacing the unconditional grants allocated to them by the Canton. After the City of Sarajevo appealed before the Constitutional Court of FBiH because it was not included in revenue-sharing mechanisms, as is the case with other LGUs, the case was positively resolved in 2015.[16] Association of local authorities in FBiH played a significant role in this process indicating the increasing negotiating power of LGUs in FBiH.

In FBiH, with the adoption of synthetic PIT from 2009, the minimum share of LGUs in PIT was increased to 34.46 per cent, and LGUs in Canton Sarajevo were given 1.79 per cent of PIT revenues. The Law on Allocation of Public Revenues in FBiH also provided for cantons to further allocate to LGUs some revenues that had been assigned exclusively to cantons, such as CIT revenues. Revenues from property taxes continue to exist as shared revenues between cantons and LGUs. These legal changes have put LGUs in FBiH in a significantly better position compared to prior periods.

In 2008, the RS government amended the Law so that the vertical share of the Road Fund was increased to 4 per cent, LGUs would receive an additional percentage point from indirect tax revenues (from 23 per cent to 24 per cent, Fig. 6.3) and the share of entity budget was decreased to 72 per cent. With the new Law from 2012, the shares and main revenues to be distributed remained the same, namely real estate tax[17] remained 100 per cent allocated to LGUs, in addition to different fees and charges that are regulated by municipality and city councils. Real estate tax is regulated at the level of RS, but the law also defines LGUs' authority in determination of market-based tax base (through zoning) and tax rates (which cannot be higher than 0.2 per cent). So, during this phase, LGUs in RS were also put in a better position in comparison to prior periods.

If we observe the share of LGUs' revenues by tax type (Figs. 6.4 and 6.5) in both entities, we can determine that the highest share of all tax revenues is that of indirect tax revenues, followed by PIT revenues. Shared taxes in FBiH (income tax, VAT, and property tax) account for the largest share of LGUs' tax revenues in FBiH. Revenues from taxes on income, profit, and capital gains[18] throughout the 14-year period were on average 6 per cent of LGUs' total revenues. Revenues from taxes on goods and services to LGUs' total revenues amounted on average to 27.3 per cent in 2003–2016 and have recorded the largest increase amongst all shared taxes (from 20 per cent in 2003 to 30 per cent in 2016). In the period of the GFC, the revenues of LGUs began to decline. LGUs compensated this decline with an increase in non-tax revenues (in a broad sense, own revenues, Fig. 6.4). The share of other revenues to total LGU revenues (mostly coming from sales of goods and services) have been steadily increasing, and, on average, amounted to 29 per cent in the period from 2003 to 2016, but with more than 40 per cent share of total LGU revenues in 2016. Revenues from property income to total LGU revenues amounted on average to 8.7 per cent (2003–2016) but have constantly declined in the third phase. Taxes on property, which are traditionally local revenues, amounted on average (2003–2016) to 10.4 per cent of LGUs' total revenues. Like revenues from property income, these revenues have been constantly falling, especially in the third phase, except for 2016. Grants (including both capital and current) account for, on average, 14 per cent of total LGU revenues (2003–2016). In 2015 and 2016, the share of grants to LGUs' total revenues dropped to 3.5 per cent and 3.9 per cent respectively. The reason for this significant fall could be explained by the position of LGUs in Sarajevo Canton prior to 2015.

A similar situation to that of FBiH can be observed in RS. Revenues from tax on income, profit, and capital gains[19] take on average (2003–2016) as little as 5.0 per cent of LGUs' total revenues. However, these have been on the increase, especially after 2011. Revenues from taxes on goods and services are the most significant source of shared taxes and have, on average, amounted to 50.3 per cent of LGUs' total revenues (2003–2016). Revenues from taxes on property take on average as little as 3.7 per cent (2003–2016) to LGUs' total revenues. This is almost three times less than the same share in FBiH. Revenues from property income to LGUs' total revenues amount to 2.4 per cent (2003–2016), but this proportion has exhibited extreme fluctuations across the three phases. Other revenues in RS (mostly from sales of goods and services) account for, on average, 27.8 per cent (2003–2016) of LGUs' total revenues. Grants as share of total LGU revenues in RS show great variations, averaging around 5.3 per cent (2003–2016), but with peaks of 15 per cent and 13 per cent of total revenues in 2007 and 2009 respectively. In absolute amounts, in 2003, LGUs' total revenues were €152 m, whereas in 2008 they had increased to €316 m, with the lowest annual total of €268 m being in 2014. LGUs in RS are much more dependent on VAT, which makes them more vulnerable to fluctuations in consumption (Fig. 6.5). This was evident in 2009 and 2010, as those years were marked by a sharp downturn in consumption, and hence VAT revenues. LGUs in RS were not able to fully compensate for these revenues, unlike in FBiH, by increasing own-source revenues.

Additionally, other revenues,[20] in addition to property income (other than Property Tax), can be assessed as own-source revenue. Through this type of revenue, LGUs can exercise some control, either by setting the rate or base, or varying collection effort. This can be said for LGUs in both entities. Property taxes include taxes on the use, ownership, or transfer of wealth (IMF GFS, 2001). In FBiH, revenues from property taxes are usually shared between cantons and LGUs, whereas revenue from real estate transfer taxes is—to the greatest extent—entirely LGUs' own revenue. Revenues from real estate transfer tax account for the bulk of revenues from property taxes, peaking in 2008. The situation of property tax reforms in RS has already been explained. However, with the abolition of real estate transfer taxes and the adoption of a real estate tax since 2013 in RS, tax revenues have remained more-or-less stable, which might indicate the government's intention to run a revenue-neutral tax reform.

If we look at LGUs' total revenues in both entities, we can determine that at no point in the post-crisis period did revenues of LGUs drop below 2006 levels, that is, prior to the introduction of the new revenue-sharing system and VAT (Figs. 6.4 and 6.5). Cities and municipalities in both entities were not given any new expenditure assignments during this period of revenue surge, so even though some vertical imbalances existed in the period preceding VAT introduction, these were corrected with the introduction of the new system. As none of the LGUs previously set responsibilities were not abolished or limited, both entity laws on revenue distribution state that the revenue transferred to LGUs can be spent entirely according to budgets approved by local councils. These facts together with increasing allocation and the size of local revenues indicate that comparing to early years of decentralisation when LGUs were mostly neglected due to state-building process, their position improved significantly up to date. This might indicate slow but a successful implementation of the ideas presented in the first generation of fiscal federalism.

Assignment of Expenditures in Both Entities in Three Phases

Throughout the observed period, LGUs' assignment of expenditures in both entities virtually did not change. Table 6.2 summarises LGUs' assignment of expenditures in both entities throughout three phases. We can determine that local expenditures stayed more or less the same and that the only change occurred in the second phase, with the strengthening of the state (BiH) level when some expenditures were rightfully transferred to a higher governmental tier, such as defence.

The shares of LGU expenditures to total expenditures in both entities were very low, especially during the first phase. For example, the share of FBiH LGUs' expenditures to FBiH total expenditures (2003–2005) amounted to 14.6 per cent and in RS 26.5 per cent in the same period. Since 2006, this share has increased in FBiH and amounted on average

Table 6.2 Changes over assignment of expenditures[a] in Bosnia and Herzegovina, 1995–2016

	Phase 1: 1996–2006						Phase 2: 2006–2008 (and post 2008)					
Assignment of expenditures	B&H level	FB&H entity	Cantons	LGUs	RS entity	LGUs	B&H level	FB&H entity	Cantons	LGUs	RS entity	LGUs
General public services	*	*	*		*		*	*	*		*	
Defence		*			*		*				*	
Public order and safety		*	*		*		*	*	*		*	
Education		*	*	*	*	*	*	*	*	*	*	*
Pre-school				*		*				*		*
Primary			*		*				*		*	
Secondary			*		*				*		*	
Higher			*		*				*		*	
Healthcare		*	*		*			*	*		*	
Social security and protection		*	*	*	*	*		*	*	*	*	*
Housing and public utilities and services			*	*	*	*			*	*	*	*
Recreation, culture & religion		*	*	*	*	*		*	*	*	*	*
Transport and communication		*	*	*	*	*		*	*	*	*	*

Source: Own interpretation

Note: Higher levels of government have a coordinating authority in some groups of expenditures or an overlapping authority with lower levels of government (LGUs)

[a]Only major types of public expenditures were considered

(2006–2016) to 16.6 per cent but remained the same in RS (average of 26.0 per cent, 2006–2016, but with significant drop in 2016, because of the integration of the extra-budgetary pension fund into the annual budget of the RS government, own calculation). This indicates that LGUs in FBiH were radically underfunded when compared to LGUs in RS, bearing in mind that LGUs' assignment of expenditures in both entities is very similar (Table 6.2).

From 2006 to the present day, LGUs in both entities have had similar assigned functions, but with some notable distinctions. In the RS entity, LGUs are assigned the so-called material expenses of elementary and secondary schools, as well as pupil transport. In three cantons within FBiH, LGUs are given the function of financing material expenses of elementary schools and pupil transport. Also, in terms of social protection, LGUs in RS were, until 2012, almost exclusively assigned the provision of all types of social assistance, while in FBiH LGUs finance the functioning of local welfare centres, but social assistance is provided either at a cantonal or FBiH level. Furthermore, LGUs in RS are mandated by the Law on Social Protection of RS[21] to earmark at least 10 per cent of their budget for social protection expenditures.

In FBiH, the share of compensation for employees and social contributions was, on average, 30.2 per cent of LGUs' total expenditures, with a declining trend since 2013. Material expenses account for, on average, 19.1 per cent of LGUs' total expenditures. Grants show strong variations, from 0 per cent of total expenditures to 8.5 per cent in 2011, but on average account for a small share of, on average, 3.3 per cent of LGUs' total expenditures (2003–2016). Subsidies and interest on average account for 2.1 per cent of LGUs' total expenditures, but other expenses account for, on average, a significant 22.6 per cent of LGUs' total expenditures (Fig. 6.6). LGUs in FBiH saw strong growth of total expenditures after 2005. In 2008, total expenditures were €416 m, which means that total expenditure grew at an annual rate of 19 per cent. The largest share of growth was generated by expenditure on non-financial assets, peaking in 2008 at €67 m, revealing the fact that LGUs invested in capital projects from the increased revenues (Fig. 6.8). In 2009, total local expenses dropped sharply by 18 per cent, which reflects the GFC and associated decrease in total revenues. It is interesting to mention that in the period

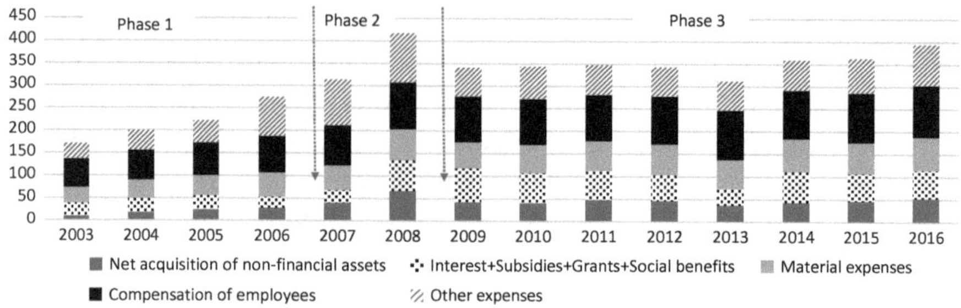

Fig. 6.6 FBiH, LGUs' structure of expenditures, in millions of EUR. Source: CBBH (2017), own calculation

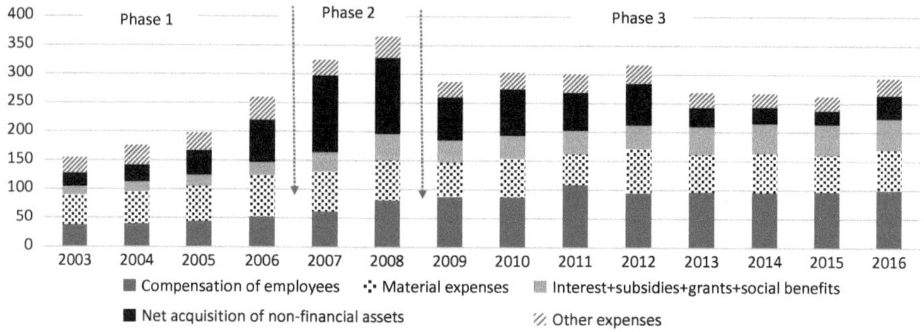

Fig. 6.7 RS, LGUs' structure of expenditures, in millions of EUR. Source: CBBH (2017), own calculation

2003–2008, the average annual growth of expenditure on employee remuneration was 11 per cent. After 2008, LGUs managed to adapt their expenditure by restraining the growth of this expenditure to a 1 per cent annual average but keeping expenditures for non-financial assets at approximately the same level nominally, albeit with sharp drops in 2009 and 2013.

Similar to cities and municipalities in FBiH, LGUs in RS increased their total expenditure from €154 m in 2003 to €365 m in 2008, at annual rate of 19 per cent, primarily to finance non-financial assets. However, in the period between 2009 and 2016, total expenses decreased at annual rate of 2 per cent, hitting an absolute minimum of €262 m in 2015 (Fig. 6.7). Expenses for employee remuneration increased until 2009 (although LGUs in FBiH had already lowered this expense by 2009) at an average annual rate of 15 per cent. Total expenses for

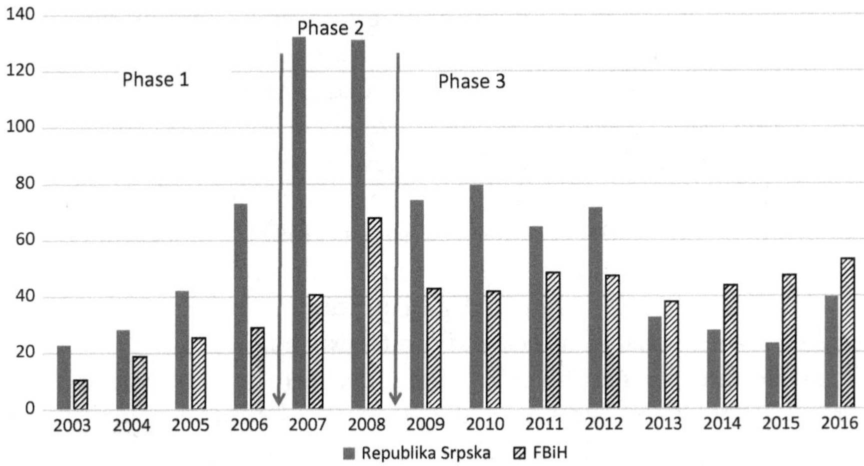

Fig. 6.8 Expenditure for non-financial assets of LGUs in BiH, in millions of EUR. Source: CBBH (2017), own calculation

Compensation for Employees and Social Contributions account for, on average, 28.6 per cent of LGUs' total expenditures. In the first phase, these expenditures witnessed a decreasing trend, but have since (second and third phases) increased significantly. Similarly, Material Expenses had a downward trend until 2008 when this expense amounted to 19 per cent of LGUs' total expenditures but have also been increasing since 2008. Other Expenses amounted, on average, to 11.8 per cent of total LGU expenditures, and interest and subsidies account for 1.9 per cent of LGUs' total expenditures. LGUs in RS do not classify grants as expenditures. Looking at the capital grants of LGUs in RS, in 2008, the total expenditure for non-financial assets was €132 m and in 2009 it stood at €131 m (Fig. 6.8). Other expenses include property expenses other than interest (e.g. dividends and rent) and miscellaneous other expenses (IMF GFS, 2001). Due to declining revenues from 2008, because of a combination of the economic crisis and the entity's foreign debt servicing issues, LGUs in RS decided to cut down on capital expenditure, but employee remuneration still increased at an annual rate of 3 per cent. The share of this expense to total expenditures also increased, because of decreasing revenue and consequentially the total expenditure of LGUs.

It was not possible to obtain numbers of employees within local administrations in either entity, but it is reasonable to assume that the numbers have increased due to increased revenues in the period 2005–2008. After 2009, and a downturn in revenues, it became almost impossible to downsize the number of local authority employees to compensate for revenue losses. Antić (2013) analysed the position of LGUs in FBiH and RS in 2008 and showed that in FBiH the local level has increased wage expenditures at the expense of the social benefits whereas in RS LGUs have retained their wage expenditures at the same level and reduced grants, social transfers, and capital expenditures.

Expenditure for non-financial assets declined sharply in the third period, 2009–2016. Because of the structure of FBiH, capital investments are financed by the cantonal and FBiH governments, making the capital expenditure of LGUs in FBiH much smaller in comparison to LGUs in RS. Those expenditures dropped sharply after the GFC in 2008 and in subsequent years because of declining revenues from indirect taxes due to foreign debt servicing reducing the funds available for LGUs (Fig. 6.8).

We can determine that even though assignment of expenditures in both entities did not change throughout the observed period, the size of local expenditures changed during three periods. During the second phase and most of the third phase, local expenditures in both entities increased significantly especially in two categories: compensation of employees and material expenses. An increase in unproductive expenditures such as compensation of employees is always debatable and might indicate inefficient spending at the local level. However, parallel to this process LGUs in both entities increased capital investments especially in the second phase but as a fall in revenues triggered fiscal stress since 2009, they began to decline up to date.

Increasing Local Public Debts: Current Issues

With the outbreak of the GFC and inability of all governmental levels to tackle high public spending in relation to falling public revenues since 2009, BiH (and both of its entities) began to increase its external public debt, which is also valid for LGUs. Growth in revenue from indirect taxes in 2006 and 2007 launched a spiral of expenses of a complex administrative apparatus and social benefits at all levels of government. Obligations created under collective agreements and laws on social rights quickly melted fiscal surpluses from 2006 and 2007. Because of the rigidity of wages and social benefits that are regulated by Entity laws, governments were not able to respond quickly to the revenue decline caused by the economic crisis and implementation of the Stabilization and Association Agreement with the European Union (EU). Stand-by arrangement with the IMF from 2009 was only partially carried out, since the government had little power to enforce austerity plans due to political aims (Antić, 2013). Similar occurred with LGUs, which is evident from Fig. 6.9.

Figure 6.9 indicates a significant increase in the public borrowing of LGUs in BiH (across both entities) after 2009. LGUs heavily borrow from the banking sector in BiH, even though some have issued bonds. Due to a lack of data availability, figures do not include possible tax arrears of LGUs' public companies. However, in the observed period (from 2008, when the first LGU securities were issued, to 2015), securities accounted for an average of 12 per cent of total borrowing. Therefore, the most pressing issue at present that both entities and LGUs face relates to increased borrowing by means of both commercial

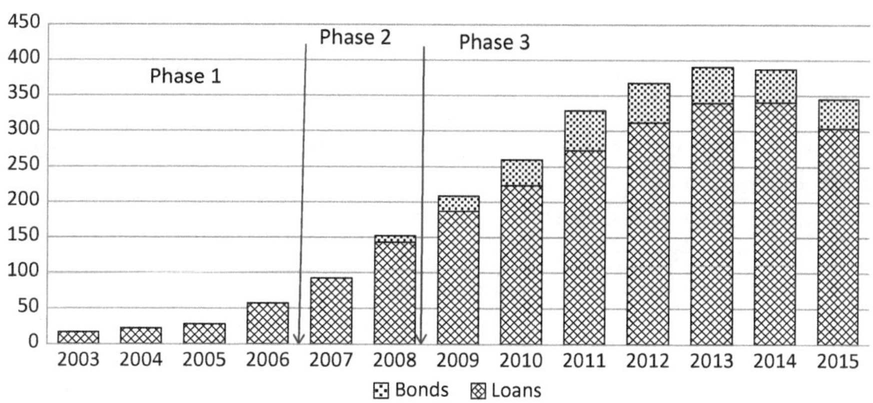

Fig. 6.9 Size and the structure of local government debt in all municipalities, 2003–2015 (millions of EUR). Source: CBBH (2017), own calculation

banks and the issuing of bonds, which imposes a threat to future capital investments (especially for LGUs). Furthermore, with greater public debt burden of all government levels, LGUs are in an especially difficult position about covering all public expenditures and efficiently providing local public goods.

LGUs' borrowing capacity is legally determined by two entity laws[22] regulating overall (consolidated) entity borrowing. Legally set limits could be assessed as a hard budget constraint as there are no legally defined bail out options. The FBiH law permits LGUs to borrow both domestically and from abroad, in local and foreign currency, but total debt is denominated in local currency (the same is regulated in RS). The FBiH law has been subjected to several amendments, but the most important legal provision deals with setting limits to LGUs' long-term borrowing (loans and securities-mostly bonds). LGUs can generate long-term debt (debt servicing longer than a year) only under the condition that, at the time of the loan's approval, debt service for each consecutive year, including servicing of the new loan and all loans for which an LGU has issued guarantee(s), does not exceed 10 per cent of revenues collected in the previous fiscal year. Short-term debt needs to be paid out within one fiscal year and cannot be refinanced or extended to beyond the end of the fiscal year. This debt cannot exceed 5 per cent of the LGU's revenues in the previous fiscal year (Basarić, 2009). In the RS, the first law regulating debt was adopted in 2007, but this was changed in 2012. Currently LGUs in RS can generate long-term debt under similar conditions as in FBiH, but the limit is set to 18 per cent of revenues. Short-term debt limits for LGUs in RS are the same as in FBiH (5 per cent). However, inter-entity differences exist in terms of approval procedures from higher tiers of government, setting guarantees, and so on as well as the entity's responsibility (or lack thereof) regarding an LGU's inability to repay and manage its public debt. Additionally, two aforementioned entity laws regulating LGUs' status in terms of the law on local self-government also define the borrowing procedure for LGUs. The greatest threat to the successful implementation of fiscal decentralisation at the level of LGUs in both BiH entities comes from the possible idea of an unleashing of LGUs' increased borrowing through changes in entity's

Table 6.3 Share of LGUs' total domestic debt to entity's total domestic debt, 2010–2015

	2010	2011	2012	2013	2014	2015
Share of LGUs domestic public debt to total domestic public debt in the Federation of Bosnia and Herzegovina (%)	2.8	2.3	2.8	5.0	4.8	4.9
Share of LGUs domestic public debt to total domestic public debt in Republika Srpska (%)	14.1	11.3	12.4	7.3	15.2	13.4

Source: BiH Ministry of Finance and Treasury (2010–2015), own calculation

laws that regulate local indebtedness. The idea of maintaining hard budget constraints on LGUs' borrowing, stemming from the second generation of fiscal federalism, might seem appropriate at present times.

The BiH Ministry of Finance and Treasury has also recorded LGUs' borrowing in terms of loans taken from commercial banks and securities issued since 2010. By their classification of domestic public debt of each entity, LGUs have different borrowing strategies: LGUs in RS rely on loans from commercial banks more heavily than LGUs in FBiH, which is also a result of the legally set limits. Table 6.3 shows the share of LGUs' domestic debt to total domestic public debt in FBiH and RS. The difference between LGU borrowing in FBiH and RS is significant, as it comes from legal provisions within the two entities, and, in the given period (2010–2015), RS LGUs' domestic public debt as a proportion of total RS domestic public debt was, on average, almost four times larger than the same share for FBiH LGUs.

Even though it is perceived that, with clear legal provisions regarding LGUs' borrowing limits, the system has become more transparent, this has only recently become a practice. In fact, LGUs' public data are only recently available, so we cannot determine the final purpose of the increased borrowing in the long run. We would assume that loans have been taken out for capital investment purposes, but they might also be used for financing current deficits or LGUs' public companies' tax arrears. Hence, it is necessary to introduce an obligatory and transparent system of reporting for all LGUs so that it is possible to evaluate and compare the actual provision of local public goods in LGUs across both entities.

Conclusion

Since 1995, the LGUs in BiH have passed through three phases. In the period 1995–2004, LGUs mostly functioned in a manner based on the former Yugoslav local governance system, meaning that mayors were elected by local councils and the scope of functions of LGUs was unclear. The introduction of the direct election of mayors in 2004 was the first major reform in this sector. This change allowed for greater accountability at the local level and has made local administration more transparent in its work. Both entities adopted new legislation on local self-governance in this period, with this clearly defining the functions of LGUs, and making them independent in their scope of work. Such legislation allowed for the possibility of delegating some functions to LGUs whereas the assignment of revenues for performing those functions was regulated by different laws. As the state-building process helped by the international aid for reconstruction and development was the primary aim during most of first phase, LGUs' needs and position were mostly neglected but began to improve with the new local legal provisions in both entities as of 2004. National data for most of the first phase (1995–2003) is non-existent, so our conclusions are drawn based upon the data from 2003 onwards.

LGUs' position improved significantly during the second phase—since 2006, as a new set of revenue-sharing laws was enacted in both entities. This came to be a necessity after RST was replaced by VAT at the state level. The new laws meant that LGUs had, for the first time, a predictable, transparent, and stable revenue source. Due to the strong growth of revenues from indirect taxes in the second phase, cities and municipalities significantly increased their revenues right up to (and slightly beyond) the GFC in 2008. In terms of local expenditures, they increased as well especially the category of compensation of employees. It was not possible to obtain data on the number of employees in LGU administrations, but expenditure on employee remuneration almost doubled in the period 2003–2008, and then remained at approximately the same level until 2015.

In terms of LGU revenues as a share of GDP, strong growth was witnessed in the period 2003–2008 in both entities. From 2009, this ratio declined, but LGUs in RS have been impacted more negatively. In fact, measured by this indicator, the position of LGUs in RS has been comparably far worse than that of LGUs in FBiH. Even though fiscal autonomy of LGUs in both entities is very low in revenue terms, LGUs enjoy autonomy in spending their budget based on local council decisions, within the mandated functions of LGUs. However, most revenues of LGUs are collected by higher tiers of government, and distributed to LGUs based on formulae, and this is especially the case in RS, where more than 60 per cent (depending on year) of LGU revenues come from indirect taxes. LGUs' spending decisions are not related to the level of effort they invest in collecting revenues, nor on deciding on tax base or rate to best suit local preferences, hence their fiscal autonomy is low. With the outbreak of the GFC, LGUs were inert in adapting the expenditure side, as they expected that upper tiers would distribute the same amount of revenues as before. However, higher tiers of government are not obliged to do so as there is no defined bail out options for LGUs in either entities. This caused budget deficits and issues related to increases in LGUs' public debt or increased fiscal stress at the level of LGUs. Increasing local public debts are currently the single most significant concern in terms of a sustainable provision of local public goods in the long run in BiH. The repayment of loans is taking a toll on local revenues. LGUs in RS are more dependent on the sharing of indirect taxes, and therefore the negative impact of foreign debt service is greater for LGUs in this entity. Furthermore, LGU's low fiscal autonomy and the fall in revenues allocated to LGUs in both entities affects their increased borrowing, both through loans (the majority) and the issuing of bonds.

Another issue is how well existing revenue-sharing laws capture the expenditure needs of LGUs. At present, there are no clear criteria for setting the expenditure standards for services delivered either by cantons or municipalities in either entity. In general, due to decentralisation of the administrative system, it has become increasingly difficult to perform coordination and oversight of the quality of services delivered. As LGUs are running deficits and as there is no criteria set for the evaluation of expenditures at the level of LGUs, locally elected representatives might act in their own self-interest. Hence, this might be a future threat to the successful implementation of fiscal federalism identified in the second generation of fiscal federalism.

The decentralisation process in the 1990s in BiH was primarily aimed at reconciling different visions of the post-war future of the country, to create a political-administrative structure which would provide for a single polity, diminishing the centrifugal forces. Assignment of functions and sources of revenue between different tiers of government, as well as introduction of a transfer system, brought to the forefront numerous opportunities for various actors at local, cantonal, entity, and state level to pursue goals under the pretence of efficiency, redistributive role or macroeconomic stability. However, even though vertical and horizontal imbalances still exist in two BiH entities, throughout three phases they have been significantly improved. There is still space for further improvements especially with growing public debt issues which sets yet another challenge for the policymakers in BiH.

In this chapter, we evaluated the position of LGUs based upon available statistical data of 14 years. We can conclude that the position of LGUs has improved during this period. Even though the process of fiscal decentralisation in BiH has been very slow in comparison to other transition countries, we would say that it is becoming more successful. Our analysis has shown that the position of LGUs has strengthened in terms of higher democratisation at the level of LGUs—the responsibilities and authorities given to mayors and local councils in both entities, the LGUs' negotiation power with the higher tiers of government improved and LGUs' position in the revenue-sharing mechanism increased. The post-war reconciliation was mostly finished during early years in the first phase and that process was speeded up by the international aid for reconstruction and development. Challenges in BiH exist in the intergovernmental fiscal relations between higher tiers of government. As these fiscal relations continue to improve, we should expect direct benefits at the level of LGUs in both entities. In terms of local economic development, LGUs began to develop during the second phase when most capital investments took place and where positive effects of fiscal decentralisation were seen the most. However, GFC brought additional problems in terms of rising public debts and questions about the success of fiscal decentralisation which remains current challenge set for all tiers of government in BiH and not only local communities.

Notes

1. In the second generation of fiscal federalism, Weingast (2007) provides an explanation of why federalism has been successful in some countries and not in the others. The reasons can be found in the decentralisation of political authority in the federal systems which aim to fulfil five necessary conditions for federalism. The first condition is hierarchy of the governments with a delineated scope of authority. The level of political authority given to subnational governments differs significantly in federal systems which defines other four conditions. The second condition relates to subnational autonomy in local regulation and local provision of public goods and services. Common market fully functioned, hard budget constraints imposed at the local level, and institutionalised political authority are the remaining three conditions (Weingast, 2007, p. 6).
2. Officially the General Framework Agreement for Peace in Bosnia and Herzegovina.
3. Such a qualification of BiH can be found in the Option of Compatibility of the Constitution of FBiH and Constitution of RS with the Constitution of BiH, written by the Venetian Commission.
4. Due to the scope of the chapter, BD will not be analysed in detail.
5. The last pre-war Census conducted in 1991 recorded a population of 4.3 million in BiH.
6. Law on Local Self-Government in RS, Official Gazette of RS, No. 101/04, 42/05, 118/05, 98/13. Current law—Law on Local Self-Government in RS, Official Gazette of RS, No. 97/16; Law on Principles of Local Self-Governments in FBiH, Official Gazette of FBiH, No. 6/95; Current law—Law on Principles of Local Self-Governments in FBiH, Official Gazette of FBiH, No. 49/06 and 51/09.
7. Law on Allocation of Revenues in FBiH, Official Gazette of FBiH, No. 26/96 i 32/98. Current law—Law on Allocation of Revenues in FBiH, Official Gazette of FBiH, No. 22/06, 22/09, 35/14, 94/15.

8. Canton Sarajevo is a special case due to its complex position in terms of the Canton-City relationship of its nine municipalities, with only four of these municipalities comprising the City of Sarajevo. The City of Sarajevo has very limited authority over expenditures (and likewise over revenues), which is not the case in cities in other Cantons. Hence, in Canton Sarajevo, most authority over expenditures and revenues lies at the cantonal level, and at the municipal level to some extent, so the case of Canton Sarajevo will not be discussed in detail.
9. Law on Budget System of RS, Official Gazette of RS, No. 96/03, 14/04, 67/05, 34/06, 128/06, 117/07. Current law—Law on Budget System of RS, Official Gazette of RS, No. 121/12, 52/14, 103/15, 15/16.
10. Since 2003.
11. Similar can be interpreted in terms of the share of total consolidated public expenditures to GDP.
12. All data are taken from the Central Bank of BiH and is in accordance with the IMF GFS (2001) methodology. Therefore, total revenues include entities' general government revenues in accordance with the definitions from IMF GFS (including extra-budgetary funds). Authors would like to thank the CBBiH statistics department and government finance statistics staff of the CBBiH for their valuable insights and explanations regarding the methodological issues.
13. Decision No. 103/03.
14. Antić (2014) refers to the operations of ITA board of directors as a type of executive federalism.
15. In FBiH, LGUs in three cantons (Herzegovina-Neretva, Canton 10 and West Herzegovina) are delegated responsibility for financing so-called material expenses of elementary schools and pupil transport. In RS all LGUs are responsible for these tasks.
16. An amount of 0.25 per cent was taken from the FBiH entity pool of funds and given to the City of Sarajevo, reducing the weight for Canton Sarajevo to 1.9658 and the canton's overall vertical share to 51.23 per cent.
17. With the adoption of the real estate tax, real estate transfer tax ceased to exist in RS.
18. In the first two phases, these taxes were classified as taxes on payroll and workforce.
19. Methodology related to taxes on payroll and workforce also applies in RS.
20. According to IMF GFS, other revenues include property income, for example, interest, dividends, rent, sales of goods and services, fines and

penalties, and miscellaneous other types of revenue. However, property income is shown separately in Figs. 6.4 and 6.5, as a major source of LGUs' own revenues.

21. Law on Social Protection in RS, Official Gazette of RS, No. 37/12; 90/16.
22. Law on Debt, Borrowing and Guarantees in FBiH, Official Gazette of FBiH, No. 86/07, 24/09, 44/10, 30/16 and Law on Debt, Borrowing and Guarantees in RS, Official Gazette of RS, No. 30/07, 29/10. Current Law on Debt, Borrowing and Guarantees in RS, Official Gazette of RS, No. 71/12, 52/14 and 114/17.

References

Analitika. (2014). *Survey results: High degree of distrust in political parties and government institutions in Bosnia and Herzegovina*. Sarajevo: Analitika—Centre for Social Research. Retrieved from http://pasos.org/wp-content/uploads/2014/11/povjerenje_fact_sheet_english.pdf

Antić, D. (2013). Multi-level fiscal system in Bosnia and Herzegovina: Evolution and coping with economic crisis. *Financial Theory and Practice, 37*(3), 279–310. Zagreb. Retrieved from http://www.fintp.hr/upload/files/ftp/2013/3/antic.pdf

Antić, D. (2014). Fiskalna koordincija kao ključni faktor funkcioniranja fiskalnog federalizma u složenim državama. *Godišnjak fakulteta pravnih nauka, 4*(4), 168–185. Banja Luka. Retrieved from http://www.gfpn-au.com/sites/default/files/GFPN-4-4/GFPN_godina_4_broj_4_Dinka_Antic.pdf

Basarić, H. (2009). *Municipal financial assessment study* (unpublished). Ministry of Foreign Trade and Relations of BiH and the World Bank.

Begić, K. (2000). A constitutional framework for fiscal federalism in Bosnia and Herzegovina. In M. Zlatić (Ed.), *The fiscal decentralisation initiative for Central and Eastern Europe: Forum on fiscal decentralisation in Bosnia and Herzegovina* (pp. 21–28). Conference proceedings, Sarajevo, 1st ed. Budapest: FDI-CEE.

BHAS—BIH Agency of Statistics. (2016). *Census of population, households and dwellings in BiH, 2013, final results*. Sarajevo: BHAS. Retrieved from http://www.popis2013.ba/popis2013/doc/Popis2013prvoIzdanje.pdf

BIH Ministry of Finance and Treasury. (2010–2015). *Informacija o stanju javne zaduženosti Bosne i Hercegovine* (different years). Sarajevo: BiH Ministry of Finance and Treasury. Retrieved from http://mft.gov.ba/bos/index.php?option=com_content&view=article&id=692&Itemid=124

Čaušević, F. (2001). The fiscal structure in BH and the problems it generates. In V. Bojičić-Dželilović et al. (Eds.), *International support policies in south-east European countries: Lessons (not) learned in BH* (pp. 101–115). Sarajevo: Müller.

Central Bank of Bosnia and Herzegovina. (2017). *Statistics web portal* (Panorama Necto). Retrieved from http://www.cbbh.ba/Content/Read/915

Eaton, K., Kaiser, K., & Smoke, P. (2010). *The political economy of decentralization reforms*. Washington, DC: The World Bank. Retrieved from http://siteresources.worldbank.org/EXTDSRE/Resources/DecentralizationReforms.pdf

IMF GFS. (2001). *Government financial statistics manual 2001*. International Monetary Fund. Retrieved from https://www.imf.org/external/pubs/ft/gfs/manual/pdf/all.pdf

ITA. (2016). *Distribution of revenues from indirect taxes*. Banja Luka: Indirect Taxation Authority. Retrieved from http://www.new.uino.gov.ba/bs/Prihodi%202016

Ivanić, M. (2000). Fiscal decentralisation and the efficiency of public institutions in RS. In M. Zlatić (Ed.), *The fiscal decentralisation initiative for central and eastern Europe: Forum on fiscal decentralisation in Bosnia and Herzegovina* (pp. 97–110). Conference proceedings, Sarajevo, 1st ed. Budapest: FDI-CEE.

Kreso, S. (2005). Fiscal decentralization in BiH. In *International symposium: Bosnia and Herzegovina from past to present* (pp. 241–259). Çanakkale: ÇanakkaleOnsekiz Mart University.

Lazović-Pita, L. (2015). *Income, personal income tax and transition: The special case of Bosnia and Herzegovina*. Bamberg: BERG-Verlag.

Lazović-Pita, L., & Štambuk, A. (2015). Professional opinions and attitudes about tax policy in Bosnia and Herzegovina with the special focus on the Federation of Bosnia and Herzegovina. *South Eastern European Journal of Economics and Business, 10*(2), 29–44.

Mujakić, M. (2010). Lokalna samouprava u Federaciji Bosne i Hercegovine—koncept, nadležnosti i organi. *Hrvatska Javna Uprava, 10*(4), 1045–1058.

Mujakić, M. (2012). Pravni aspekti financiranja lokalne samouprave u Bosni i Hercegovini. *Hrvatska i komparativna javna uprava, 13*(2), 611–623.

Oates, W. E. (1972). *Fiscal federalism*. New York: Harcourt Brace Jovanovich, Inc.

RS Institute of Statistics. (2016). *Statistički godišnjak 2016—drugo izmjenjeno izdanje*. Banja Luka: RS Institute of Statistics. Retrieved from http://rzs.rs.ba/front/article/2240/

Savezni zavod za statistiku. (1989). *Statistical yearbook of Yugoslavia, 36*. Belgrade: Federal Institute for Statistics.

Transparency International. (2014). *Percepcija javne uprave Bosna i Hercegovina 2014*. Retrieved from https://www.cin.ba/wp-content/uploads/2014/09/TI-BIH-Percepcija-Javne-Uprave-BiH-2014.1.pdf

USAID. (2005). *Reordering intergovernmental fiscal relations in Bosnia Herzegovina: Local government finance reform and the implementation of VAT* (pp. 1–30). Sarajevo: USAID.

Weingast, B. R. (2007). *Second generation fiscal federalism: Implications for decentralized democratic governance and economic development*. Retrieved from http://policydialogue.org/files/events/Weingast_Second_Generation_Fiscal_Federalism.pdf

Part III

Local Governments in Transition and the Political Economy of Ethnicity

7

Macedonia: Local Government Efficiency and Ethnic Fragmentation

Marjan Nikolov

Introduction

At its independence in 1991, Macedonia was founded as a parliamentary democracy with a single-tier local self-government, and elected mayors and municipal councillors. Three periods can be identified in the process of decentralisation in its post-independence period (CEA, 2006). The first of these periods from 1991 to 1995 was one of centralisation, which left municipalities without competencies and with an inefficient system of financing. During this period, the government was focused mainly on achieving macroeconomic stability and liberalisation, deregulation, and privatisation.

During the second period, lasting from 1995 to 2005, macroeconomic stabilisation was achieved, but overall economic performance was relatively poor. A new Law on Local Government[1] and a new Law

M. Nikolov (✉)
Center for Economic Analyses, Skopje, Macedonia

International Slavic University, Skopje, Macedonia

W. Bartlett et al. (eds.), *Fiscal Decentralisation, Local Government and Policy Reversals in Southeastern Europe*, https://doi.org/10.1007/978-3-319-96092-0_7

on Territorial Organisation[2] were adopted in 1996, introducing 123 municipalities, a fragmentation of the 34 municipalities that had been inherited from the Former Yugoslavia. Both laws were products of a highly ethnically and politically motivated process (Popovski & Panov, 1998).

Macedonia signed the European Charter of Local Self-Government in 1996 and ratified it in the following year. In 1998, the Ministry of Local Government was established. The process of decentralisation was further supported by two important documents adopted in 1999, namely the Government Programme and the Government Strategy for Reforming the Public Administration. As a result of these two initiatives, a working team within the Ministry of Local Government was established in March 1999 to start the process of decentralisation.

In 1999, the Kosovo conflict further complicated ethnic tensions in Macedonia and led to an armed interethnic conflict in 2001. The crisis ended with the signing of the Ohrid Framework Agreement (OFA) in 2001 and the decentralisation initiatives of 1999 thus gained new momentum, introducing preferential policies for ending the crisis and calming ethnic unrest. These policies were implemented through the new Constitution of Macedonia in 2001, which introduced equitable representation of communities and established a new institution for support of consensus democracy—the Council for Interethnic Relations within the Parliament. This allowed for the official use of a language that is spoken by at least 20 per cent of the population of a municipality, and introduced higher education opportunities for minority communities. Soon after, in 2002, a new Law on Local Self-Government[3] was adopted, which regulates the competencies of the local governments.

The third period of decentralisation in Macedonia started in 2005 (and is still ongoing) when the government adopted a detailed plan for the transfer of competencies and resources to municipalities. This plan, together with the new legislation from 2004 (the Law on Territorial Organisation[4] and the Law on Financing Local Government[5]), provided an effective legal framework enabling a new and modern process of decentralisation in Macedonia to begin.

Patterns of Decentralisation Development

On independence, the system of government was based on the principle of the division of powers among the legislative, executive, and judiciary branches. The right to local government was one of the fundamental values stated in the Constitution[6] from 1991, as well as in the post-OFA Constitution of 2001.

Territorial Organisation

The evolution of decentralisation in the post-independence period has involved a mixture of political inefficiency and ethnic disputes. The 1991 Constitution guaranteed the right to one-tier local self-government, but it referred the detailed regulations to subsequent laws, which never allowed for true decentralisation. In fact, after independence and the start of transition, power was concentrated and centralised. The only competencies municipalities had were in the area of communal services. This period was a period of basic economic transition reforms that changed the economy to a market economy based on liberalisation, privatisation, deregulation, and the achievement of macroeconomic stability (Svejnar, 2002).

In that period up to 1996, Macedonia inherited the territorial organisation of the former socialist system of 34 municipalities. A new Law on Territorial Organisation[7] that was adopted in 1996 introduced 123 municipalities, of which 52 municipalities (42 per cent) had fewer than 6,000 inhabitants and 46 (38 per cent) had fewer than 5,000 inhabitants. The increasing economies of scale were evident in municipalities of up to 6,000 inhabitants, comparable to the Slovenian average municipality size of 5,000 inhabitants and the Bulgarian average of 6,000 inhabitants, which was the most efficient and smallest size of municipality (Nikolov, 2004).

With the new Law on Territorial Organisation[8] adopted in 2004, local governments in Macedonia were restructured into 84 municipalities (15 of which have fewer than 5,000 inhabitants), with the city of Skopje being a special unit comprising ten municipalities in accordance with a separate Law on the City of Skopje.[9] This law created new amalgamation dynamics in a number of municipalities. Thus, in 2013 one urban municipality (Kicevo) merged with four rural municipalities (Zajas, Oslomej, Vranestica, and Drugovo) due to an ethno-political agreement based on the OFA. Since 2013, Macedonia has had 80 municipalities plus the capital City of Skopje.

Using a Data Envelopment Analysis-Variable Returns to Scale (DEA-VRS) and a Stochastic Frontier Analysis (SFA) I find a robust estimate that the most efficient municipalities in Macedonia are those with around 10,000 inhabitants (Nikolov, 2013). Municipalities with fewer inhabitants (less than 10,000) show increasing returns to scale and lower technical efficiencies because they must provide the same amount of services for a smaller number of inhabitants compared to larger municipalities due to the influence of fixed costs on current expenditures. On the other hand, municipalities with more than 10,000 inhabitants have decreasing returns to scale and higher technical efficiencies due to the effect of negative agglomeration externalities.

Decentralisation of Functions

In the first and second period of decentralisation, that is, from 1991 and until 2005, the Law on Limiting Public Consumption and the Budget Execution Law were used to define the system of local government finances and the budget process (beside the organic Budget Law). In 2005, the government adopted a detailed plan for the transfer of competences and resources. Administrative decentralisation was planned in April 2005 in terms of the transfer of institutions, assets, employees, and documentation. In this plan, the deconcentrated units of line ministries were transferred to the local level as well. The plan, together with the new legislation, provided an efficient legal framework for the new modern process of decentralisation.

The 2002 Law on Local Government[10] regulates the competencies of the local governments. A wide range of responsibilities is listed in the provisions of Article 22 of this law, which includes: urban planning and space arrangement; environmental and nature protection; local economic development; communal services; cultural development, in accordance with the national programme for culture; sports and recreation; social care and child protection; foundation of education, financing and management of primary and secondary schools in cooperation with the central government; organisation of transport and food supplements for students and student housing; health care, managing the system of public health organisations and primary health care; undertaking measures for the protection and rescue of citizens and material goods in the case of destruction in war, natural disasters and other accidents; fire protection provided by the local fire departments; and supervision over activities regarding the municipality's responsibilities and other matters determined by law.

In accordance with the Law on Financing Local Government there were two phases of the decentralisation process. The first phase started on 1 July 2005, while the second phase started on 1 July 2007, but only for local governments that satisfied certain criteria as presented in Table 7.1.

Phase I was related only to the construction, maintenance, and operation of premises for education, social services, and culture. This phase coincided with the introduction of earmarked grants from the central government, intended to cover the costs of operating and maintaining existing buildings and tangible assets, comprising utilities, heating, communication and transport, materials and tools, repairs, current maintenance, and contractual services.

Phase II was initiated in 2007 with the devolution of teacher and other personnel salaries and the introduction of block grants. During this second phase, block grants were still to be paid for operation and maintenance costs, but additionally including salaries and employee benefits.

The phased approach to fiscal decentralisation was closely connected to transfers from the central government. The major principles of this phased approach were to ensure a gradual devolution of responsibilities proportional to the capacity of local governments to undertake those responsibilities, as well as to providing an equitable and adequate transfer of funds for an efficient and ongoing execution of transferred competencies.

Table 7.1 Illustration of the two-phased approach to fiscal decentralisation in Macedonia

Phase	Starting date	Assignment of responsibility	Conditional upon
Phase I	1 July 2005 (with amendments on 30 December 2004)	1. Transferring own revenues from tax sources (the PIT sharing) to municipalities (GOV); 2. Developing a methodology for transferring the capital grants and earmarked grants (GOV); 3. Local governments to begin implementing the plan for resolving the arrears before 31 January 2001 (local governments)	90% of total municipalities comprising 90% of the total population providing: 1. At least two financial officers; 2. At least three tax experts
Phase II	Conditional	Assignment of responsibilities (for block transfers): 1. Culture; 2. Social welfare and child protection (kindergartens and homes for the elderly); 3. Education (primary and secondary schools); 4. Healthcare (public health organisations and primary care)	1. All conditions from phase I being satisfied; 2. The proper capacity of financial officers (also in phase I); 3. Viable results after 24 months for on time and regular reporting confirmed by the Ministry of Finance; 4. There being no accounts payable other than the usual ones (up to 90 days); 5. The phase commission will evaluate if all the conditions have been satisfied; 6. There being a written request from municipalities to the relevant ministry and the Ministry of Finance to grant block transfers after all the conditions have been satisfied

Source: The Law on Financing Local Self-government

However, under the third period of decentralisation that began in 2005, the devolution of revenue preceded the transfer of competencies. The fiscal needs or of the fiscal capacity of municipalities were not estimated. Budget planning was based on a historical analysis, and sometimes some cost drivers were taken into account. Some calculations of the cost of services were based on unit prices, such as for kindergartens (EAR, 2007).

Transition costs related to the demographic, economic, and institutional changes that took place during the transition created additional expenditure needs, but the design of the intergovernmental transfers did not take these changes into account when addressing the fiscal gap for local governments. At the same time, the central government appeared to be unwilling to compensate municipalities for any of the following costs: (a) transition expenditures (including those stemming from the lower purchasing power and changes in the relative prices that took place after the fall of socialism); (b) administrative overheads, incurred hitherto by departments of the central government for the now transferred competencies; (c) geographical (and other) distinctions among various municipal jurisdictions; (d) diseconomies of small-scale service delivery by municipalities in which these may occur; (e) the potential for social disruption resulting from small-scale or more localised choices of service delivery; (f) macroeconomic instability (inflation); (g) demographic changes; (h) underinvestment during the transition and before decentralisation; and (i) insufficient maintenance during the transition and before decentralisation (EAR, 2007).

Table 7.2 shows the consolidated local government expenditures (the total of the administrative budget and the local government's fund budget) for the period 2000–2006 in millions of euros. Note also that the third period of decentralisation began in 2005 with the new Law on Financing Local Government from 2004 and the expenditures were immediately reflected by an increase in their ratio to gross domestic product (GDP). Total local government expenditures as a percentage of the GDP continuously increased in the period 2000–2006, especially after the start of the third period of decentralisation in 2005. Thus, expenditures in 2006 as a percentage of the GDP, increased by 37 per cent in 2006 compared to 2005.

Table 7.2 Local government expenditures for the period 2000–2006 in millions of euros

	2000	2001	2002	2003	2004	2005	2006
Total expenditures	14.13	42.34	54.54	48.29	77.33	78.77	117.04
Total as % of GDP	0.37	1.10	1.36	1.18	1.79	1.57	2.14
Wages and salaries	6.87	7.48	8.19	5.29	9.06	11.38	19.61
Goods and services	4.45	19.94	20.76	18.27	21.49	25.36	56.56
Transfers and subsidies	1.50	3.61	5.90	2.97	2.97	0.00	0.00
Interest payment	0.00	0.30	0.16	0.10	0.24	0.00	0.00
Capital expenditures	1.03	9.44	18.99	21.14	43.04	3.85	3.80
Capital transfers	0.25	1.01	0.07	0.17	0.22	0.00	0.00
Borrowing	0.03	0.56	0.47	0.35	0.31	38.18	37.07

Source: Ministry of Finance data. Author's calculations

After 2006, during the third period of decentralisation, expenditures increased especially under Phase II when block grants began to be transferred from the central government. As explained previously, Phase II was initiated in 2007, with the devolution of teacher and other personnel salaries through block grants (see Table 7.3).

The challenge for local government expenditures is the relatively high costs for salaries and other remuneration and small expenditures for investment in relation to other comparable countries. It should be noted that such comparisons depend on the manner in which expenditures are presented, since in some countries capital transfers to public enterprises are presented as investment, while in others they are presented as subsidies; and salaries in some countries are presented as salaries and other remuneration, while in others as goods and services (NALAS, 2016).

The structure of expenditures reveals that almost half of the expenditures related to education (Table 7.4), of which around 78 per cent cover wages, salaries, and social contributions for teachers. The second highest share of local government expenditures is related to public utility services (mostly public lightning, public hygiene, maintenance and protection of local roads and streets, and regulation of the traffic regime and public parks) making up 19 per cent of total expenditures in 2012–2015, while municipal administration accounted for 13 per cent of expenditures. Social security and child protection expenditures mostly relate to kindergartens.

Table 7.3 Local government expenditures for the period 2008–2015 in millions of euros

	2008	2009	2010	2011	2012	2013	2014	2015
Total expenditures	301.75	341.11	381.00	422.94	473.43	451.09	447.57	470.77
Salaries and other remuneration	145.29	170.78	190.45	202.82	216.64	219.40	222.55	233.73
Reserves and non-defined expenditures	0.54	0.58	0.67	0.49	0.49	0.38	0.51	0.53
Goods and services	80.47	91.95	98.64	100.41	116.97	113.45	114.89	120.00
Interest payment	0.02	0.03	0.02	0.05	0.40	0.64	0.89	0.94
Subsidies and transfers	11.31	10.76	12.18	14.63	19.46	20.25	18.97	19.49
Social benefits	0.23	0.34	0.36	0.41	0.53	0.53	0.52	0.59
Capital expenditures	63.89	66.66	78.68	104.14	118.92	96.46	89.23	95.51
Principal payment	0.02	0.07	0.10	0.17	0.54	0.95	2.48	4.02
Total as % of GDP	4.46	5.04	5.36	5.61	6.24	5.56	5.25	5.18
Local expenditures as % of general government expenditures	11.69	13.08	14.10	14.89	15.76	14.86	14.16	13.94

Source: Ministry of Finance data. Author's calculations

Revenue Decentralisation

In the first and second period of decentralisation, from 1991 and until 2005, the Law on Limiting Public Consumption and the Budget Execution Law were used to define the system of local government finances and the budget process. In that period, the responsibility for the administration and collection of taxes at both central and local levels lay with the central government. At that time, the centralised public revenue office used low quality data from the cadastre system for property taxes and lacked a good statistical information system. It should be noted that

Table 7.4 Programme expenditures of local governments in Macedonia for the period 2012–2015 in millions of euros and average structure for the period 2012–2015

Competency	2012	2013	2014	2015	Structure
A—Municipal council	10.73	11.34	10.97	10.90	2
D—Mayor	4.95	4.75	4.39	4.41	1
E—Municipal administration	55.38	55.65	57.28	63.65	13
F—Urban planning	17.68	15.24	17.38	16.64	4
G—Local economic development	12.25	12.90	11.05	5.93	2
J—Public utility services	92.71	81.65	82.48	96.24	19
K—Culture	22.97	15.91	9.97	10.08	3
L—Sports and leisure	4.11	4.06	3.48	4.69	1
M—Development programmes	0.61	0.96	1.60	1.35	0
N—Education	217.22	214.35	215.06	222.07	47
R—Environmental protection and nature conservation	1.40	1.37	1.37	1.23	0
T—Healthcare promotion	0.09	0.08	0.08	0.17	0
V—Social security and child protection	27.33	27.30	28.69	30.81	6
W—Fire protection	6.55	6.50	6.24	6.62	1
Total	473.97	452.04	450.05	474.78	100

Source: Ministry of Finance data. Author's calculations

tax revenues at that time were not directly allocated to those local governments on whose territory they were collected but were transferred into the treasury system and distributed among local governments in accordance with a formula. Total local government revenues as a percentage of the GDP continuously increased in the period 2000–2006, as can be seen from Table 7.5, which shows the consolidated local government revenues (the total of the administrative budget and the local government's fund budget) for this period.

The ratio of local government revenues to GDP was high in 2001 due to the higher revenues received after the privatisation of Macedonian Telecom. In April of that year, a strong multi-ethnic delegation from Macedonia signed an agreement in Luxembourg with the European Union (EU) calling for new political and economic relations with the then 15-nation EU. However, in 2001, ethnic Albanians clashed with government forces. Following these clashes, much was done through the OFA to grant ethnic Albanians the rights

Table 7.5 Local government revenues in Macedonia for the period 2000–2006 in millions of euros

	2000	2001	2002	2003	2004	2005	2006
Tax revenues	11.73	20.35	37.02	36.32	51.99	53.73	56.60
Non-tax revenues	0.12	16.09	3.70	1.84	5.06	3.09	18.51
Capital revenues	0.00	0.14	0.30	0.73	1.79	0.09	1.35
Transfers and donations	3.40	34.78	15.64	12.01	20.49	33.78	55.18
Domestic borrowing	0.02	0.04	0.00	0.75	2.28	0.22	0.00
Surplus	0.70	28.86	3.80	3.40	2.92	9.29	8.69
Total	15.97	100.25	60.46	55.04	84.53	100.20	140.32
Total as % of GDP	0.41	2.61	1.51	1.34	1.95	1.99	2.56

Source: Ministry of Finance data. Author's calculations

they had claimed since independence (Nikolov, 2013). The OFA was in effect a peace treaty that brought the ethnic clashes to a halt and also brought a new momentum to the decentralisation process. The OFA was written in Ohrid and signed in Skopje on 13 August, 2001 after a period of conflict that had lasted for seven months. The negotiators, who were the leaders of four political parties, two Macedonian and two Albanian, went through a procedure in the spirit of consensus democracy, which was, however, neither transparent nor democratic (Siljanovska-Davkova, 2007).

A major change brought on by new legislation in the third post-OFA period of decentralisation after 2005 was the assignment of property-related taxes to the local level (property and property transaction tax and inheritance and gift tax). Moreover, it was not only the revenue from these taxes that was assigned to local governments, but also the power to determine the rate and base as well as the power to collect these taxes. Thus, local governments began to exercise devolution in the fiscal sphere by administering their own-source revenues.

In 2009, the global financial crisis hit Macedonian GDP indirectly through the channel of international trade, and industrial production began to decline with a time lag of about one year as shown in Fig. 7.1 (see Nikolov, 2016).[11] The crisis had little effect on the financial sector because Macedonia was not integrated into the global capital market, and the banks mainly used domestic deposits for issuing credits. Local

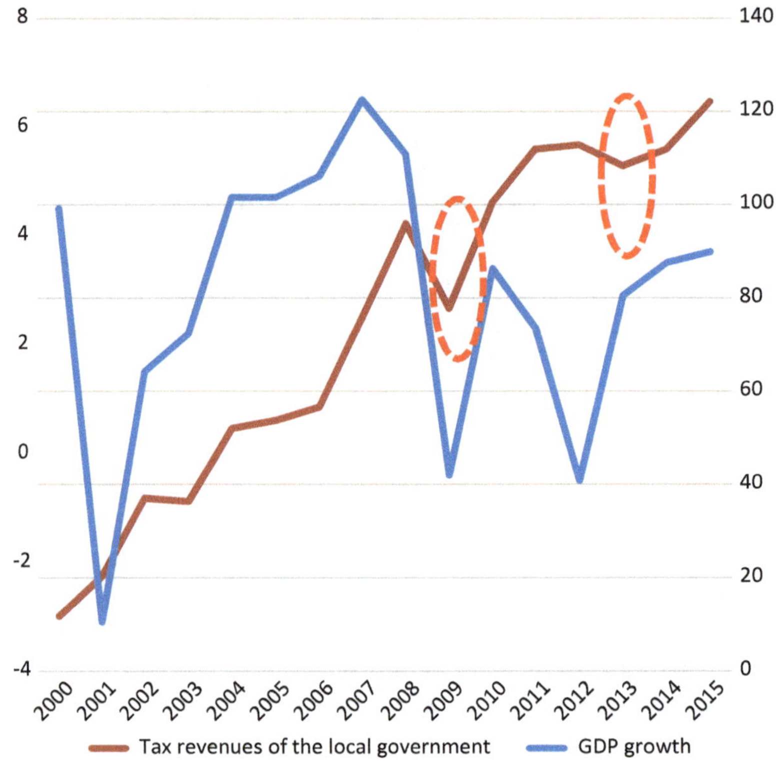

Fig. 7.1 Real GDP growth and tax revenues of local government, 2000–2015 in millions of euros. Source: State Statistical Office and Ministry of Finance Treasury, author's calculations

government tax revenues declined in both 2009 and in 2013, making a double-dip impact on GDP as shown in Fig. 7.1. However, tax revenues of local governments recovered in 2014 and 2015.

The structure of local government revenues in Macedonia is a mixture of own-source taxes, shared taxes, and transfers from the central government. Own-source revenues are derived from the property tax, a share of the personal income tax (sharing PIT), non-tax revenues from communal taxes and administrative taxes, capital revenues from the sale of assets, and the share from the value-added tax (unconditional value-added tax (VAT) transfer). Their structure is shown in Table 7.6.

Table 7.6 Local government revenues in millions of euros by source for the period 2008–2015

	2008	2009	2010	2011	2012	2013	2014	2015
Own source	144	132.86	168.55	187.03	216.6	188.24	195.67	219.61
Donations	1.67	1.28	3.00	2.77	4.41	5.23	6.62	8.47
Loans	0.41	0.00	0.58	7.59	8.55	10.93	9.71	8.26
Self-financing	14.77	14.26	14.9	14.36	15.14	14.08	14.49	14.89
Transfers	156.16	194.31	205.68	213.68	230.9	232.94	231.87	237.86
Total	317.01	342.7	392.71	425.43	475.6	451.42	458.36	489.08
Total as percentage of GDP	4.68	5.06	5.52	5.64	6.27	5.56	5.37	5.38
Local revenue as % of general government revenue	12.50	14.09	15.45	16.02	17.49	16.54	16.22	15.75

Source: Ministry of Finance Treasury data. Author's calculations

Donations, as a source category, mostly come from foreign aid donors, especially in the education sector. Self-financing activities are a source of revenue that are derived from the users of local government budgets (schools and kindergartens), through the financial participation of parents and the organisation of excursions. Transfers from central government are mostly tax revenues for block and earmarked grants for wages/salaries for teachers and employees in education, kindergartens, and libraries; and the maintenance of schools, kindergartens, and cultural institutions that come from the relevant line ministries.

Table 7.6 shows that own-source revenues declined by 8 per cent in 2009 compared to 2008 because of the first dip of the global financial crisis. However, own-source revenues increased by 27 per cent in 2010. In 2009, the decline of own-source revenues was matched by higher transfers from the central government, thus, keeping the positive trend of growing total local government revenues during the year in question. Furthermore, fiscal dependency of the local government on the central government's transfers declined in the period 2008–2015, eventually reaching less than 50 per cent in 2015.

The 27 per cent increase of own-source revenues in 2010 was a result of the increased tax effort of local government, but also a result of the fact that property tax collection from legal entities started in 2009. The increase was also due to a new policy that charged business fees in 2009, whereby producers of energy from fossil fuels were forced to pay compensation for pollution to local governments. It should also be noted that credit expanded in 2011, a topic that will be discussed in the section on Local Government Borrowing.

Own-source revenues of the local government declined by 13 per cent in 2013 compared to 2012 as a consequence of the second dip of the global financial crisis. Total revenues still increased in 2013 compared to 2012 because of the 28 per cent increase in borrowing, the 19 per cent increase in donations, and the 1 per cent increase in central government transfers.

It is also evident that the level of decentralisation is increasing as measured by the share of total revenues in GDP. However, if transfers from the central government are removed, over which the central government makes decisions, the level of decentralisation related to revenues over which local governments exercise discretion is reduced by about half as shown in Fig. 7.2.

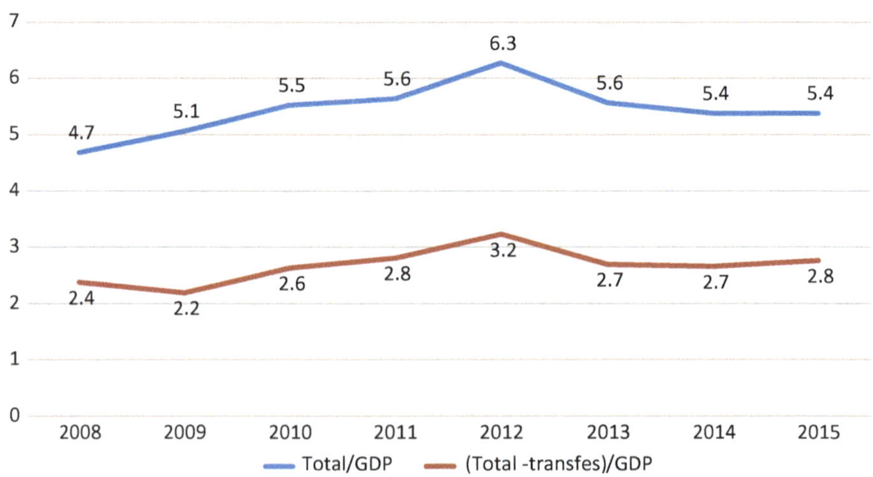

Fig. 7.2 Local government revenues over GDP, 2008–2015. Source: Ministry of Finance Treasury data, author's calculations

Horizontal Equalisation

Before 2005, centrally administered revenues from the property tax, the property transaction tax, the inheritance and gift tax, and communal fees were not directly distributed to those local governments on whose territories they were collected, but rather transferred into the treasury system. They were then distributed to local governments in accordance with a formula consisting of three variables: 80 per cent was distributed according to population size, 10 per cent according to area, and 10 per cent according to the number of settlements. All the revenues that were above a legislated cap were placed in an equalisation fund. It was common for the excess revenues above the cap to start to accumulate in the second half of the year and then to be redistributed back to the municipalities in the form of general or earmarked grants upon government decision. The criteria for redistribution of the resources above the cap were not very transparent and the purpose of the equalisation mechanism was not very clear (Nikolov, 2005). As a result, the discussion concerning the design of the new Law on Financing Local Government in 2004 was heavily based on how to abolish the cap system and design a new modern equalisation mechanism (Nikolov, 2004).

After 2005, an implicit horizontal equalisation system was introduced through the mechanism of VAT transfer. The revenues from VAT to be distributed to local governments were planned as a total fund equal to 3 per cent of VAT collections in the previous fiscal year. This is an unconditional transfer, and is distributed by a formula that states that at least 50 per cent of the transfer will be distributed according to population and not more than 50 per cent according to other criteria. These other criteria are stipulated in a methodology to be defined by the government in agreement with the commission to monitor the development of the financing system. The central government sees VAT as an unconditional transfer for equalisation purposes even though it is defined in law as own-source revenue for local governments. In 2009, amendments to the Law on Financing Local Government were adopted in which VAT transfers was envisaged to gradually increase from 3.4 per cent of GDP in 2010 to 3.7 per cent in 2011, to 4 per cent in 2012, and to 4.5 per cent in 2013.

Local Government Borrowing

Local governments can borrow in accordance with the Law on Financing Local Government after consent from the government, which is based upon an opinion from the Ministry of Finance. Public enterprises established by local governments can also borrow, but first a guarantee should be issued upon the decision adopted by the local government's council.

There can be short-term and long-term local government borrowing with clear and explicit borrowing rules adopted by law. Short-term non-interest borrowing is provided from the central budget to overcome liquidity problems during the fiscal year. There can also be long-term non-interest borrowing from the central budget, with a term of no more than five years.

In general, local governments can borrow short term, but they must pay back the loan within 12 months from the moment of signing the short-term borrowing contract. In this case, total short-term debt in the fiscal year cannot be higher than 30 per cent of the realised total revenues of the current operational budget from the previous fiscal year.

Local governments can take long-term loans for financing capital projects and investments, but also to refinance debts, cover for guarantees issued and in cases of natural or environmental disasters. The local government council can only approve long-term borrowing following a public hearing. Local governments can take long-term loans after a decision from the council that is valid only in the same fiscal year in which it is adopted. The total cost of a long-term loan cannot be more than 30 per cent of total revenues of the current operational budget of the previous fiscal year. The debt due, including guarantees issued, cannot be higher than the total revenues of the current operational budget of the previous fiscal year.

Financial instability is defined as occurring if a local government account is blocked for more than six months or if contingent liabilities rise above a threshold. Local governments do not have a rich experience with borrowing, as credit expansion started domestically only in 2011 with a credit line under the World Bank's Municipal Service Improvement Programme (MSIP) administered by the Ministry of Finance. Borrowing has made up a relatively small share of the total

Table 7.7 Borrowing at the local government level in Macedonia for the period 2008–2015 in millions of euros

Borrowing in euros	Domestic	In % of total revenues	Foreign	In % of total revenues
2008	0.41	0.01	0.00	0.00
2009	0.00	0.00	0.00	0.00
2010	0.58	0.01	0.00	0.00
2011	7.58	0.10	0.00	0.00
2012	6.42	0.08	2.13	0.03
2013	7.55	0.09	3.38	0.04
2014	8.82	0.10	0.89	0.01
2015	8.10	0.09	0.16	0.00

Source: Author's calculation based on Ministry of Finance Treasury data

revenues of local governments, and foreign borrowing started with the World Bank's MSIP in 2012 (see Table 7.7).

The borrowing capacity of local governments is relatively low given the scarce managerial skills, lack of basic project and proper strategic documents, and non-existent creditworthiness. The low absorption capacity was confirmed with a study of 13 municipalities that comprise nearly half of the population (Nikolov & Stojkov, 2007). Thus, there is little risk to macroeconomic stability of the country in the near future arising from local government borrowing.

The Role of EU Pre-accession, Accession, and Structural Funds

It is important to note that in Macedonia, as a candidate country for EU accession, the set of rules that ensures sound public finances and coordination of fiscal policies with those of the EU through the Stability and Growth Pact is not binding. The only requirement Macedonia has as a candidate country for EU accession is to prepare and implement the national programme for economic reforms following the Stabilisation and Association Agreement that was signed in April 2001 (Nikolov, 2016). No significant material benefits were received in this period from the EU Instrument for Pre-accession Assistance (IPA) at the local level, except the change in the budget presentation format in order to separately account for IPA funds in the capital part of the budget presentation. In terms of improved project preparation and management the only serious developments have been the Urban Planning Project of the World Bank Institute and the World Bank's MSIP. Macedonian local governments should take the time to improve their administrative capacity and ability to network and partner with civil society, especially by increasing their fiscal transparency (CBM, 2013).

Ethno-political Impact on Decentralisation

The evolution of decentralisation in the post-independence period has been accompanied by political inefficiency and ethnic disputes. Because of the political and ethnic impact on the efficiency of the provision of local public services, this section considers the ethno-political impact of decentralisation. We base the discussion on the observation that ethnicity becomes politicised when political coalitions are organised along ethnic lines, or when access to political or economic benefits depends on ethnicity, as is the case in Macedonia.

As already discussed, the third period of decentralisation started in 2005 with the newly enacted post-OFA laws on the financing and territorial organisation of local government in Macedonia. These laws were a direct result of the new momentum gained for decentralisation in the post-OFA period. While the political elite was already considering decentralisation, the speed and the depth of structural changes in society were of a wider scale with the new momentum provided by the OFA.

The basic reason to support decentralisation after 2005 was its potential to satisfy the demands of the minority ethnic groups, mainly the Albanians, for autonomy over their own affairs and resources. On the other hand, decentralisation can also legitimise, and thus strengthen ethnic divisions, leading to more antagonism between ethnic groups (Lipset, 1983). Such a development may make ethnic fragmentation a factor in the inefficient delivery of public services at the local level.

In 1999, the Kosovo conflict complicated ethnic tensions in Macedonia and led to an armed interethnic conflict in 2001, ending with the signing of the OFA in 2001. It is difficult to identify the roots of the ethnic conflict in Macedonia. Was it due to the different socio-economic status of the ethnicities? Was it because of the constitutional arrangements? Or was it just a result of fighting for territory? In any event, the disintegration of Yugoslavia provided plenty of opportunities for international organisations to experiment with the decentralisation option, especially in Bosnia and Herzegovina, Kosovo, and Macedonia (Nikolov & Brosio, 2015).[12]

There are two views on the reasons for this interethnic conflict. One view is that the root of the conflict lay in the territorial aspiration of the Macedonian Albanians (Arsovski, Kuzev, & Damjanovski, 2006) and that their final goal was the creation of a Greater Albania (also see Joseph, 2006). However, Siljanovska-Davkova (2007) argues that a survey carried out in 2001 showed that the main reasons for the insecurity were unemployment (57.2 per cent of the respondents), low family income (16 per cent), and insufficient social security (6.2 per cent). Only a small proportion of the respondents (5 per cent) felt insecure due to interethnic relations. The second view is based on the effect of the constitutional arrangements in Macedonia. At the promulgation of the new 1991 Constitution, representatives of the Albanian political party PDP-NDP abstained from voting in order to protest the preamble of the Constitution, which formally declared Macedonia to be the national state of the Macedonian people (MAR, 2012).[13] Following the OFA, the preamble of the new 2001 Constitution reads as follows: "The citizens of the Republic of Macedonia, the Macedonian people, as well as citizens living within its borders who are part of the Albanian people, the Turkish people, the Vlach people, the Serbian people, the Romany people, the Bosnian people and others". Thus, in a way, the post-OFA Constitution institutionalised ethnicity in Macedonia. The post-OFA constitutional amendments removed the notions of "nationality" and "minority", which were seen by Albanians as a sign of inferior status. Albanians were included in the government as an ethnic group even though it was already a "tradition" after the independence of Macedonia to have one Albanian political party in the government coalition in power.[14] Albanians were also always represented in the Macedonian Parliament. Moreover, in 2007, the Law on the Committee for Communities' Relations[15] was adopted, which regulates and makes parliamentary decisions on, among other things:

culture, language, education, personal identification documents, and symbols.

In Macedonia it could be argued that decentralisation was introduced mainly to increase ethnic cohesion rather than to enhance the efficiency of local governments. However, there are a few factors that may work to dampen the efficiency impact of decentralisation. The first one is the prevalence of national issues over local ones in local elections. During the local election campaigns in 2009 and 2013, mayors and opponents referred more to national problems than to local problems in the media (Nikolov & Brosio, 2015). A second reason might be that the Macedonian system is in reality closer to a deconcentrated system than to a decentralised system, and there are a few examples of this. It has been empirically confirmed that the population between the ages of 5 and 19, that is, elementary and secondary schoolchildren, significantly negatively influences municipal expenditures (Nikolov, 2013). This phenomenon is understandable as elementary and secondary schools are completely financed by the central government. The explanation for the findings here is that the more pupils there are of that age (and the greater the demand for schools), the less expenditures the municipalities will plan from their own-source revenues because their current own expenditures will be allocated to other priorities, leaving the central government to pay for the schools and for the transportation of pupils. This situation clearly shows that even though primary and secondary education is a devolved function, municipalities still consider that it is the central government's responsibility to take on the financial burden for these. Another example is the low number of municipalities (10 per cent of them) that have a higher property tax rate voted in the council. Many mayors consider asking the councils for a higher tax rate, but would not prefer to address the proper councils because of the political sensitivity. They thus pressure the Ministry of Finance to amend the law and the central government to introduce higher tax rates in legislation. The third example is the water tariff amendment, which is similar to the property tax rate example. The water supply was always a local government competency even in former Yugoslavia. Public utility companies and the local government pushed the central government to introduce an independent regulatory commission for setting water tariffs just because they thought that setting higher tariffs to reflect the full costs of the services would be too politically sensitive.

In such a set-up, one of actual deconcentration rather than devolution and of fiscal dependency of around 50 per cent, it is the central government that to a large extent actually determines the provision of services at the local level (the preferences are not yet revealed at the local level) in Macedonia. This set-up also facilitates clientelistic practices, particularly in those municipalities where the mayors share the same political affiliation of the central government, while it represents a great obstacle to good administration in those municipalities where mayors do not have the same political affiliation of the central government (Nikolov & Hrovatin, 2013).

Through the OFA, Macedonia has chosen relatively expensive preferential policies over electoral policies in order to reduce ethnic conflict (Horowitz, 2000). These may have a negative impact on costs and might reduce efficiency of public services. Electoral policies can accommodate ethnic harmony by encouraging the formation of multi-ethnic coalitions, inducing ethnic groups to engage in interethnic bargaining and fragmenting the support of one ethnic group to prevent it from achieving permanent domination. In contrast, preferential policies view ethnic conflict as a result of economic differences, and see ethnic disharmony as being caused by disproportional distribution. Ethnic fragmentation has a negative impact on Macedonian municipalities when it comes to providing efficient public services since Data Envelopment Analysis (DEA) and SFA show that ethnic fragmentation has a negative impact on efficiency in the provision of public services in ethnically fragmented Macedonian municipalities (Nikolov, 2013). The explanation is that if there is a greater ethnic balance between ethnic groups in a municipality, political power is more equally distributed, and ethnic groups may prolong making decisions that would bring about a more efficient operation of municipal services.

Where preferences for specific public policies are strongly correlated with ethnic origin, political conflicts over public policies may be fought more often along ethnic lines. In polarised societies interest groups may become political actors, and ethnic groups may then favour rent-seeking spending programmes and the patronage of their respective groups, thus undervaluing the public goods that benefit the whole community. In Macedonia the political affiliation of the mayor with that of the central government coalition has a positive impact on municipal efficiency, not because of the mayor's additional effort but because of patronage activities (Nikolov & Brosio, 2015). This is due to the relative lack of devolved competencies, and so many decisions about the provision of local services depend on the central government. In contrast, it is common practice in Macedonia for a mayor of the opposite political affiliation to that of the central government to have his or her local projects delayed because of the adverse influence of the central government on local matters.

Further, our findings support the view that in Macedonia the element of ideology is missing in political parties. They are catch-all parties that nurture the ideologies of North Atlantic Treaty Organization (NATO) and EU membership (Vankovska, 2007). In such an environment, the patronage of the central over the local government with a mayor of the same political affiliation can guarantee the support for, and realisation of local projects. This set-up has nothing to do with behaviour in a representative democracy. This situation presents great risks for the provision of effective local services in Macedonia, especially if politicians continue to exercise political patronage in implementing the OFA, and if the international community that supported the OFA does not help with more resources to underpin the OFA's expensive preferential policies (Nikolov, 2013). Macedonia is also at risk because of great socio-economic stratification (Bartlett, Cipusheva, & Shukarov, 2010). This stratification is replicated amongst the electorate and might make it more difficult for political actors to make promises about public service provision to large sections of the voters. Macedonian voters might only believe promises made by candidates belonging to their own ethnic or religious group. Those promises are therefore necessarily narrow and mainly target members of the respective ethnic groups (Nikolov, 2013).

Conclusion

After independence in 1991, the process of transition involved centralisation in order to provide better management of macroeconomic stability and ensure the institutional change needed to deliver the transition to a private market economy. That is why the period from 1991 to 1995 was one of centralisation. In 1995, the second period of decentralisation started and lasted until 2005. This was a period not only driven by the socio-economic requirements, but even more so by the ethno-political requirements that would calm the ethnic unrest after the OFA. The third period started in 2005 and is ongoing.

Macedonia inherited a territorial organisation of 34 municipalities after its independence in 1991. Then in 1995, the ethno-political fragmentation introduced a territorial division of Macedonia into 123 municipalities. Finally, immediately after the OFA in 2001, the territorial consolidation resulted in 80 municipalities. Given the existing legislation, the most cost-efficient municipalities are those with around 10,000 inhabitants.

In the first and second period of decentralisation, that is, from 1991 and until 2005, the Law on Limiting Public Consumption and the Budget Execution Law were used to define the system of local government finances and the budget process in Macedonia. During these two periods, the Constitution guaranteed the right to local self-government, but proper legislation to allow for decentralisation was not enacted until the third period of decentralisation. Thus, since independence, power was concentrated and centralised and the only competencies municipalities had were in the area of communal services until 2005.[16]

The new Law on Financing Local Government of 2004 was introduced in phases that devolved specific responsibilities conditioned upon administrative and financial readiness of municipalities. This approach led to negative results due firstly to the devolution of revenue preceding the assignment of competencies. Secondly, expenditure needs, cost of services, and fiscal capacities were never properly calculated. Finally, the demographic, economic, and institutional changes that have taken place created additional expenditure needs that were not taken into account.

While the share of expenditures of local governments in GDP has reached more than 6 per cent of GDP, the measurement of real decentralisation is at most 3 per cent of GDP taking into account the expenditures over which local governments have discretionary power. Further, about half of all local government expenditure is for salaries and only 20 per cent for investments. In the last four years about half of local expenditures was on education, of which around 78 per cent was for wages and salaries, while public utility services account for almost 20 per cent of the total expenditures. One of the major reforms within the structure of public finances was the devolution of the administration of the property taxes to the local government level. This resulted in higher revenues from property taxes, which helped local governments become more resilient to the global financial crisis.

The evolution of decentralisation in the post-independence period has witnessed a mixture of political inefficiency and ethnic disputes. A main reason for the rising interest in decentralisation in many countries, as also in Macedonia, has been the quest for political stability rather than economic efficiency. The post-OFA Constitution brought a new momentum to the decentralisation process, an equitable representation of communities, the use of additional official languages, and access to higher education for minority communities. However, the emphasis on deconcentration rather than devolution, ethnic fragmentation, and political patronage have negatively affected efficiency on the delivery of local public services.

Notes

1. Law on Local Government, Official Gazette of the Republic of Macedonia, No. 60/1995.
2. Law on Territorial Organisation, Official Gazette of the Republic of Macedonia, No. 49/1996.
3. Law on Local Self-Government, Official Gazette of the Republic of Macedonia, No. 05/2002.
4. Law on Territorial Organisation, Official Gazette of the Republic of Macedonia, No. 55/2004.
5. Law on Financing Local Government, Official Gazette of the Republic of Macedonia, No. 61/2004.
6. The first post-independence Constitution of the Socialist Republic of Macedonia (Official Gazette of the Socialist Republic of Macedonia 1991/52) was promulgated at the session of the Macedonian Assembly on the 17 November 1991. Retrieved October 20, 2016 from http://www.slvesnik.com.mk/Issues/67DD2F3F5BB14EB4ADB0BB89FBFC9522.pdf.

7. Law on Territorial Organisation, Official Gazette of the Republic of Macedonia, No. 49/1996.
8. Law on Territorial Organisation, Official Gazette of the Republic of Macedonia, No. 55/2004.
9. Law on the City of Skopje, Official Gazette of the Republic of Macedonia, No. 55/2004.
10. Law on Local Government, Official Gazette of the Republic of Macedonia, No. 05/2002.
11. The 2001 GDP decline was due to the ethnic clashes.
12. There is a growing literature on ethnicity and decentralisation in these countries (Ackermann, 2001; Bojicic-Dzelilovic, 2011; Koneska, 2012; Loew, 2013; Lyon, 2011; Monteux, 2006; Siljanovska-Davkova, 2007).
13. Previously, under the Yugoslav Constitution of 1974, the preamble had defined Macedonia as a nation of the Macedonian people, as well as that of the Albanian and Turkish minorities.
14. The practice of a government established by the winning ethnic Macedonian political party and the winning ethnic Albanian political party in Macedonia together with minorities having the right to veto laws related to culture, language, and education; the equitable representation principle in the public administration gives Macedonian democracy characteristics of a consociational democracy (Vankovska, 2007).
15. Law on the Committee for Communities' Relations, Official Gazette of the Republic of Macedonia, No. 150/2007.
16. Even though the new Law on Local Self-Government was enacted 2002, the proper finances came to be defined and regulated with the new Law on Financing Local Self-Government in 2004.

References

Ackermann, A. (2001). *On the razor's edge: Macedonia ten years after independence.* Retrieved from http://www.core-hamburg.de/documents/yearbook/english/01/ackermann.pdf

Arsovski, M., Kuzev, S., & Damjanovski, R. (2006). *Vojnata vo Makedonija vo 2001 godina* [The war in Macedonia in 2001]. Skopje: Matica Makedonska.

Bartlett, W., Cipusheva, H., & Shukarov, M. (2010). The quality of life and regional development in Macedonia. *Croatian Economic Survey, 12*(1), 121–162.

Bojicic-Dzelilovic, V. (2011). *Decentralization and regionalization in Bosnia-Herzegovina: Issues and challenges*. LSE papers on Decentralization and Regional Policy, Research paper no. 2.

Center for Economic Analyses (CEA). (2006). *The future of local public finances*. Retrieved from http://www.cea.org.mk/documents/studii/CR_ANG_WEB.pdf

Coalition for budget monitoring (CBM). (2013). Retrieved from http://kbm.mk/

European Agency for Reconstruction (EAR). (2007). Estimation of the costs of the transferred competences to local government units. *EuropeAid to Macedonia, No. 05MAC01/07/11/001*.

Horowitz, D. (2000). *Ethnic groups in conflict*. Berkeley: University of California Press.

Joseph, R. (2006). *Politics and ethnicity: A comparative study*. New York: Palgrave Macmillan.

Koneska, C. (2012). Vetoes, ethnic bidding, decentralisation: Post-conflict education in Macedonia. *Journal on Ethnopolitics and Minority Issues in Europe, 11*(4), 28–50.

Lipset, S. M. (1983). *Political man: The social bases of politics* (2nd ed.). London: Heinemann.

Loew, D. (2013). *Decentralization as a model for conflict: The case of Kosovo*. CCS Working Papers, 16.

Lyon, A. (2011). Municipal decentralisation in the Republic of Macedonia: Preserving a multi-ethnic state? *Federal Governance, 8*(3), 28–34.

Minorities at Risk (MAR). (2012). *Chronology for Albanians in Macedonia*. Retrieved from http://www.mar.umd.edu/chronology.asp?groupId=34301.

Monteux, C. (2006). Decentralization: The new delusion of ethnic conflict regulation. *International Journal of Multicultural Societies, 8*(2), 162–182.

Network of Associations of Local Authorities of South-East Europe (NALAS). (2016). *Fiscal decentralization indicators for South-East Europe: 2006–2014*. Retrieved from http://www.nalas.eu/Publications/Books/2016_FD_Report

Nikolov, M. (2004). *Fiscal decentralization in Macedonia: Recent developments and challenges*. Centre for Economic Analysis (CEA). Retrieved from http://pdc.ceu.hu/archive/00002625/01/Fiscal_Decentralization.pdf

Nikolov, M. (2005). An assessment of fiscal decentralization reform in Macedonia. In United Nations Development Programme—UNDP (Eds.), *Fiscal decentralization in transition economies: Case studies from the Balkans and the Caucasus*. Retrieved from http://www.cea.org.mk/documents/studii/FiscalDecentralization2005%20UNDP.pdf

Nikolov, M. (2013). *Cost efficiency of municipalities in service delivery: Does ethnic fragmentation matter?* Ljubljana: Lex Localis. https://doi.org/10.4335/978.961.6842.16.7(2013).

Nikolov, M. (2016). Accession states. In E. Ahmad, M. Bordignon, & G. Brosio (Eds.), *Multi-level finance and the euro crisis*. Cheltenham, UK; Northampton, MA: Edward Elgar Publishing.

Nikolov, M., & Brosio, G. (2015). Efficient delivery of ethnic public services in ethnically fragmented municipalities. *Lex Localis—Journal of Local Self-Government, 13*(3), 299–319.

Nikolov, M., & Hrovatin, N. (2013). Cost efficiency of Macedonian municipalities: Does ethnic fragmentation matter? *Lex Localis—Journal of Local Self-Government, 11*(3), 743–775.

Nikolov, M., & Stojkov, A. (2007). *Study on the role of local government in economic development and macroeconomic stability—The case of Macedonia*. Centre for Economic Analysis (CEA). Retrieved from http://cea.org.mk/documents/proekti/CEA%20Final%20Report%20F%20dec%20mac%20stability%20growth%20REV%20Final.pdf

Popovski, V., & Panov, M. (1998). *Opštinite vo Republika Makedonija* [The municipalities of the Republic of Macedonia]. Skopje: Misla.

Siljanovska-Davkova, G. (2007). *Globalisation, democracy and constitutional engineering as mechanism for resolving ethnic conflict*. Athens: VII World Congress of Constitutional Law.

Svejnar, J. (2002). Transitional economies: Challenges and perspectives. *Journal of Economic Perspectives, 16*(1), 3–28.

Vankovska, B. (2007). *Politichki system* [Political system]. Skopje: Bomat Grafiks.

8

Kosovo: Can Decentralisation Resolve Ethnic Conflict?

Adem Beha and Anton Vukpalaj

Introduction

The reform of local government commenced immediately after the Kosovo war, which ended with a military intervention and the establishment of the international civilian and military administration. Overall, local government reform and the initiation of the decentralisation project were deemed as political tools of the international community to build a democratic, peaceful and tolerant society, considering inter-ethnic divisions between Albanians and Serbs in post-conflict Kosovo. Thus, decentralisation became a key tool for addressing ethnic coexistence and providing security for local Serbs.

In 1989, as a result of the discriminatory policies pursued by the former President of Yugoslavia, Slobodan Milošević, the autonomy of Kosovo as one of the units of the Yugoslav federation was abolished and direct rule from Belgrade was imposed (Malcolm, 1999). This was

A. Beha (✉) • A. Vukpalaj
Department of Political Science, University of Pristina, Pristina, Kosovo
e-mail: adem.beha@uni-pr.edu; anton.vukpalaj@uni-pr.edu

W. Bartlett et al. (eds.), *Fiscal Decentralisation, Local Government and Policy Reversals in Southeastern Europe*, https://doi.org/10.1007/978-3-319-96092-0_8

followed by the installation of a thoroughly Serb administration in Kosovo, despite the fact that its population was mostly Albanian. In terms of territorial organisation, two developments occurred after the abolition of Kosovo's autonomy. On 2 July 1990, in response to this policy, the delegates of the Kosovo Assembly approved a Constitutional Declaration, which proclaimed Kosovo to be a republic within the Yugoslav Federation. On 7 September 1990, Kosovo adopted its Constitution.

The September 1990 Constitution, also known as the 'Kaçanik Constitution', organised the territory of Kosovo into municipalities as territorial units. Despite the fact that these documents displayed the Kosovo Albanians' aspirations for self-government and autonomy within Yugoslavia, they did not gain international legal recognition. The Republic of Serbia refused to recognise the claims of Albanians. With the 1992 decree issued by the Republic of Serbia, its territory was divided into 29 districts, while Kosovo territory was divided into 5 districts, such as the District of Kosovo, District of Peja, District of Prizren, District of Mitrovica, and the District of Morava.

After the abolition of Kosovo's autonomy, a civil resistance movement was launched by the Democratic League of Kosovo, a political party that aimed to address the unresolved problem of Kosovo through peaceful means. Despite this civil resistance against the discriminatory measures taken by Milošević, the risk of war increased. Judah (2000, p. 59), commenting on civil resistance in Kosovo, argued that it was an 'extraordinary experiment' that failed. The brushing aside of the issue of Kosovo in the Dayton Agreement of 1995 resulted in increased frustration amongst Kosovo Albanians, in Kosovo and in the Diaspora. A military response was organised by the newly formed Kosovo Liberation Army (KLA). The increasingly bitter conflict eventually led to intervention by North Atlantic Treaty Organisation (NATO) in spring 1999 with the aim of imposing a solution by force as a last resort after exhausting all diplomatic means to resolve the conflict, following failed negotiations at Rambouillet, in France.

Following the end of the armed conflict, an international civil administration, the United Nations Mission in Kosovo (UNMIK) was established on the basis of the Resolution 1244 of the United Nations Security

Council.[1] After its deployment, UNMIK rearranged the territorial organisation in Kosovo with municipalities as basic units of autonomous local self-government under its supervision. United Nations international officials established new local administrations in 20 municipalities (IDEA, 2004).

Resolution 1244 did not set out an exit strategy for UNMIK and consequently the political status of Kosovo was indefinitely undefined. UNMIK, as an international civil administration in Kosovo, established new Kosovo institutions through its regulations. Thus, the process of decentralisation was, since its inception, linked with the undefined political status of Kosovo. After building an institutional basis, pursuant to Regulation 2000/39[2] on the Municipal Elections in Kosovo in October 2000, UNMIK organised the first municipal elections in which a proportional electoral system was adopted. Despite the municipal elections and the establishment of legitimate local institutions, the supreme authority in Kosovo, as defined by UNMIK Regulation 1999/1,[3] remained with the Special Representative of the Secretary-General (SRSG), who was the supreme authority of the executive, legislative, and judiciary in Kosovo. Local elections were held instead of general ones in order to deflect the discourse of political parties away from Kosovo's status, while the proportional electoral system aimed at achieving an adequate representation of women and minorities. After the generally successful local elections, UNMIK began drafting one of the main documents, called the Constitutional Framework for Provisional Institutions of Self-Government in Kosovo, through which central institutions were to be established and the groundwork for a new territorial organisation in Kosovo would be set (King & Mason, 2006).

From a theoretical point of view, decentralisation can take several forms: administrative, political, fiscal, and economic (see Chap. 1). Various scholars have argued that decentralisation of power increases the quality of public services, good governance, accountability, transparency, and local economic development (Faguet, 2012). Others stress the importance of local autonomy and discretion in raising own-source revenues (Martínez-Vázquez, 2008). It is commonly held that fiscal decisions made at the local level better reflect the citizens' preferences. In countries with high levels of cultural, ethnic, and linguistic diversity, there is even more justification for giving different communities more control over their political and economic affairs (Tanzi, 2002). At the same time, decentralisation is considered to be a political instrument for the democratisation of local government. As an instrument for the delivery of local self-government, decentralisation aims to reduce ethnic divisions and to establish lasting peace in conflict-troubled countries. Ulrich Schneckener (2004, p. 30) considers decentralisation to be a constructive political strategy aimed at the alleviation of inter-group conflict. As he puts it, 'the potential for group conflicts is diminished by the fact that each group in its own region makes its own decisions, leaving only very few issues to be resolved by cooperation between groups (or between majority and minority).'

This chapter will tackle how political and fiscal decentralisation of power in Kosovo has been used as a strategy and policy instrument to mitigate conflict and increase security for the Serb community. Despite the fact that the political decentralisation is considered a successful story in Kosovo, the financial decentralisation still remains unconsolidated as the newly established municipalities do not sufficient fiscal autonomy and mainly rely on central government funds.

Local Government Reforms and Decentralisation

Since 1999, Kosovo has gone through two stages of local government reform. The first stage, which lasted from 2000 to 2008, established the institutional base of local governance through the Constitutional Framework for Provisional Self-Government in Kosovo[4] and UNMIK regulations. The second phase includes the period from 2008 to 2015. This phase is characterised by the beginning of the implementation of decentralisation, the creation of new Serb-majority municipalities, with the exception of the establishment of the municipality of northern Mitrovica. After the verdict of the International Court of Justice that the declaration of independence was not in contradiction with international law, and since 2010, under the leadership of the European Union (EU),

Kosovo and Serbia have begun a new process of negotiations on normalising their relations, an effort that was materialised with the agreement on the normalisation of relationships between Kosovo and Serbia signed on 19 April 2013. Under this agreement, additional autonomy is granted to the Serb municipalities in northern Kosovo, which are allowed the creation of the Association of Serb-Majority Municipalities.

The decentralisation process in Kosovo differs from other cases in Southeastern Europe. Three factors should be taken into account. First, decentralisation in Kosovo started before the international settlement of the country's political status, meaning, before the centralisation of authority in the provisional self-governance central institutions. Second, after the deployment of NATO troops and the UNMIK administration, Kosovo Serbs created parallel institutions in breach of Resolution 1244 and refused cooperation with the UNMIK administration and the interim self-governing institutions in Kosovo. Third, in order to attract them into Kosovo institutions, decentralisation became a key tool to address inter-ethnic strife in Kosovo, establish lasting peace, and provide assurances that after independence Kosovo Serbs would not be persecuted, but would enjoy self-governance and extensive autonomy in their municipalities. In other words, the decentralisation of power in Kosovo aimed at legitimising Kosovo's international state building on the one hand, and local peace building between Serbs and Albanians on the other. Despite both goals being legitimate, from the outset the costs and financial viability of such decentralisation were neglected.

The Political Dynamics Before Independence

The UNMIK international administration was installed with the aims of stopping the conflict in Kosovo, enabling refugee return, restoring order, and consolidating a democratic and multi-ethnic society. In order to achieve these objectives, UNMIK established the institutional framework, initially at the local level. UNMIK was aware that the issue of independence would be the number one topic of the election campaign of the political parties. UNMIK delayed the announcement of the election date for as long as possible in order to minimise the success of the political forces that emerged from the KLA (Mitchell, 2000; Tansey, 2009). UNMIK did not want the generals of the KLA, as had happened in Bosnia, to become politicians and lead the country. Their policy was based on the perception of the Democratic Party of Kosovo (PDK) as a more radical party, while the Democratic League of Kosovo (LDK) was perceived as a more moderate party.

While this classification may have had some value in terms of the background, manner of establishment, as well as programmatic and rhetoric approaches of both parties, when it came to the independence of Kosovo, all Albanian political parties were at least as 'nationalist' as the PDK itself. All political parties, including Ibrahim Rugova's LDK, considered Kosovo's full independence as the only option for compromise. Paris (2004, p. 216) noted that the concept of political moderation is a relative concept in Kosovo. However, UNMIK's greatest fears related to the tools used to realise the political demands of Kosovo Albanians, that is, the allegedly peaceful LDK tools or the non-peaceful ones of the PDK. On the other hand, Kosovo Serbs refused to cooperate with UNMIK and established parallel structures providing public services in education and health in breach of Resolution 1244 (OSCE, 2007, p. 24). Over time, these parallel structures were strengthened, especially in the northern part of Kosovo.

Before organising the elections, UNMIK put in place a set of consultative mechanisms. UNMIK established the legal infrastructure for the smooth running of elections,[5] constructing democracy from the ground up. This implied a new administrative and territorial organisation. UNMIK Regulation 2000/43 on the number, names, and boundaries of municipalities in Kosovo[6] laid out the composition of Kosovo into 30 municipalities: Deçan, Gjakovë, Gllogovc, Gjilan, Dragash, Istog, Kaçanik, Klinë, Fushë Kosovë, Kamenicë, Mitrovicë, Leposaviq, Lipjan, Novobërd, Obliq, Rahovec, Pejë, Podujevë, Prishtinë, Prizren, Skenderaj, Shtime, Shtërpce, Suharekë, Ferizaj, Viti, Vushtrri, Zubin Potok, Zveçan, and Malishevë. Municipal boundaries were drawn based on cadastral zones.

The UNMIK Regulation on Municipal Elections in Kosovo specified that 'the elections for municipal assemblies will be held under the system of proportional representation based on lists of candidates of political parties, citizens' initiatives and coalitions and independent candidates' and that 'each list of candidates must include at least 30 per cent women candidates within the first 15 candidates' (Chesterman, 2004). In July 2000, the Central Election Commission headed by UNMIK unilaterally imposed an electoral system based on proportional representation. In accordance with Lijphart's (1969, 2004) idea on consociational democracy, after the elections political parties were forced to sit with each other, build post-electoral coalitions, and cooperate among themselves, whether they liked it or not. In other words, the proportional electoral system was one of the key methods used by UNMIK to engineer political representation, political culture, and construct democratic and multi-ethnic institutions.

The organisation of the first elections was probably UNMIK's most important political activity after its deployment. Linz and Stepan (1992) argue that in post-conflict societies general elections must precede local ones. This did not happen in the case of Kosovo, where general elections were not on UNMIK's agenda. From UNMIK's perspective, five advantages were expected from holding local elections before general elections: first, they would serve as a 'pilot project' to test the procedures, infrastructure and institutions that would manage the elections; second, a counterbalance to the political legitimacy of political structures emerging from the KLA would be created; third, the participation of Kosovo Serbs would change their negative prospects after 1999; fourth, local governments would become functional and would begin to provide services; and fifth, local elections would enable UNMIK to assess the configuration of power after the conflict in Kosovo (Beha, 2017; Taylor, 2002).

In October 2000, UNMIK organised local elections in Kosovo and although the electoral platforms of the political parties should have dealt with economic development and local democracy, the electoral platforms of the Albanian political parties focused on a demand for independence. Despite international concerns that the local elections would be won by the PDK, 58 per cent of the electorate voted for the LDK, and only 27 per cent for the PDK. Kosovo Serbs boycotted the local elections, which was seen by many as a failure of the UNMIK administration. UNMIK, under the leadership of Michael Steiner, began negotiations with local Serbs on the decentralisation of power on condition that they participated in the next general elections. Resolution 1244 had authorised UNMIK to establish the Provisional Institutions of Self-Government and build a multi-ethnic society and the Serb boycott hampered the realisation of this mission. Thus, decentralisation turned into a major political priority for UNMIK in order to attract Serbs to Kosovo's institutions. The logic behind decentralisation in Kosovo and the establishment of institutional structures of local government before the formation of central institutions was based on the idea of building democracy from the ground up.

> When UNMIK took over the administration of Kosovo in 1999, it decided to create local government institutions before central institutions in order to build democracy from the ground up. These legal acts divide Kosovo into 30 municipalities with the boundaries of each municipality 'delineated by its component cadastral zones' rather than on the basis of the pre-conflict local government units (USAID, 2007, p. 9)

After the adoption of the Constitutional Framework, general elections were held in 2001. Although the Kosovo Serbs had boycotted the local elections of 2000, the fall of the Milošević regime opened the possibility of cooperating with Serbia, so that it would not appeal for a boycott of the elections to be organised in 2001. Many Serbs had deep reservations about participating in these elections. Those who were displaced in northern Kosovo were most reluctant, as they had already created de facto several 'parallel institutions' and enjoyed the direct support of Serbia. The Serbs living in Graçanicë/Gračanica were more pragmatic over their participation in the elections (Sörensen, 2013, p. 275). Serb participation in the general elections became possible after an agreement was signed on 5 November 2001, between the UNMIK Special Representative, Hans Haekkerup, and the President of the Federal Republic of Yugoslavia Coordination Centre for Kosovo, Nebojša Čović. The LDK emerged as the winner of the election, with 45.7 per cent of the total vote. Compared to the 2000 local elections, when the LDK received 58 per cent of the votes, the results marked a decline in the general support for this political party. The LDK, entered a coalition with the PDK and the Alliance for the Future of Kosovo to form the central government. Soon after the creation of the institutions, tensions between Albanian political parties and the UNMIK administration surfaced. These tensions were related to the fact that UNMIK had no clear exit strategy from Kosovo.

In lieu of an 'exit strategy', UNMIK set a number of standards that Kosovo had to meet before opening discussions on its final status. Incidentally, this policy known as 'standards before status' was used as a strategy to delay the talks on Kosovo's status, rather than to provide a clear exit strategy. Meeting these standards, especially in relation to the return of displaced Kosovo Serbs and their integration into Kosovo institutions through free and fair elections, was hostage not only to the policies of the institutions of Kosovo, but also to the insistence of Serbia that Kosovo Serbs boycott the elections and refuse to participate in Kosovo institutions. UNMIK, under the leadership of Michael Steiner, promised to Serbs decentralisation for the northern Kosovo if they would accept to participate in the 2002 local elections. Northern Kosovo was almost beyond the control of UNMIK, and Steiner proposed a seven-point plan to establish local authorities there. In this plan, Steiner argued that there would be no decentralisation of power without political participation and 'there would be no investments without legitimate institutions' (Beha, 2013, p. 271).

Despite the Serb boycott of the second local elections and of all the other elections up to Kosovo's declaration of independence in 2008, Steiner invited the Council of Europe to lead the process of decentralisation. In February 2003, The Council of Europe sent to Kosovo a mission composed of experts on decentralisation. Besides many other options, this mission recommended the creation of new municipalities within the existing ones (Osmani & Manaj, 2014, p. 57). In 2005, the Kosovo Assembly adopted the Framework Document on Local Government Reform. The document foresaw the creation of five additional municipal units: two of them for Kosovo Albanians, two for Kosovo Serbs, and one for the Kosovo Turks. These municipalities will be known as the 'pilot municipal units.' Graçanica/Gračanica and Partesh/Parteš will be the Serb municipalities, Mamusha the Turkish one, and Hani i Elezit/Elez Han and Junik the Kosovo Albanian ones. Previous to the negotiations on the future status of Kosovo that were going to take place in Vienna, the international community engineered decentralisation as a policy that aimed to improve the inter-ethnic relations and the integration of minority communities into Kosovo institutions (Tahiri, 2008, p. 31).

Legal Framework

The founding document upon which the whole institutional architecture of post-war Kosovo has been built is the Constitutional Framework for Provisional Self-Government in Kosovo, signed on 15 May 2001 by the UNMIK SRSG, Hans Haekkerup. The provisional executive, legislative, and judicial institutions of Kosovo were established through this document, and Kosovo was considered an 'indivisible territory' and an 'entity under interim international administration.' However, the Constitutional Framework did not define the final political status of Kosovo. This document protected individual and collective rights of national communities (i.e. minorities) in Kosovo. Serbs and other minorities were guaranteed 20 seats in the Kosovo Assembly, regardless of the number of votes they would be able to win in elections. Likewise, they were guaranteed representation at government and municipal levels and at the institution of the President (Beha, 2014).

The fundamentals of local self-government in pre-independence Kosovo were set in the Constitutional Framework and UNMIK Regulations.[7] Under the Constitutional Framework, 'Kosovo is composed of municipalities, which are the basic territorial units of local self-government with responsibilities as set forth in UNMIK legislation in force on local self-government and municipalities in Kosovo.'[8] The municipal responsibilities were established with UNMIK Regulation No. 2000/45. The UNMIK Regulation on Local Self-Government of Kosovo Municipalities was the first to regulate local self-government based on the European Charter on Local Self-Government, the European Conventions for the Protection of Human Rights and Fundamental Freedoms and its Protocols, and the European Charter for Regional or Minority Languages. For the municipalities, as basic territorial units of self-government, this regulation devolved powers that were not expressly reserved for central bodies. According to this regulation, 'central power' was vested in UNMIK.

First of all, the regulation determined that municipalities should promote coexistence between their inhabitants and create conditions for all communities to express, preserve and develop their ethnic, cultural, religious and linguistic identities.[9] According to this regulation, members of national communities had the right to use their own language in all municipal bodies, and public meetings were to be held in two languages: Albanian and Serbian. Likewise, the names of cities, towns, villages, streets, and public places were to be displayed in both languages.

This regulation gave municipalities 16 powers. Inter alia, municipalities were responsible within their territory for the provision of the basic local conditions for sustainable economic development, urban and rural planning and land use, licencing of construction works and other development, local environmental protection, provision of local utilities and infrastructure, including water supply, sewers and drainage, sewage processing, maintenance of local roads, local transportation, management of local assets, preschool, primary and secondary education, primary health care, social services and housing, and the safety and maintenance of parks.

The highest representative body of the municipality was the Municipal Assembly, whose members were directly elected. The Assembly was responsible, inter alia, for the adoption of the budget, approval of the statute of the municipality, adoption, amendment or repeal of local laws, election of the president and deputy president of the municipality, appointment of the chief executive officer and the appointment of the board of directors. The meetings of the Assembly were to be chaired by the president. The president and deputy president were elected by secret ballot by the members of the Municipal Assembly and could be removed from the same body by a vote of more than two-thirds of the elected members. In connection with municipal financial management, this regulation established the general principles that the municipal budget should cover all activities undertaken within each fiscal year and that it should be drafted transparently. Also, it provided that municipal financing was to be achieved through central government financial transfers to municipalities as well as municipal revenues collected through licences and fees set by the municipality, the proceeds from municipal assets and a share of fines or penalties.

In order to monitor the activities of municipalities, UNMIK Regulation 2000/45 provided two methods of supervision. First, oversight was to be provided by UNMIK, which supervised the implementation of the regulation in accordance with the legal framework. Second, the SRSG could overrule any decision of a municipality that clashed with Resolution 1244 of the Security Council and the applicable law. Specifically, the regulation provided that every activity that did not take into account the rights of non-majority communities a municipality would be repealed by the SRSG.

The last UNMIK Regulation on local government before Kosovo's declaration of independence was Regulation 2007/30, which amended the previous Regulation 2000/45. Unlike the Law on Local Government, which was approved immediately after the declaration of independence, the two prior regulations on local government did not refer explicitly to own and delegated powers. The terminology of own and delegated powers appeared for the first time in 2005, in an administrative instruction of the Ministry of Local Government that tried to fill the gaps in UNMIK Regulation 2000/45 (OSCE, 2008, p. 10). Under UNMIK Regulation 2007/30, the powers of municipalities did not differ from those of the previous regulation and were divided into activities that the municipalities 'shall be responsible for' and activities that the municipalities 'may take action'. The first included public services, management of municipal assets, primary health care, preschool, elementary, and secondary education, housing, and naming roads, while the latter included tourism, cultural activities, sports, and youth activities. This second regulation established three types of committees to be established within the Municipal Assembly: a Policy and Finance Committee, a Communities Committee, and a Mediation Committee. The Policy and Finance Committee proposes the municipal budget and was chaired by the mayor of the municipality.

Unlike the previous regulation, Regulation 2007/30 directly empowered the mayor (Schultze-Kraft & Morina, 2014), who was elected by the direct votes of citizens rather than by the Municipal Assembly. This regulation restricted the service of the mayor to two terms. The mayor has the authority to appoint municipal directors, chairs the Board of Directors, proposes the annual budget to the municipal assembly, and reports every three months to the municipal assembly. Municipalities could establish a number of municipal directorates, including, inter alia, the Administration and Personnel Directorate, the Health and Social Welfare Directorate, the Education and Culture Directorate, the Finance, Economy and Development Directorate, the Urbanism, Cadastre, and the Environmental Protection Directorate. Directors appointed by the mayor were considered political staff.[10]

After two rounds of general elections and the establishment of central institutions, the Ministry of Local Government Administration, established in 2005, was tasked with directly supervising the activities of municipalities. According to UNMIK Regulation 2007/18, the executive powers of the Ministry were extended to allow it to suspend or set aside any municipal decision or action that did not comply with the law.[11] The new regulation, Regulation 2007/30 enabled UNMIK to invalidate any decisions of municipalities opposed to Resolution 1244 of the Security Council.

Fiscal Decentralisation

Fiscal decentralisation was deployed as a policy for the first time in Kosovo in 1999. Fiscal policies were established by the central banking authority. Initially, municipalities had the right to tax small businesses and collect a levy on agricultural land. Initially, local government revenues constituted only 0.35 per cent of state revenues, distributed to local authorities through unconditional grants (MLGA, 2012). In 2001, local municipalities spent 6 per cent of the total budget of Kosovo, rising to 27 per cent in 2003; thereafter the expenditure share stabilised at 24 per cent of the budget (see Table 8.1). The main municipal expenses were education (47.6 per cent of total municipal expenditure), health (12.4 per cent), and general municipal administration (37.7 per cent).

Table 8.1 Expenditure by different government levels (€ millions)

	UNMIK	PISG	Municipalities	Total	% Municipalities in total
2000	49.8	152.8	0.0	202.6	0
2001	70.7	154.3	14.6	239.5	6
2002	144.1	169.0	89.0	402.1	22
2003	138.5	234.5	141.8	514.9	27
2004	167.5	430.8	188.9	786.9	24
2005	0.0	531.6	164.5	696.1	24

Source: Péteri and Vaillancourt (2007, p. 25)

Table 8.2 Revenue of municipalities by function (per cent of total municipal revenues)

	2003	2004	2005	2006	2007
General grant	27.6	28.9	21.9	22.7	24.2
Education grant	42.2	41.6	46.3	45.4	47.4
Health grant	10.6	10.1	11.2	10.9	11.4
MOSR (municipal own-source revenues)	19.6	19.3	21.5	21.1	17.0
Total	100.0	100.0	100.0	100.0	100.0

Source: USAID (2007), Municipal budget allocation 2003–2007, p. 43

The largest grant municipalities receive from the central level is the Education Grant, followed by the General Grant and the Health Grant (see Table 8.2). The total revenues increased from €142 million in 2003 to €164 million in 2007. These grants account for almost 90 per cent of the financial resources of the municipalities.

Over the period 2000–2008 Kosovo municipalities had little financial autonomy, but relied heavily on the financial resources of the central government. While the municipalities accounted for a quarter of total general government expenditures and employed half of all government employees, they increased their own-source revenues within the municipality by only 4 per cent (USAID, 2007). Collecting taxes at municipal level is one of the main problems facing the municipalities. Larger municipalities like Pristina, Prizren, Peja, Gjilan, Gjakova, Fushë Kosova, Ferizaj, and Kaçaniku have collected more revenues than other municipalities. During the period 2003–2006, the municipality of Pristina collected €79.8 million on average, the municipality of Prizren collected €5.1 million, and the municipality of Peja €4.1 million from income taxes and value-added tax (VAT) (see Table 8.3).

Table 8.3 Large municipalities' share of all municipal income taxes and VAT (2003–2006)

Municipality	Share (%)	Million euros
Pristina	72.0	79.9
Prizren	4.6	5.05
Peja	3.7	4.07
Ferizaj	2.3	2.57
Fushë Kosova	2.3	2.55
Gjilan	2.1	2.29
Gjakova	2.0	2.22
Kaçanik	1.8	2.05
Eight largest municipalities	90.8	100.58

Source: USAID (2007), Municipal budget allocation 2003–2007, p. 16

Local Government after Independence

Political Dynamics

As a result of the dissatisfaction of the local population with the international administration of Kosovo and a lack of economic growth, major riots took place in 2004 (Beha, 2011). In March, Albanian crowds attacked UNMIK assets and facilities and Serb Orthodox religious sites. These events accelerated the discussion on the status of Kosovo, and in 2005 the UN appointed a special envoy to launch negotiations on Kosovo's status. These events transformed the debate on the decentralisation of government and the creation of new Serb municipalities into discussions about providing security for Serbs, and on Kosovo's future status. In October 2005, the Contact Group for Kosovo adopted the 'Ten Guiding Principles on the Future Status Talks of Kosovo'. These included the principles that the existing territory of Kosovo could not be divided, that there would be no return to the situation before 1999 and that Kosovo could not join any other state. The principles also included the decentralisation of power as a substantial element in future talks on status and that the decentralisation process should support the coexistence of different communities (Gjoni, Wetterberg, & Dunbar, 2010). After nearly two years of negotiations between the international community, Kosovo and Serbia in Vienna, mediated by the UN chief negotiator Martti Ahtisaari, the latter recommended supervised independence for Kosovo, in February 2007.

The essence of the Vienna talks centred on the decentralisation of power and the establishment of Serb-majority municipalities in Kosovo (Perrit, 2010), as the instruments through which minority communities in Kosovo, especially the Serbs, would feel protected. Considering it a political project rather than an instrument for reform and democratisation of local governance, 'Kosovo's authorities seem to have adopted the position that accepting the Ahtisaari Plan, including its core provisions on decentralisation, was the price they had to pay for independence from Serbia' (Schultze-Kraft & Morina, 2014, p. 6). Decentralisation, besides being initially rejected by the Serb side, was accompanied by dilemmas and scepticism from the opposition parties. For example, the Self-Determination Movement opposed decentralisation, arguing that it is based on principles of ethnic division and therefore it fails to integrate the delivery of services to the citizens.

On 17 February 2008, unilaterally Kosovo declared its independence in accordance with the Ahtisaari Plan. Ahtisaari proposed a new system of local government that turns Kosovo into a highly decentralised state. His plan proposed the creation of five new Serb-majority municipalities (Graçanica/Gračanica, Ranillug/Ranilug, Partesh/Parteš, Kllokot/Klokot, and Mitrovice/Mitrovica North) and the expansion of the territory of another municipality (Novobërd/Novo Brdo) (Beha, 2011). The Ahtisaari Plan foresaw the withdrawal of UNMIK from Kosovo and its replacement with a European Union Rule of Law Mission (EULEX) as well as an International Civilian Office (ICO) that would oversee the independence of Kosovo.[12]

Two months after the declaration of independence of Kosovo, in May 2008, Serbia organised local elections in Kosovo in 23 municipalities out of a total of 30, in breach of Resolution 1244. By organising these elections, Serbia openly opposed Kosovo's independence and challenged the authority of Kosovo institutions. With the support of Serbia, Serb parallel structures refused to cooperate with local and international institutions for the implementation of decentralisation under the Ahtisaari Plan for the creation of new Serb municipalities with extended powers. At the same time, Serbia continued to financially support Serb parallel structures, allocating €500 million to fund them. Municipalities in northern Kosovo have continued to refuse to cooperate with Kosovo institutions, EULEX and ICO.

One of the main challenges in Kosovo after the declaration of independence has been the implementation of decentralisation and the creation of new municipalities under the Ahtisaari Plan. On 15 November 2009, under the auspices of the ICO, Kosovo held its first local elections after independence in 38 municipalities, including the former pilot municipal units and new Serb municipalities that were to be established in accordance with the Ahtisaari Plan. These elections were of exceptional importance since new municipalities would be established through them, and the lack of Serb participation would have marked a backward step in the consolidation of statehood and democracy. Serbs participated in the elections and won in four municipalities: Graçanica/Gračanica, Kllokot/Klokot, Ranillug/Ranilug, and Novobërd/Novo Brdo. On 20 June 2010, elections were organised for the establishment of the municipality of Partesh. Serb participation in these elections was very high. However, in the three northern Kosovo municipalities, they boycotted the elections. In 2010, the ICO, in cooperation with the institutions of Kosovo, drafted a document called 'Strategy for the North of Kosovo', which aimed to integrate the Serbs of northern Kosovo into the Kosovo institutions, dissolve the parallel structures, and carry out elections in the municipalities as a prelude to the implementation of the Ahtisaari Plan (Visoka & Beha, 2013).

After the establishment of the new municipalities and the transfer of powers from the central level to the local level, the main challenge was financial decentralisation. The estimated cost of implementation of decentralisation was around €30 million. Mayors of Albanian municipalities complained that the new powers of municipalities, through the Law on Local Self-Government, were not accompanied by sufficient funds (KLGI, 2009). Likewise, since 2010, the five new Serb-majority municipalities with the exception of the municipality of North Mitrovica, which is yet to be established in accordance with the Ahtisaari Plan, have continued to receive general grants from the central budget of the Kosovo government including capital investments (see Table 8.4).

Table 8.4 Financing Serbian municipalities in Kosovo (€ million)

	MLGA capital investments during 2010	Grants by central govt. budget (2011)	Own-source revenues 2011	Capital investments (2011)
Graçanica	766,478	4,138,780	400,00	1,486,688
Novobërd	285,668	2,121,265	29,063	522,653
Ranillug	230,000	957,071	40,000	92,791
Kllokot	230,000	847,355	8,390	211,446
Partesh	230,000	905,424	0	228,306
North Mitrovica	86,000	N/A	N/A	N/A

Source: Tahiri (2011, p. 18). Available at: http://library.fes.de/pdf-files/bueros/kosovo/09762.pdf

Legal Framework

Kosovo's new Constitution of June 2008 established the general principles and the organisation and functioning of local self-government.[13] It is based on the European Charter of Local Self-Government, as were the various laws and by-laws adopted later. Two fundamental principles underpin local government under this Constitution: providing local public services based on the principles of good governance, transparency and effectiveness and addressing the concerns of the minority communities.

Municipalities have remained the basic units of local self-government, the boundaries of which are regulated by the Law on Municipal Administrative Boundaries.[14] This law regulates the territorial organisation of local self-government and establishes new municipalities and their territory. Eight new municipalities were established under this law, in addition to the 30 municipalities that were established immediately after the conflict by UNMIK. The territory of the Novo Brdo municipality was to be expanded, while two new municipalities were to be established from the territory of the municipality of Mitrovica: the municipality of Mitrovica North and the municipality of Mitrovica South. Also, this law turned the Pilot Municipal Units that had operated since 2005 into the municipalities of Junik, Mamusha, and Hani i Elezit. In addition, three new laws were approved from the package of laws that were adopted under the Ahtisaari Plan: the Law on Local Self-Government,[15] the Law on Inter-Municipal Cooperation,[16] and the Law on Local Government Finances.[17]

The Law on Local Self-Government was adopted only three days after the declaration of independence of Kosovo under an accelerated procedure. It bases its principles on the European Charter of Local Self-Government and the Framework Convention for the Protection of National Minorities. Under this law, the assembly and the mayor comprise the municipal authorities. The highest body of the municipality is the Municipal Assembly, whose delegates are directly elected for a four-year term. It approves the statute and rules of procedure, approves the budget and investment plans, and defines municipal fees, among other functions. The mayor is elected directly, and municipal directors are political staff directly appointed by the mayor. The new legislation provided mayors with substantial powers and turned them into key political figures over whom the Municipal Assembly lacks sufficient mechanisms to hold the mayor accountable to the citizens of the municipality. The Municipal Assembly cannot dismiss the mayor unless a call for his or her dismissal receives a majority of the votes of all potential voters, making removal from office almost impossible given the low turnout in local elections (Tahiri, 2012). This has created some ambiguities concerning the division of responsibilities in the municipalities.

Kosovo municipalities exercise their powers based on the principle of subsidiarity including own, delegated and enhanced powers. Own powers are the full and exclusive powers of the municipalities, of which there are 18 covering areas such as local economic development, urban and rural planning, land use and development, implementation of construction regulations and construction control standards, provision of primary health care, public health care, naming of roads and public places and public housing. The powers that are delegated by the central government include cadastral notes, civil registration, voter registration, business registration and licencing, distribution of social assistance payments, and protection of forests.

Meanwhile, Serb-majority municipalities have been awarded enhanced municipal powers that include secondary health care, higher education, and selection of local police commanding officers. For example, the municipalities of Mitrovica North, Graçanica/Gračanica, and Shtërpca/Strpce have enhanced powers to provide secondary health care, including registration and licencing of health care institutions, recruitment, payment of salaries, and training of health care personnel and administrators (Article 20). The municipality of Mitrovica North has enhanced powers in higher education, including the licencing of educational institutions (Article 21). The new law, just as the previous UNMIK Regulation 2007/30, provided for the direct election of mayors for four-year terms. Mayors lead the municipal government and oversee the financial management of the municipality. Unlike the previous UNMIK regulations, the law gives the mayor greater responsibility and increases his or her autonomy to make decisions. Under the same law, individual municipalities have the right to cooperate under representative associations that provide services such as training and increasing the technical capacities of municipalities. They may cooperate with other international associations, but do not have executive powers.[18]

The Law on Inter-Municipal Cooperation and partnership[19] regulates relationships between municipalities as well as international municipal cooperation. According to this law, inter-municipal cooperation can be conducted through joint working groups, joint administrative bodies, joint public institutions, public joint enterprises, and joint public-private partnerships.

Two laws governing local finances: the Law on Public Financial Management and Responsibilities and the Law on Local Government Finances.[20] The latter determines the financial resources of the municipalities, including revenues, grants, and other financial resources. It regulates the financial independence of the municipalities in accordance with their powers, but restricts this independence by to the collection of the tax on immovable property within its borders (Article 3). Municipal financial resources consist of municipal revenues, grants for enhanced powers, transfers for delegated powers, extraordinary grants, financial assistance from Serbia (for Serb municipalities) and proceeds from municipal borrowing. Municipal own-source revenues are divided into eight categories including municipal taxes, rents on immovable property, proceeds from the sale of municipal assets, revenues from undertakings wholly or partly on the municipal property, and grants or donations from foreign governments (except for financial assistance from Serbia). Municipalities are also financed through operational grants from the Kosovo Consolidated Budget. The so-called Operational Grants include General Grants, Specific Grants for Education, and Specific Grants for Health.

According to the Law on Local Government Finances, municipalities are entitled to receive a General Grant that they may use to finance any of their municipal competencies. It is meant to provide stability of municipal income, a measure of equalisation between municipalities, be proportionate to the provision of public services, and provide an adequate allocation of resources for the minority communities. The General Grant accounts for about 10 per cent of central government revenues. In order to equalise low own-source revenues of the smaller municipalities, each such municipality receives €140,000 per annum less one euro for each member of the population, or zero euro for municipalities with populations equal to or greater than 140,000. The Specific Grant for Education is allocated to municipalities according to a formula based on effective student enrolment and the normalised number of teachers. It takes into account the national curriculum, special needs education, non-wage operating expenses, class size norms, and location. Minority students are given higher weights. The Specific Grant for Health is allocated to municipalities according to the age and gender distribution of the population registered with primary health care providers, and the number of elderly persons and of persons needing special health care.

Fiscal Decentralisation

After declaring independence, Kosovo became the most decentralised state in the region in terms of the transfer of powers from the central to the local level. However, the financial stability and autonomy of municipalities remain problematic. Most municipalities rely on grants and financial transfers from the central government. During 2015, €421 million out of €1.2 billion, that is, 33 per cent of the total budget, was planned to be distributed to the municipalities of Kosovo (INPO, 2015). According to NALAS, 'in 2014, Kosovo local government derived 40 per cent of their revenues from block grants for Education (31 per cent), and Primary Health Care (nine per cent). They also receive a General Grant which in 2010 constituted 40 per cent of their revenues. Of the rest, about 15 per cent comes from own-revenue, and 15 per cent from the shared Property Transfer Tax' (NALAS, 2016, p. 76). Two of the most important taxes collected by municipalities as own-source revenue are Construction Permits and the Property Tax. Between 2006 and 2014, 'the yield of the property tax remained stable and generated revenues equal to about 0.32 per cent of Gross domestic product (GDP). In 2014, the property tax constituted about 30 per cent of local government own-revenue and about 3.5 per cent of total revenues' (NALAS, 2016, p. 77). The municipal tax rate for property is charged in three bands, from 0.05 per cent to 0.15 per cent, from 0.15 per cent to 0.20 per cent, and from 0.20 per cent to 0.30 per cent.

From 2010 to 2015, the share of municipal revenues in total government revenues averaged 4.2 per cent. The share fell from 4.2 per cent in 2010 to 3.7 per cent in 2011, and then increased gradually to 4.2 per cent in 2014. From the internal point of view, the share of own-source revenues in general municipal revenues averaged 16.5 per cent from 2010 to 2014. The highest share of own-source revenues in the total municipal revenues was achieved in 2010, and the lowest in 2012.

The average share of own-source revenues in total municipal ranges from 35.8 per cent in Pristina to 2.5 per cent in Partesh/Parteš (MLGA, 2015). Four of the five newly created municipalities of the Ahtisaari Plan are in the group of municipalities with the lowest share of own-source revenues in total municipal revenues. The exception is the municipality of Graçanica/Gračanica, which is in the group of municipalities with the largest share of own-source revenues in total municipal revenues.

From 2010 to 2014, the trend of direct revenues collected by municipalities increased by 3.5 per cent on average and that of indirect revenues by 23 per cent. In 2010, direct revenues collected by municipalities were €46.2 million, increasing to €52.5 million in 2014. The trend of own indirect municipal revenues has also increased from €5.9 million in 2010 to €8.5 million in 2014 (see Table 8.5).

Table 8.5 Direct and indirect own-source revenues

	Revenues (€ million)					Change in revenues (%)					
	2010	2011	2012	2013	2014	2011/10	2012/11	2013/12	2014/13	2014/10	Average 2010/14
Direct revenues	46.2	49.8	55.8	52.2	52.5	7.9	12.2	−6.5	0.5	13.7	4.5
Indirect revenues	5.9	6.0	3.6	3.7	8.5	−0.5	−38.0	1.4	131.2	44.4	14.7
Total	52.0	55.6	59.4	55.6	61.0	6.9	6.9	−6.1	9.1	17.2	5.8

Source: MLGA (2015), Collection of own-source revenues and trends by year for period 2010–2014, p. 17

Local government revenues increased on average by 4.5 per cent per annum from 2010 to 2014. However, own-source revenues have been low as a percentage of GDP, reducing the potential financial autonomy of municipalities, a crucial aspect of fiscal decentralisation. The composition of own-source revenues changed over the period 2010–2014, being dominated by property taxes, construction permits, fines, and fees of property registration in the earlier years. In 2013, restrictions on construction permits were reduced, leading to a growth of this category (see Fig. 8.1).

While over half of municipal expenditure is devoted to salaries, municipalities have dedicated a substantial 35 per cent of their total expenditure to investments (NALAS, 2016). The composition of municipal expenditure between investment, wages, goods and services, grants and transfers, and other items of expenditure changed little over the period from 2006 to 2012 (see Fig. 8.2).

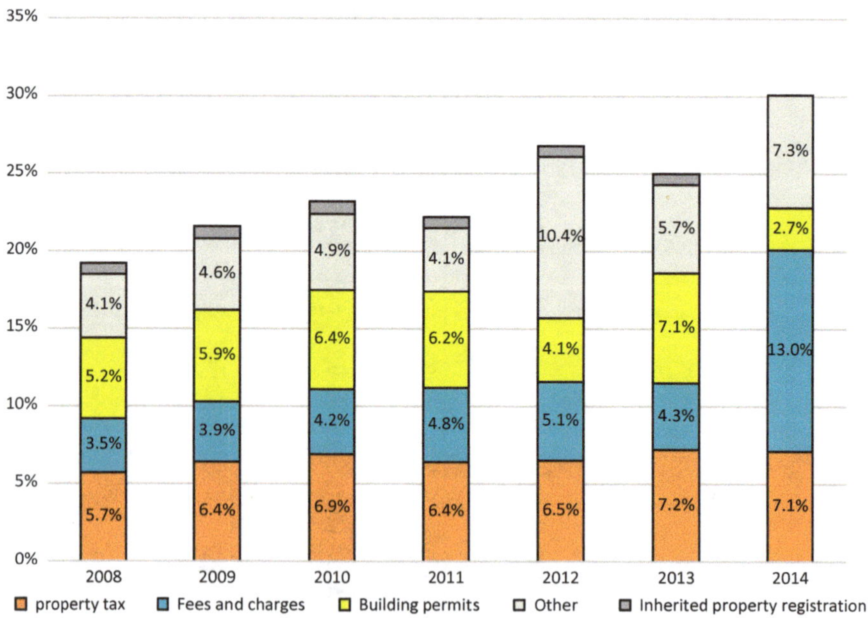

Fig. 8.1 Composition of own-source revenues, 2010–2014 (per cent of total revenues). Source: NALAS (2016, p. 82)

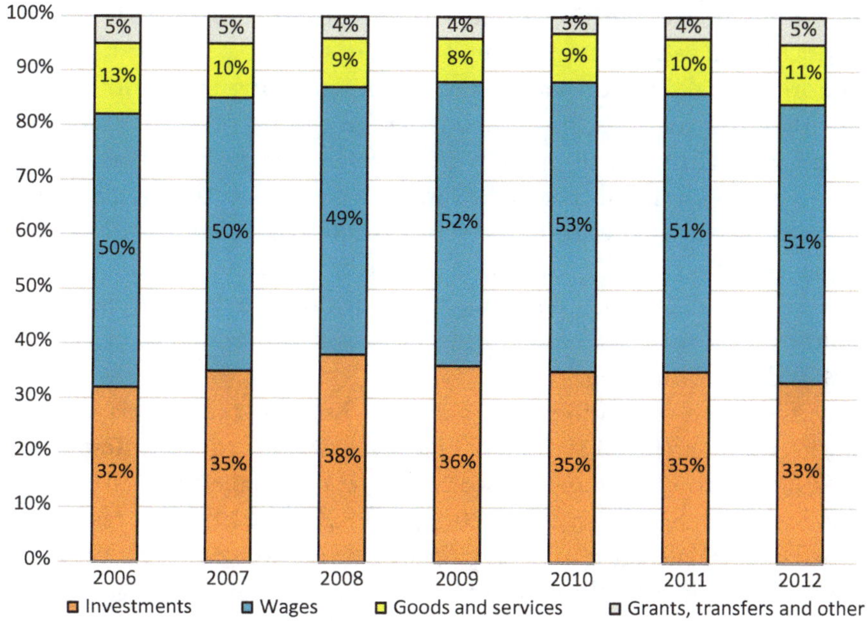

Fig. 8.2 The composition of municipal expenditure (2006–2012). Source: NALAS (2016, p. 82)

Challenges Ahead

Establishment of the Association of Serb-Majority Municipalities

The first challenge remains the creation of the Association of Serb-Majority Municipalities and the implementation of decentralisation in northern Kosovo. After the declaration of independence, in addition to EULEX, which was deployed to increase capacities in the field of rule of law, the ICO was also installed in Kosovo. The latter was intended to oversee the implementation of the Ahtisaari Plan, including the adoption of new legislation on local self-government and the protection of minorities, which derived from this plan. In September 2012, ICO concluded its mission on the grounds that the Kosovo authorities met most of the obligations that derived from the Ahtisaari Plan, especially those pertaining to the creation of new Serb municipalities. Even so, the Ahtisaari Plan was not implemented in full in some respects. First, Kosovo authorities had and still have difficulty in extending their authority in northern Kosovo, which has been out of their control since 1999. Second, the municipality of Mitrovica North, which was to be established in accordance with the Ahtisaari Plan, was not created because of the refusal of Serbs to participate in the November 2009 and 2010 elections. The implementation of decentralisation in northern Kosovo and the installation of local democracy remain a test, not only for international state building in Kosovo but also for the successful consolidation of democracy and peace building.

Unfortunately, relationships between Kosovo and Serbia remain blocked. In March 2011, the UN General Assembly adopted Resolution 64/298, which obliges the EU to facilitate a dialogue between Kosovo and Serbia (Beha, 2015; ICG, 2013; KIPRED, 2013). This resolution aimed at normalising relationships between the two countries. With the mediation of the EU, Kosovo and Serbia held ten rounds of negotiations. In April 2013, Kosovo and Serbia signed the 'First Agreement on Principles Governing the Normalisation of Relations'. The deal has 15 points and is intended to address the concerns of northern Kosovo Serbs in Zveçan/Zvečan, Mitrovice/Mitrovica North, Leposaviq/Leposavič, and Zubin Potok who have refused to accept the authority of the Kosovo Government in that area. According to the agreement, northern Serbs will be allowed to establish an Association/Community of Municipalities, with a membership mechanism open to other Serb municipalities in southern Kosovo. Representatives of the association will have a seat on the Communities Consultative Council, which is not the case with the Association of Kosovo Municipalities. In addition, the agreement provides that the regional commander of the police in the four northern municipalities will be a Serb. The agreement was ratified by the Assembly of Kosovo and was established in law.[21]

One of the points of the April agreement was the organisation of elections in the four Serb municipalities in northern Kosovo. For the first time since 1999, Serbs took part in the local elections, which were held in November 2013. The Serb Civic Initiative, directly supported by Serbia, won in four northern Serb municipalities: Mitrovica North,

Zubin Potok, Zveçan/Zvečan, and Leposaviq/Leposavič and in five municipalities in other parts of Kosovo, including Graçanica/Gračanica, Raniullug/Ranilug, Partesh/Parteš, Shtërpc/Strpce, and Novobërd/Novo Brdo. The Serb Liberal Party in Kosovo, which had been supported by the government since the local elections of 2008, emerged as the loser. The main concern of civil society and opposition parties is that the Serb Civic Initiative may legally sabotage and render dysfunctional the state by blocking decisions of the Assembly of Kosovo, since important decisions in the Assembly require a two-thirds majority and also support of two-thirds of the minority communities.

In August 2015, two years after signing the April agreement, Kosovo and Serbia agreed and signed a document that would precede the implementation of the April agreement. The Office of the President of Kosovo challenged the signed document called 'Association/Community of Serb-Majority Municipalities in Kosovo—General Principles/Main Elements' in the Constitutional Court. In its decision, the Constitutional Court stated that the document violates the following constitutional principles: equality before the law, human rights and fundamental freedoms, and the rights of communities and their members. In other words, the Constitutional Court contested the mono-ethnic character of the Association of Serb-Majority Municipalities and its executive powers. Since the Constitutional Court listed the unconstitutional parts of the August agreement, what remains to be done is for the drafters of the Statute of the Association of Serb-Majority Municipalities to take into account the assessment of the Constitutional Court. Four years after the signing of the April agreement, the statute of the Association of Serb-Majority Municipalities has not been drafted and the mechanism has not been established. The creation of this association in accordance with the Constitution of Kosovo and the laws on local self-government is one of the main challenges in relation to local government.

Demand for New Municipalities and Financial Self-Sustainability

The second largest challenge to local government relates to increased demands for the creation of new municipalities and their budgetary implications. Based on the Law on Administrative Boundaries of Municipalities of Kosovo, 11 communities of villages have applied for the status of municipality (Has of Gjakova, Has of Prizren, Hogosht, Janjeva, Llapjasi, Komorani, Krusha e Madhe, Orllani, Zhegra, Pozherani, and Reçan). These communities of villages justify their requests by the lack of capital investment in their locations and the distance from existing municipal administrations and difficulties in obtaining municipal services. For most of these claims, no financial sustainability or feasibility studies have been carried out. However, one study that shows that the creation of new municipalities would reduce the general budget of all municipalities, since the total grant allocated to municipalities by the central government would be shared with the potential new municipalities.

> The establishment of new municipalities will reduce the overall budget allocated to municipalities. The impact will be greater in the municipalities within which new municipalities will emerge. The establishment of new municipalities will significantly increase the number of civil servants, thus increasing expenditures for salaries and consequently decreasing the budget for capital investments and subventions. Each new municipality will have at least 55 civil servants. The majority of potential new municipalities have relatively small number of households and businesses, thus the base for their own source revenues is very small. Consequently, new municipalities will remain largely dependent on government grants. (GAP, 2013, p. 3)

In the case of establishing new municipalities, the difference as a percentage of the current grant for existing municipalities may be as much as 41 per cent for the Drenas municipalities where the Komorani municipality may be created, −21 per cent for Gjakova where the Has municipality may be created, and −21 per cent for Kamenica where the municipality of Hogosht may be created. On the other hand, the general grant that would be received by the new municipalities would be insufficient for their financial sustainability. The only justifiable request from all potential new municipalities comes from Komorani, since this municipality could potentially generate more own-source revenues since 903 businesses are registered there.

In 2017, the total budget planned for municipal expenditures is €18 million more than in 2016, reaching €440 million. However, the municipalities expect around one million euros less in own-source revenues than in the previous year. This goes against a recommendation by the International monetary fund to reduce municipalities' dependence on the central budget (GAP, 2017).

Conclusion

The decentralisation of power and the establishment of new municipalities were two of the explicit requirements of the international community in order to build a multi-ethnic and democratic society in Kosovo. Decentralisation sought to legitimise international state building from the top down and peace building and democratisation from the bottom up. All UNMIK regulations on local government sought to provide more effective and efficient services to the citizens of Kosovo and to promote and protect the rights of minority communities.

After its declaration of independence, Kosovo became one of the the most decentralised countries in Southeastern Europe. The Ahtisaari Plan was accepted by Kosovo institutions, which provided the basis for the declaration of an independent and sovereign state, and for the establishment of six Serb-majority municipalities. Kosovo adopted new legislation accepting international commitments to establish new Serb municipalities, the expansion of their powers, and the provision of their security.

Although decentralisation in Kosovo has proven to be relatively successful in political terms, since so far five of the six municipalities planned by the Ahtisaari Plan have been established, the financial support for enhanced municipal powers has been insufficient. Even though the international community has invested in the decentralisation process in Kosovo over the past 15 years and the autonomy of local governments has significantly increased, local government remains unconsolidated and does not enjoy sufficient financial autonomy since Kosovo municipalities still rely heavily on central government funds. The implementation of decentralisation in northern Kosovo and the poor prospects for the financial sustainability of many municipalities remain two of the main challenges facing local government in Kosovo.

Acknowledgements We are grateful to Roland Gjoni from Columbia University and to Gëzim Selaci and Arben Hajrullahu from the University of Pristina for their continuous support during the drafting of this chapter.

Notes

1. Security Council Resolution 1244, 10 June 1999, S/RES/1244.
2. UNMIK Regulation No. 2000/39 on Municipal Elections in Kosovo, UNMIK/REG/2000/39, 8 July 2000.
3. UNMIK Regulation/1999/1 on the Authority of the Interim Administration in Kosovo, UNMIK/REG/1999/1, 25 July 1999.
4. UNMIK Regulation No. 2001/9 on a Constitutional Framework for Provisional Self-Government in Kosovo, 15 May 2001.
5. UNMIK Regulation 2000/16 on the Registration and Operation of Political Parties in Kosovo, UNMIK/REG/2000/16. 21 March 2000; UNMIK Regulation 2000/21 on the Establishment of the Central Election Commission, UNMIK/REG/2000/21. 18 April 2000.
6. Section 2 of the UNMIK Regulation 2000/43 on the Number, Names and Boundaries of Municipalities, UNMIK/REG/2000/43. 27 July 2000.
7. UNMIK/Regulation 2000/45 on Self-government of Municipalities in Kosovo, UNMIK/REG/2000/45. 11 August 2000 and UNMIK Regulation 2007/30 amending Regulation 2000/45 on Self-government of Municipalities in Kosovo, UNMIK/REG/2007/30, 16 October 2006.
8. Basic Provisions 1.3 of the UNMIK Regulation 2001.
9. Article 2.3 of the UNMIK/Regulation 2000/45, 11 August 2000.
10. Article 30 of the UNMIK Regulation 2007/30 Amending UNMIK Regulation No. 2000/45 on Self-Government of Municipalities in Kosovo, UNMIK/REG/2007/30, 16 October 2006.
11. Section 1 of the UNMIK Regulation 2007/18 amending UNMIK Regulation No, 2001/19 on the Executive Branch of the Provisional Institutions of Self-Government in Kosovo, UNMIK/REG/2007/18, 9 May 2007.

12. This whole scenario was complicated by the fact that the Russian Federation refused to accept this development in the Security Council.
13. Chapter X of the Constitution of Kosovo, Articles 123 and 124 on Local Government and Territorial Organisation in Kosovo.
14. Law on Municipal Administrative Boundaries, Kosovo Official Gazette, No. 26/2008.
15. Law on Local Self-Government, Kosovo Official Gazette, No. 28/2008.
16. Law on Inter-Municipal Cooperation, Kosovo Official Gazette, No. 7/2011.
17. Law on Local Government Finances, Kosovo Official Gazette, No. 27/2008.
18. Law on Local Self-Government, Kosovo Official Gazette, No. 28/2008.
19. Article 9 of the law No. 04/L-010, on Inter-municipal Cooperation and Partnerships, Kosovo Official Gazette, No. 7/2011.
20. Law No. 03/L-049 on Local Government Finance, Kosovo Official Gazette, No, 27/2008.
21. Law No. 04-L-199 on the ratification of the first international agreement for the normalisation of relationship between The Republic of Kosovo and The Republic of Serbia, available at: https://gzk.rks-gov.net/ActDetail.aspx?ActID=8892

Bibliography

Beha, A. (2011). Decentralisation in Kosovo: A challenge to deal with. *Journal of Peace, Conflict and Development, 17*, 23–42.

Beha, A. (2013). Contested statebuilding in Kosovo: The nature and characteristics of Serbian parallel structures. In C. Giordano & N. Hayoz (Eds.), *Informality in Eastern Europe: Structures, political cultures and social practices* (pp. 261–279). Peter Lang.

Beha, A. (2014). Minority rights: An opportunity for adjustment of ethnic relations in Kosovo. *Journal on Ethnopolitics and Minority Issues in Europe, 13*(4), 85–110.

Beha, A. (2015). Disputes over the 15-point agreement on normalization of relations between Kosovo and Serbia. *Nationalities Papers, 42*(1), 1–20.

Beha, A. (2017). *Between stabilisation and democratisation: Elections, political parties and intra-party democracy.* Friedrich Ebert Stiftung & Centre for Political Courage.

Chesterman, S. (2004). Imposed constitutions, imposed constitutionalism, and ownership. *Connecticut Law Review, 37*(2), 947–954.

Faguet, J. P. (2012). *Decentralization and popular democracy: Governance from below in Bolivia*. Ann Arbor, MI: University of Michigan Press.

GAP Institute. (2013). *The establishment of new municipalities in Kosovo*. Pristina.

GAP Institute. (2017). *Municipal budget according to the 2017 draft budget*. Pristina.

Gjoni, R., Wetterberg, A., & Dunbar, D. (2010). Decentralization as a conflict transformation tool: The challenge in Kosovo. *Public Administration and Development, 30*, 291–312.

Initiative for Progress (INPO). (2015). *Municipal financial (un)sustainability*. Pristina.

Institute for Democracy and Electoral Assistance (IDEA). (2004). *Developing local democracy in Kosovo*. Pristina.

International Crisis Group (ICG). (2013). *Serbia and Kosovo: The path to normalization*. Europe Report No. 223.

Judah, T. (2000). *Kosovo: War and revenge*. New Haven, CT: Yale University Press.

King, I., & Mason, V. (2006). *Peace at any price: How the world failed Kosovo*. Ithaca, NY: Cornell University Press.

Kosovar Institute for Policy Research and Development (KIPRED). (2013). *The implementations of agreements of Kosovo-Serbia: Political dialogue*. Policy Paper, No. 4/13. Pristina.

Kosovo Legal Government Institute (KLGI). (2009). *Implementation of the decentralization process in Kosovo: One year after the constitution*. Pristina.

Lijphart, A. (1969). Consociational democracy. *World Politics, 21*(2), 207–225.

Lijphart, A. (2004). Constitutional design for divided societies. *Journal of Democracy, 15*(2), 96–109.

Linz, J., & Stepan, A. (1992). Political identities and electoral sequences, Spain, the Soviet Union and Yugoslavia. *Daedalus*, (121), 123–139.

Malcolm, N. (1999). *Kosovo: A short history*. London: Harper Perennial.

Martínez-Vázquez, J. (2008). Revenue assignments in the practice of fiscal decentralization. In N. Núria Bosch & J. M. Durán (Eds.), *Fiscal federalism and political decentralization: Lessons from Spain, Germany and Canada*. Cheltenham: Edward Elgard.

Ministry of Local Government Administration (MLGA). (2012). *Progress report on decentralization implementation in the Republic of Kosovo*. Pristina.

Ministry of Local Government Administration (MLGA). (2015). *Analysis on own-source revenues in the municipalities of the Republic of Kosovo*. Pristina.

Mitchell, I. R. (2000). The ambiguities of elections in Kosovo: Democratisation versus human rights? *The International Journal of Human Rights, 43*(4), 246–262.

Network of Associations of Local Authorities of South-East Europe (NALAS). (2016). *Fiscal decentralization indicators: South-East Europe 2006–2014*.

Organisation for Security and Cooperation in Europe (OSCE). (2007). *Parallel structures in Kosovo 2006–2007*. Pristina.

Organisation for Security and Cooperation in Europe (OSCE). (2008). *Relationships between central and local authorities in Kosovo: Legal, administrative and fiscal aspects*. Pristina.

Osmani, J., & Manaj, R. (2014). *Administrative-territorial division of Kosovo 1944–2010 (documents)*. Pristina: Academy of Sciences and Arts of Kosovo.

Paris, R. (2004). *At war's end: Building peace after civil conflict*. Cambridge: Cambridge University Press.

Perrit, H. (2010). *The road to independence for Kosovo: A chronicle of the Ahtisaari plan*. Cambridge: Cambridge University Press.

Péteri, G., & Vaillancourt, F. (2007). Local government in Kosovo. In R. Ebel & G. Péteri (Eds.), *The Kosovo decentralization: Briefing book*. Kosovo Foundation for Open Society & Local Government and Public Service Reform Initiative. Retrieved from http://pdc.ceu.hu/archive/00005307/01/decentralization__4_.pdf

Schneckener, U. (2004). Models of ethnic conflict regulation: Politics of recognition. In U. Schneckener & S. Wolfe (Eds.), *Managing and settling ethnic conflict: Perspectives on success and failures in Europe, Africa and Asia*. London: Hurst & Co.

Schultze-Kraft, M., & Morina, E. (2014). Decentralisation and accountability in war-to-peace transitions: The case of Kosovo. *IDS Bulletin, 45*, 92–104.

Sörensen, S. J. (2013). International statebuilding in Kosovo. In D. Chandler & T. Sisks (Eds.), *Handbook of international statebuilding*. London: Routledge.

Tahiri, B. (2008). *Decentralization policy in Kosovo*. Pristina.

Tahiri, B. (2011). *Decentralization a heavy weight to be carried out, struggling to move from consolidation of local democracy to better service delivery*. Pristina. Retrieved from http://library.fes.de/pdf-files/bueros/kosovo/09762.pdf

Tahiri, B. (2012). *Mayor—Representative or dominant?—A contribution to the strengthening of institutional accountability at local level: Kosovo case*. Kosovar Institute for Local Governance & Friedrich Ebert Stiftung.

Tansey, O. (2009). *Regime-building: Democratization and international administration*. Oxford: Oxford University Press.

Tanzi, V. (2002). Pitfalls on the road to fiscal decentralization. In E. Ahmad & V. Tanzi (Eds.), *Managing fiscal decentralization*. London and New York: Routledge.

Taylor, A. (2002). This election was never going to be perfect: The Kosovo municipal election of October 2000 as post-conflict election. *Civil Wars, 5*(3), 65–118.

USAID. (2007). *Municipal budget allocation 2003–07*. Pristina.

Visoka, G., & Beha, A. (2013). *Clearing up the fog of conflict: Actor-based mapping of the disputes in the North of Kosovo*. Forum 2015 & Kosovo Institute of Peace.

Part IV

Albania: Struggling with the Legacy of Extreme Centralisation

9

Albania: Aligning Territorial and Fiscal Decentralisation

Elton Stafa and Merita Xhumari

Introduction

Traditional normative theory suggests that decentralisation is key to good governance and the democratisation of political, social, and economic life, particularly in countries with a history of severe totalitarianism, such as Albania. From this perspective, decentralisation refers to the process of redistributing authority and responsibility for certain functions from central governments to autonomous local government units (LGUs). Nowadays, the main aim of decentralisation is increasing both the efficiency and effectiveness of delivering public services, based on the hypothesis that local governments have a better understanding of

E. Stafa (✉)
USAID Albania, Tirana, Albania

The Network of Associations of Local Authorities of South-East Europe, Skopje, Macedonia

M. Xhumari
University of Tirana, Tirana, Albania

W. Bartlett et al. (eds.), *Fiscal Decentralisation, Local Government and Policy Reversals in Southeastern Europe*, https://doi.org/10.1007/978-3-319-96092-0_9

community needs than central governments and, as a result, they may use scarce public financial resources more efficiently (Oates, 1993, 1999). However, for decentralisation to be successful, any transfer of responsibilities should be followed by a transfer of fiscal power from central to local government as well as any institutional arrangements that enable its implementation. The literature argues that the key issue is fiscal autonomy, i.e. control over sufficient resources to plan and manage the provision of local public services according to citizens' preferences without continuous interference from higher authorities (Bahl & Linn, 1992). One of the underlying ideas is that if local governments raise substantial amounts of revenue from their own local communities, they are likely to be subjected to increased demands for accountability and for increased citizen participation in deciding how the resources will be used.

Based on the above conceptual framework, this chapter provides an overview of the process and political economy of decentralisation reforms undertaken in Albania over the last 25 years. It describes commonalities and differences with the normative theory of decentralisation and the political and policy incentives and circumstances that have characterised the passing and implementation of such decentralisation reforms. The chapter focuses also on the current challenges facing Albanian LGUs, and the need to develop and implement a thorough fiscal decentralisation reform.

Since the early 1990s, Albania has undertaken structural reforms as part of the processes of the political, economic, and social transition from socialism to democracy. During 1992–1994, the focus of decentralisation reforms was to establish democratically elected local self-governments and define their functional responsibilities. In terms of administrative divisions, the central government's deconcentrated structures operating at the local level that were inherited from the socialist system were abrogated and 393 autonomous LGUs were established: 314 communes and 43 municipalities that constituted the first tier of local governments and 36 districts that constituted the second tier of local governments, in total 393 LGUs.[1] The administrative division was based on the urban and rural patterns where a municipality meant an urban administrative zone, a commune covered a rural administrative zone, and a district was composed of the main municipality and surrounding communes. As a result,

LGUs were very diverse in terms of size, capacity, and economic potential. However, despite such substantial diversity, they were assigned uniform functional responsibilities, which led smaller LGUs to face significant challenges to deliver services that citizens were entitled to receive (Council of Europe, 2011).[2]

With the ratification of the European Charter for Local Self-Government and the adoption of a new Constitution in 1998, Albania entered a new and more successful phase of decentralisation: (a) A new law on the organisation and functioning of local governments sought to consolidate local governments' rights and responsibilities; (b) The territorial and administrative division was revised to create 385 local LGUs out of which 373 first-tier LGUs (308 communes and 65 municipalities) and 12 regions (the regions replaced 36 districts of the second-tier LGUs); (c) A new law on local taxes was introduced to strengthen local government taxing powers; and (d) A general-purpose intergovernmental transfer was introduced, phasing out the high and direct level of control from the national government. These reforms were undertaken in parallel with a broader public administration reform through the enactment of the Law on Civil Servants of 1999.

Fragmentation was a characteristic of Albanian LGUs prior to 2014, when the government adopted a major Territorial and Administrative Reform (TAR) that reduced the number of first-tier LGUs from 373 communes and municipalities to just 61 larger municipalities. The second tier of local governments was not affected by the TAR. This reform eliminated the previous urban-rural separation and, by unifying the LGUs in terms of size, has created an opportunity to increase administrative efficiency and improve service delivery. This major territorial consolidation was followed by other decentralisation reforms: (a) a new National Crosscutting Strategy for Decentralisation and Local Governance (NCSDLG) 2015–2020 was adopted to serve as the main decentralisation roadmap; (b) a new Law on Local Self-Government (LLSG) enacted at the end of 2015 to consolidate local governments' rights and responsibilities and further decentralise a number of new and costly functions to the local level; (c) in 2017, a Law on Local Self-Government Finance (LLSGF) and a property tax reform were adopted.

Overall, there has been substantive progress in creating the necessary legal and policy framework to advance decentralisation. Yet, there remain significant challenges to fully unleash the benefits of decentralisation. The instruments the national government has employed to promote decentralisation are similar across the different periods or waves of decentralisation, while the scope and outcome of such decentralisation reforms are very diverse and have been greatly impacted by the political circumstances or incentives of the national government.

To analyse the decentralisation framework in Albania, we conducted a review of the legal framework, government strategic documents, and existing research studies, and we collected statistical data on local finances until 2017. The normative analysis aims at understanding the evolution of local government rights, roles and responsibilities, and how they have varied over time to reflect different priorities or political interests. The quality of norms was assessed vis-à-vis outputs in terms of local fiscal autonomy, especially after the ratification of the Council of Europe's Charter on Local Self-Government.

A detailed analysis of the evolution of local government rights, responsibilities, and financial resources was provided across the four time periods identified. Analysis of decentralisation from the fiscal dimension uses detailed information on the level and composition of local government revenues for the period 2000–2017, expressed both in terms of gross domestic product (GDP) and general government revenues. The analysis places particular emphasis on the following ratios: total local revenues over GDP; total local revenue over general government revenue; and structure of local government revenue in terms of general government revenues. Such analysis shows that local governments in Albania continue to suffer from weak fiscal and financial autonomy. This is related to the decisions of the national government to continuously amend and mostly reduce local competences to collect own-source revenues (OSRs), ongoing restrictions on their revenue raising capabilities, refusal of central government agencies to cooperate and share relevant fiscal data with local governments, and last but not least, insufficient institutional capacity development. The frequent amendments of the legal framework have resulted in confusion over rights and responsibilities and have discouraged local governments from putting particular effort or investment in specific local taxes. In other instances, it appears that in specific cases, certain local governments have overlooked taxing powers they were given by law, in the presence of abundant tax revenues from the business sector or transfers from the national government.

Our analysis builds on work carried out by international organisations such as United States Agency for International Development (USAID), the World Bank, the Network of Associations of Local Authorities in South-East Europe (NALAS) and the Council of Europe. The specific sources of documents prepared by the Albanian Government and independent organisations have been used accordingly.

This chapter is composed of five sections. Following this introduction, the four sections focus on an analysis of the decentralisation process in Albania over the last 25 years. Each section covers major decentralisation reforms: the early stage between 1992 and 1997, focusing on establishing democratically elected local governments; the second phase between 1998 and 2008 that consolidates local governments' functional responsibilities and revenue assignments; the third phase between 2009 and 2013, focusing on decentralisation policy during the economic crisis that coincides the global economic crisis; and Chap. 5 is dedicated to the major decentralisation reforms that are undertaken in recent years by the new government. Particular focus is given to the challenges the recently consolidated 61 municipalities face in managing their increased functional responsibilities, including an analysis of the major achievements in the fiscal dimension of decentralisation and some concluding remarks on next steps to implement the fiscal decentralisation reform.

The Early Stage of Governance Decentralisation: 1992–1997

After more than half a century of an extremely centralised government, Albania entered the path of political, administrative, and fiscal decentralisation in 1992, with the amendment of the Constitutional Dispositions[3] and the adoption of the Law on the Organisation and Functioning of Local Governments (LOFLG).[4] Local elections were organised immediately after the adoption of the LOFLG and Albania established of 393 "elected local government units" functioning under the principles of self-government and local autonomy.[5] The 393 local governments have been organised in two tiers: 314 communes and 43 municipalities (which constituted the first tier), situated in 36 districts (the second tier) and "controlled" by 12 Prefectures, which constituted the largest territorial organisation in Albania.[6]

Under the LOFLG framework, local governments were supposed to perform a wide array of public functions such as: administering public properties; guaranteeing public order and the fundamental freedoms of people; organising local transport, road maintenance, and postal services; implementing urban development programmes; maintaining health and education facilities; taking measures for the employment and shelter of citizens; preserving environment; ensuring free trade and competition by incentivising free-market initiatives; organising local charity institutions; organising public markets; and managing local public enterprises. Although not directly mentioned in the LOFLG, LGUs had also certain responsibilities with regard to water supply and sewerage systems. Notwithstanding the impressive number of responsibilities, the 1992 LOFLG did not define how these responsibilities would be financed, nor how the responsibilities for each function would be shared across the levels of government.

Local governments' legal powers to tax were sanctioned in the Law on the Tax System in the Republic of Albania of 1992.[7] This law prescribed that LGUs had the right to charge a tax for stamps on legal acts (certificates), a registration tax for automobiles and certain business activities, a waste disposal tax, a public space occupation tax, and finally a hunting tax. LGUs did not have any discretionary power to influence tax bases or rates. Local taxes were collected by the central government tax offices and transferred to the local budgets as many local governments did not have their own tax offices. Although substantial issues in administering taxing powers, the most profound problem was related to the fact that the fiscal and financial resources given to local governments were inadequate when compared to their functional responsibilities (Banks & Pigey, 1998). As a result, many of the public services under the responsibility of local authorities were poorly provided and even when provided, local governments were very much dependent on the central government both in terms of regulatory authority and financial resources (World Bank, 1994).

Recognising these challenges, Albania initiated a reform process with the adoption of a law regulating local budgets in 1993[8] and one year later, a separate law regulating property taxation on buildings and agricultural land.[9] The Law on Local Budget defined revenue sources of LGUs as: (a) OSRs from taxes and fees; (b) intergovernmental transfers from the state budget consisting mainly in earmarked grants and shared taxes; and (c) revenues from local borrowing,[10] foreign aid and other donations. The Law on Property Tax sanctioned that 60 per cent of the yield of property taxes charged and collected by the central government would be shared with local governments.

In 1994, the World Bank stated: "Overall, during these years the main successes were the creation of the legal framework for the functioning of local governments and to a lesser degree their revenue sources" (The World Bank, 1994). On the side of LGUs expenditures, the decisions were strongly influenced or directly made by the central government. Most resources used locally were earmarked transfers and local authorities were left with insignificant, uncertain OSRs. During this first phase of decentralisation, revenues from local taxes and fees financed only 5 per cent of local expenditures, whereas 95 per cent was financed through non-transparent and unpredictable conditional grants from line ministries (Brahimi et al., 2013). In 1997, intergovernmental transfers constituted 80 per cent of total local revenues whereas OSRs constituted only 20 per cent (Ministry of Finance, 2015).

During this period, local public administration was weak and it lacked the necessary capacities to deal with the new challenges of an open-market economy and autonomous self-government. Further, political instability was affecting local administrations. High levels of turnover weakened local capacities and demotivated qualified professionals. Particularly after the 1997 pyramidal scheme crisis, the need for institutional development and capacity building both at the central and local government level was evident. Thus, during the first phase of decentralisation, the main success was the design of the basic infrastructure for local governance, after 50 years of severe central planning and control. Obviously, further substantive efforts were necessary to strengthen local autonomy, to make LGUs less dependent on the central government and increase their political, fiscal, and administrative capacities (Hoxha, 2002).

The Second Phase of Decentralisation: 1998–2008

One of the most important factors influencing the decentralisation process in Albania was the ratification of the European Charter of Local Self-Government[11] and the adoption of a new Constitution in 1998.[12] The Charter's principles were incorporated in the new Constitution, which sanctioned that local government in Albania would be based on the principle of decentralisation of powers and exercised according to the principle of local autonomy. The Constitution also established the main concepts and principles regarding local self-governments. The new Constitution was followed in 2000 by the National Strategy on Decentralisation, as well as three new laws supporting decentralisation: the 2000 LOFLG,[13] which became the main pillar of decentralisation reforms until 2014, the 2000 Law on Territorial and Administrative Division,[14] and the 2002 Law on the Local Tax System (LLTS).[15]

The new LOFLG aimed at improving the definition of local functions: the types of authority local governments could exercise to fulfil their responsibilities, the relationship between the two levels of governance by assigning responsibilities according to three categories: *exclusive*, *shared*, and *delegated* functions. First, exclusive functions were those functions over which LGUs exercised full administrative, service, investment, and regulatory authority. Public services related to infrastructure and utilities formed the core of exclusive functions of local governments in Albania, including water supply, waste management, sewage and drainage systems,[16] local road infrastructure, urban planning, land management and housing, public transport, public markets, social services (including orphanages, day care centres, and elderly homes), protection and development of local forests, pastures and natural resources, civil protection and law enforcement through municipal police and other services. Second, when it comes to shared functions,[17] LGUs exercised partial responsibility, while the share of responsibility was to be assigned by the central government. Third, delegated functions were authorised to LGUs by the central government through specific laws, which regulated the procedures in detail. Unfortunately, the exact competences and the accompanying financial resources for shared functions were never clarified, constituting an area of ongoing conflict between the local and central government.

Another major development to the political and administrative dimension of decentralisation was the adoption of the Law on Civil Service,[18] which applied both to the central government and to municipalities. The aim was to create a more sustainable and professional public administration, avoiding political bias. This led to the creation of several central-level institutions: Department of Public Administration, responsible for civil service management; the Civil Service Commission, responsible for monitoring the implementation of the Law on Civil Service; and the Training Institute for Public Administration, responsible for training public servants.

In 2000, the new Law on the Administrative-Territorial Division led to the reorganisation of LGUs in Albania in 65 urban municipalities and 309 rural communes,[19] to a certain degree reflecting the mobility of population from rural to urban areas. The reform abolished the 36 districts and established 12 regions as the second tier of local government. Albania inherited and preserved a fragmented administrative structure for historical reasons—228 LGUs, each with less than 5,000 inhabitants. Further, about 61 per cent of the LGUs had jurisdiction over only 19 per cent of the population, and, on average, generated only 8–10 per cent of total local government revenues, while receiving about 30 per cent of the transfers from the central government (Hoxha, 2002).

Such reforms had a direct impact on the fiscal dimension of decentralisation, improving it substantially during the period 2001–2006. For the first time, the Law on 2001 Budget adopted the concept of unconditional transfers (general-purpose transfers) from the state budget to local governments. LGUs were given full discretion in the use of this transfer to finance their responsibilities. However, the size of the unconditional grant would be determined every year by policymakers, and there was no rule anchoring it to any macroeconomic indicator. The allocation criteria were determined every year in the annual budget laws and were based mainly on the size of population and geographic area, with extra coefficients given to mountainous or fiscally distressed LGUs. The unconditional grant allocation formula also provided for some fiscal equalisation between jurisdictions with different fiscal capacities as measured by the per capita yield of certain local and shared taxes. While the new legal framework certainly improved local government autonomy and discretion over resources, it did not address the issue of the year-to-year unpredictability of the size of the grant. As prescribed by the so-called second-generation theories of decentralisation (Oates, 2005, 2008; Weingast, 2009, 2014), national political actors preserved power over local government finances. As a result, one of the most important sources of local financing had to be negotiated every year with the national government, therefore substantially undermining the principles of autonomy and local governments' ability to adequately plan and implement their budgets.

In 2002, to expand local taxing powers and advance fiscal decentralisation, the Government of Albania adopted the LLTS,[20] which gave powers to LGUs to administer local taxes. With this law, the existing property tax and the tax on small-business activity, both previously collected by the central government and shared with LGUs, were defined as exclusive local taxes. The law increased also local governments' discretion over tax bases and tax rates. LGUs were authorised to establish more detailed categories of centrally determined tax bases and had the power to increase or decrease the centrally determined tax rates by ± 30 per cent.

Until 2006, central government funding for local investments were allocated by sectoral ministries in the form of conditional grants. Project selection procedures were controversial (World Bank, 2008). In 2006, conditional grants were replaced by competitive grants where funding allocations were to be made by "inter-ministerial committees for evaluation" based on criteria set in law. In 2009, competitive grants were replaced with the Regional Development Fund (RDF) while maintaining a similar structure of fund allocation.[21] Also in this case, LGUs were asked to compete against each other with projects to receive funding from a Committee chaired by the Prime Minister, and composed of a number of ministers and heads of central agencies, and a very small number of representatives from local government associations. General and specific criteria to allocate funds were enshrined again in legislation.[22] Overall, even though allocation criteria are regulated and published with every call for proposals, the actual allocation has been and continues to be subject to criticism by local governments and their associations arguing the lack of transparency and political favouritism.[23] Such concerns are reinforced by the fact that there are no mechanisms in place that explain rejections or that would allow local governments to appeal the Committee's decisions. As a result, there is a general perception that subsequent national governments prefer to maintain a high level of control over local government investments, eventually putting first their own party interests managing the largest investment instrument at the local level, rather than objective criteria set to reduce regional and local disparities between expenditure needs and revenue capacities.

The central government patronage of municipal financing sources continues with local borrowing. While both the LOFLGs of 1992 and 2000 sanctioned the right of LGUs to borrow resources, it was only in 2008 that the Government of Albania enacted a Law on Local Borrowing (LLB) that defined the criteria, process, roles, and responsibilities for local borrowing.[24] The enactment of this law promised to provide LGUs with the necessary resources to finance long-term capital investments but, because of the country's high level of public debt, the Ministry of Finance issued administrative orders that have made it virtually impossible for LGUs to borrow resources.

During this period there was significant progress in establishing the framework that would promote a democratic and decentralised system of governance in Albania. Local responsibilities were expanded to include more social functions, and this led to increased expenditure needs, while local government revenue assignments were improved with the new LLTS and intergovernmental transfers. Figure 9.1 shows general government revenues and local government revenues as a percentage of Albania's GDP and local government revenues as a percentage of general government revenues for the period 1998–2008. Between 1998 and 2008, general government revenues averaged 25 per cent of GDP, while local government revenues increased from 0.4 per cent of GDP in 1998 to 2.7 per cent in 2008.

The structure of local government revenues improved as well: as of 2008, revenues from local taxes and fees constituted about 42 per cent of local revenues, up from 26 per cent in 2002 or 0.8 per cent in 1998

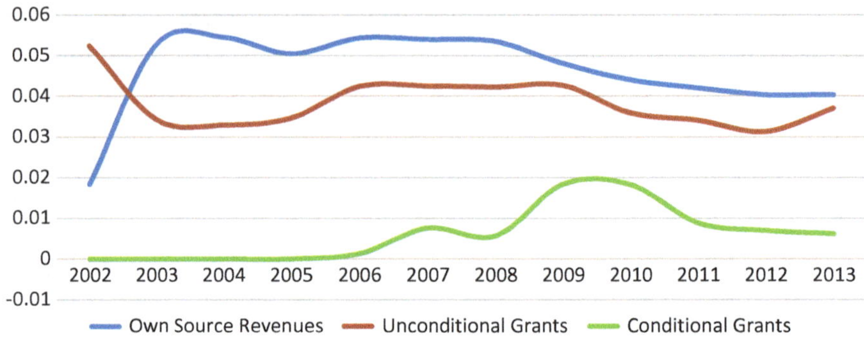

Fig. 9.1 General and local government revenues, 1998–2008. Source: Ministry of Finance of Albania, author' calculations

(Hoxha, 2007; Ministry of Finance, 2017). Overall, local government revenues increased, showing that in the second stage of the decentralisation policies, policymakers put emphasis on strengthening local government finance, although the central government continued to maintain a relatively high degree of discretion over some of the local finance instruments. Nevertheless, despite these improvements, expectations for greater fiscal decentralisation have been strongly affected by the global economic crisis and by measures that the central governments undertook to (supposedly) counter economic downturn.

Decentralisation in Times of Crisis: 2009–2013

Between 2009 and 2010 the legal framework regarding LGUs' functional responsibilities and assigned revenues experienced several amendments. To implement commitments under the LOFLG, the process of transferring ownership over the assets of water utilities advanced and local governments became fully responsible for their management. Additionally, local governments became responsible also for running certain social service functions. These new functions were in part financed through subsidies and transfers from the line ministries that were previously responsible for them. However, the calculation and allocation of such subsidies has been quite debatable, with concerns that local governments have received less than 40 per cent of the funds that the national government was previously spending on these functions (USAID, 2016b).

As part of the Government's reaction to the 2008 global financial crisis, the Law on the Local Tax System was amended in April 2009, about one month before national elections of June 2009.[25] The justification for the amendment of the law was to alleviate small businesses from the "excessive" burden of local taxes and fees. Obviously, this measure adversely affected local revenues and LGUs saw their taxing powers and fiscal autonomy diminish substantially. Until 2009, local governments had the authority to increase or decrease centrally set indicative tax rates for local taxes by 30 per cent. With the new measure, local governments could still cut the indicative tax rate by 30 per cent but could only increase it by 10 per cent. Further, and more important, local governments' powers to charge fees for local services (and temporary taxes) on all businesses taxpayers were constrained to only 10 per cent of the indicative tax rate prescribed by law for the small business tax. These constraints resulted in an immediate drop of local government revenues from the small business tax and the property tax by 52 per cent in 2009, whereas non-tax revenues and fees fell by 19 per cent in 2010 (USAID, 2016a, 2016c).

The decline in revenues from local taxes was coupled with a decline in the unconditional grant. In 2010, the unconditional grant was reduced by 12.6 per cent in annual terms.[26] The LGUs then experienced additional cuts when the government ruled to use a part of LGUs' unconditional grant to clear the past-due obligations towards third parties (mainly to the Energy Distribution Company) of the public utilities they owned (basically water utilities).[27]

While local government freely disposable revenues from taxes and the unconditional grant have been curtailed, the central government increased funding from competitive grants from the RDF. Figure 9.2 shows the development in the composition of local government revenues as a per cent of general government revenues.

The threefold increase in the size of the centrally controlled competitive grants, while crowding out freely disposable revenues showed a clear preference of the national government to influence investments at the local level. However, the new size of the RDF grants was difficult to maintain as Albania's public finances started to suffer from the slowdown

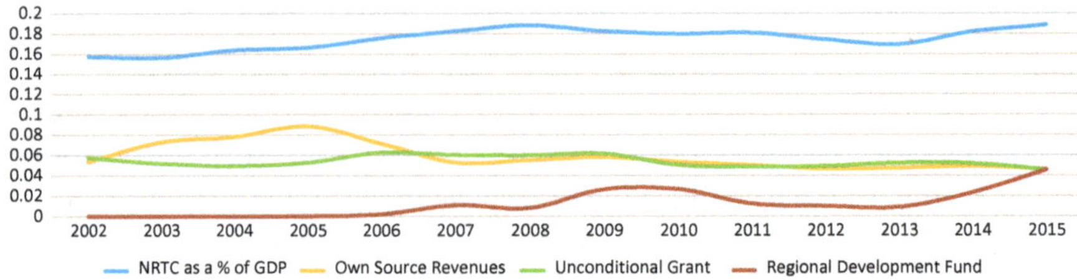

Fig. 9.2 Local government revenues (NRTC), in per cent of general government revenues, 2002–2013. Source: Ministry of Finance, author' calculations. (Competitive grants mean transfers from the RDF)

of economic activity. As a result, competitive grants were halved in 2011 (returning to the pre-crisis levels) and it would be only in 2014 that they would again reach the same level as that of 2009/2010. Obviously, these affected local governments' capacity to finance their functions in general and local investments in particular.[28]

The LLB of 2008 started to be implemented during 2009–2010 with USAID support. Several LGUs successfully borrowed financial resources from the banking sector. However, the possibility to access debt capital to finance costly long-term capital investments vanished quickly as Albania was approaching the self-imposed fiscal rule limiting public debt to 60 per cent of GDP. In this framework, the relationship between central and local government borrowing became much more problematic as rules that allowed local governments to borrow were treated subjectively. At the end of 2010, only 5 of the 373 local governments had successfully completed a loan procedure to banks, with a total stock of local debt of 0.06 per cent of GDP. After 2010, the Government made it virtually impossible for LGUs to borrow, by adopting administrative ordinances that greatly impacted the final approval of loans and their annual disbursements.

The weaknesses in fiscal decentralisation were recognised also by Albania's long-standing partners in local governance. While recognising the progress made by Albania in establishing a framework that would promote a democratic and decentralised system of governance, the 2012 White Paper on Fiscal Decentralisation prepared by USAID states that "particularly important is the dimension of fiscal decentralisation and ensuring that local governments have a predictable and equitable financial basis and the capacity to provide essential public services". In fact, while local government responsibilities have increased, their revenue assignments have been mostly downwardly unstable, with continuous interferences from the central government both on local government taxing powers and intergovernmental transfers. Overall, in 2012 local government OSRs and the unconditional grant were respectively 14 per cent and 16 per cent lower than the pre-crisis period of 2008.

Renewed Impetus for Decentralisation Reforms: 2014–2018

Albania's new national government, elected in 2013, made decentralisation a key priority, starting with the promise to address the historical fragmentation of local governments, which was considered a systemic weakness and one of the main impediments to effective delivery of local public services. The new government enacted the TAR, which reorganised the previous 373 first-tier LGUs (municipalities and communes) to 61 new municipalities, eliminating the rural-urban division.[29] This TAR constitutes a major milestone in the country's effort to improve the effectiveness and efficiency of public administration and the quality of public services. The reduction in the number of LGUs should increase the efficiency of local government by lowering administrative costs. The concentration of human and financial resources in a smaller number of larger LGUs should increase the effectiveness of public services by enhancing the ability of local governments to respond to the preferences of their electorates. And the transfer of additional responsibilities for delivering day-to-day public services to larger LGUs should allow the national government to focus more of its energies on the strategic, legislative, and policy-making functions of the state—including the goal of balanced territorial development (USAID, 2015).

The 2014 TAR was followed by the 2015–2020 NCSDLG, which laid down a new decentralisation agenda with key roles, responsibilities, actions and deadlines. The central objectives of NCSDLG are to improve the efficiency and effectiveness of public administration at both the national and local levels, to improve the quality of local public services, and to encourage more balanced socio-economic development.[30]

The NCSDLG was followed by a new LLSG[31] that was approved by Parliament in December 2015. The LLSG reflects the new reality created by the TAR and sets forth both the new functions, responsibilities and authorities of Albania's 61 newly created municipalities. One of the innovations of the LLSG is the elimination of the concept of shared functions, and the additional decentralisation of several new functions to the local level, such as: preschools, fire protection, forestry, and irrigation and drainage. In terms of finances, the LLSG sanctions for the first time that: (a) the size of the unconditional grant shall be anchored as a certain percentage of public revenues; and (b) that a certain percentage within the annual public borrowing limit would be allocated for local government borrowing.

The new Law on Civil Service[32] extended its scope of application to all levels of local government administration by focusing on increased quality, professionalism, political neutrality and accountability. Such principles are crucial for successful provision of local public services, especially those regarding education, infrastructure, and water supply. Referring to a study conducted by the Council of Europe, most of the Albanian LGUs had no capacities to meet the requirements of the Law on Civil Service on managing human resources.[33]

The administrative and political decentralisation initiated with the TAR, the NCSDLG, and the new LLSG were followed also by reforms in the fiscal dimension of decentralisation, which addressed many of the structural weaknesses in the intergovernmental finance system. In April 2017, after a lengthy and complex process, the Government of Albania adopted the first-ever comprehensive law regulating LLSGF.[34]

The political, economic, and institutional context in which the LLSGF has been developed, discussed, and approved and has played a major role in its final scope and political economy instruments. To better understand the context in which the LLSGF has been developed it is important to have the full picture of the status and development of the Albanian local government finances until the end of 2015 and 2016 when the Law was being drafted and discussed. Figure 9.3 shows local governments' main sources of revenues as a percentage of central government's revenues from taxes and customs. Figure 9.3 can help us better understand the key challenges and pressures that Albanian national and local policymakers faced in the process of drafting the LLSGF.

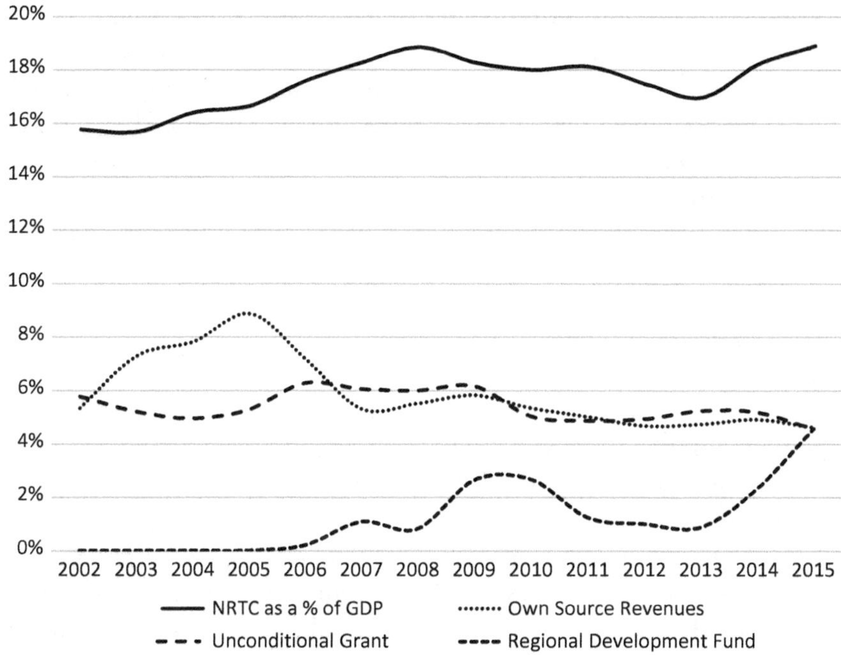

Fig. 9.3 Local government revenue in percent of general government revenues, and its components, 2002–2015. Source: Ministry of Finance of Albania, Consolidated Fiscal Indicators, author' calculations

Local finances in Albania have always been dominated by intergovernmental transfers in the form of freely disposable unconditional grants and competitive grants for local infrastructure. This is not uncommon when compared to the other countries in the South East Europe (SEE) region, where about 65 per cent of local expenditures are financed through intergovernmental transfers, in the form of shared taxes and unconditional and conditional grants (NALAS, 2015). Intergovernmental transfers in Albania have financed about 55 per cent and 64 per cent of local expenditures respectively in 2014 and 2015 (USAID, 2016b, 2017).

Even with the territorial consolidation, the unconditional grant accounted for more than 50 per cent of revenues for 43 out of the 61 new and larger municipalities in 2015. And despite its historical importance for local budgets, the unconditional grant has been continuously underfunded. Further, not being anchored to any macroeconomic variable, the unconditional grant has also been downwardly unstable. In fact, between

2013 and 2015 the unconditional grant fell from 5.2 to 4.5 per cent of general government revenue the lowest since this instrument was introduced in 2002. Further, the downward instability of the unconditional grant has been coupled with a striking increase in conditional and competitive investment grants under the RDF, that have increased from 0.9 to 4.6 per cent of general government revenue, therefore the approximately same size of the unconditional grant. The most important issues that needed to be addressed in the area of unconditional and conditional intergovernmental transfers was their systemic unpredictability in terms of size and criteria for allocation of funds.

Over the years, the instability of intergovernmental transfers has been coupled with the frequent amendment (mostly reductions) of LGUs' taxing powers. The LLTS adopted in 2006 has been amended more than 18 times since its introduction until 2016, curtailing and depressing LGUs' efforts to improve collection of revenues. In 2014, the government eliminated some of the limitations imposed in 2009 on local governments' ability to alter centrally set tax rates by ±30 per cent and the restraints on local fees. On the other hand, they centralised the collection of one of the most important local taxes—the small business tax, but most importantly they cut the tax rate first by half and then by two thirds and while exempting its major taxpayers. As in the case of 2009, the government again argued the necessity of such measures on the grounds of reducing the fiscal burden on small business to promote economic activity and to reduce the informal economy. The financial consequences have been devastating from local governments, which in 2016, received from the small business tax only 17 per cent of the amount they were receiving in 2005 (USAID, 2016a, 2016c).

Despite the number of amendments to the LLTS, unfortunately policymakers have never addressed the systemic weaknesses in local taxation—there is insufficient investment from both the national and local governments in the technical, regulatory, and political infrastructure necessary for the effective implementation of local tax powers. The main issues here remain the lack of accurate registers of tax payers and tax bases, the lack of tax administration systems, and the lack of effective tax enforcement powers (USAID, 2016b).

Other pressures that have accompanied the discussion and finalisation of the LLSGF are related local government debts. Because of the lax public finance management systems, as the national government a few years earlier, local governments too had accumulated substantial payment arrears. This issue became particularly evident with territorial consolidation. In most cases, the new and larger municipalities have inherited substantial payment arrears from the abolished communes in their jurisdictions. Tax arrears have never been quantified or accurately reported. The local arrears accumulated till 2015 amounted 11.6 billion Albanian Lekë (ALL) or 0.7 per cent of the GDP, constituting up to 90 per cent of the unconditional grant allocated for the year 2016. During the period January–September 2016, 4.5 billion ALL of new arrears were accumulated, which is about 0.3 per cent of the GDP. In total, in September 2016, the payment arrears totalled 16.1 billion ALL or 1 per cent of GDP. By the end of 2016, local governments had cleared 6.2 billion ALL.[35] However, about 9.9 billion ALL of payment arrears remain to be cleared in the upcoming coming year(s). The Ministry of Finance has clearly stated that local governments need to deal with their own payment arrears, as they have inherited both rights and responsibilities with territorial reorganisation.

From an institutional point of view, the process of drafting the LLSGF was led by the Ministry of Finance of Albania, with the lead support USAID's Planning and Local Governance Project in Albania. The Ministry's Public Finance Management Strategy adopted in late 2014, limited the scope of upcoming LLSGF to a new formula with criteria for the allocation of unconditional grants, establishing a fiscal cadastre of properties for the purposes of the local property tax, and tighter public finance management rules related to local budget planning, implementation, reporting, and auditing. Many of Albania's international partners agreed to the importance of this perspective. Tighter rules for local public finance management, a property tax reform, and a new formula for unconditional grants were also foreseen under the new National Cross-cutting Strategy on Decentralisation and Local Governance led by the Minister of State for Local Issues. However, this latter Strategy called for a more thorough reform of the local finance system, including: (a) strengthening local government taxing powers in terms of setting tax bases and rates; (b) anchoring the size of the unconditional grant to a macroeconomic variable; (c) revising the unpredictability, lack of transparency, and eventually the politisation of the RDF, as the major instrument supporting local investments from the national government; and (d) more opportunities for local borrowing for creditworthy municipalities. All these elements were missing in the Ministry of Finance's Strategy.

It is clear, therefore, that the process of drafting the LLSGF has been a subject to many pressures and complexities which have impacted the final shape of the draft law that has been approved in April 2017, after more than a year and a half of discussions. Because of these political, economic, and institutional complexities, the final adopted version LLSGF does not address all strategic objectives outlined in the Public Finance Management Strategy or the National Cross-Cutting Strategy on Decentralisation and Local Governance for the fiscal decentralisation reform. Nevertheless, this Law constitutes a major milestone in Albania's progress towards fiscal decentralisation. It addresses many of the historical structural weaknesses and introduces a number of internationally recognised best practices in municipal finance, such as:

- addressing the historical underfunding of the unconditional grant—through increasing its size by 36 per cent when compared to the average of the past five years;
- addressing the instability and unpredictability of the unconditional grant by anchoring its annual size to a macroeconomic variable, 1 per cent of the GDP;
- defining the criteria to be used for the allocation of the unconditional grant;
- introducing clear and specific rules for financing the new, decentralised functions, in order to avoid unfunded mandates;
- defining clear and specific rules for consultations between the national and local governments on legislation and decisions that affect local government revenues and expenditures;
- sharing 2 per cent of the centrally collected personal income tax revenues with local governments on an origin basis;
- increasing the local share of revenues from the national tax on vehicles, from 18 per cent to 25 per cent;

- introducing rules for the diligent, sustainable and accountable budget planning, implementation, reporting, and auditing;
- introducing rules for the prevention and management of cases of financial distress and insolvency.

These are all substantive improvements. However, it is important that the fiscal decentralisation reform initiated with the Draft Law on Local Government Finance is accompanied by additional fiscal policy reforms (USAID, 2017). The government's measures in late 2017 and early 2018 towards a value-based policy of property taxation, while long overdue, is a good step ahead.[36] The revised Law on Local Tax System introduces a market value-based property tax system and promises the establishment of nationally managed cadastre of properties and tax bases. Nevertheless, additional efforts are necessary to make sure that local governments can implement this new policy and that they have the systems in place for an effective administration of all local taxes and fees. Establishing the technical and infrastructural systems, in particular a fiscal register (cadastre) of real estate, is critical for achieving the overarching goals of decentralisation—to improve the efficiency and effectiveness of public administration at both the national and local levels, improve the quality of local public services, and encourage more balanced territorial and socio-economic development.

Additionally, the government needs to stop the practice of frequent legal amendments of local tax and fiscal powers, which has been accompanied by conflicting policy priorities, inconsistencies, and confusion regarding the implementation. Simultaneously with the adoption of the 2018 fiscal package that introduced the property tax reform, the central government reduced local government tax powers (on rather unclear political economy basis), by granting substantial exemptions to specific categories of payers of the property tax and the tax on the infrastructure impact of new investments.

Overall, the last wave of decentralisation initiated in 2013 is characterised by substantive improvements in the policy and legal framework for decentralisation. The LLSG consolidates local governments' rights and responsibilities, while the implementation of both the TAR and the LLSGF creates the pre-conditions necessary for creating a stronger local government that are also able to provide and improve local service delivery.

Concluding Remarks

Using 1992 as a baseline, major decentralisation reforms have taken place almost every ten years in Albania and similar features have been identified in each phase: (a) definition or redefinition of local governments' rights and responsibilities; (b) revision of territorial and administrative boundaries; (c) amendments of local fiscal powers and intergovernmental transfers for the fulfilment of the LGUs' functions; and (d) efforts to establish and maintain a professional and responsible local public administration.

Despite these similarities, the three waves of decentralisation differ substantially from one another in their objectives, scope of intervention, instruments, expectations, and outcomes. This is particularly true for the fiscal dimension of decentralisation policies. In the early stage of the 1990s, the focus was on creating a basic legal framework for democratically elected local governments. In the 2000s, the focus was on clarifying LGUs' rights and responsibilities and complying with the principles of European Charter of Local Self-Government. In 2009, the focus was supposedly on adjusting local tax burdens to the country's fiscal policy measures responding to the global crisis and economic downturn. The new wave of reforms that took place after the 2013 focused on increasing and consolidating LGUs' responsibilities, and on meeting increased expectations for good governance, efficient local administration, and economic development.

Similarly, looking through the lens of territorial and administrative reorganisation, the purpose of decentralisation in the early 1990s was to get rid of Albania's socialist heritage. In 2000, the goal of decentralisation was to replace the second tier of local government without any substantive change in the first tier. In 2014, the goal was to consolidate the very fragmented first tier local governments into larger municipalities that would be able to provide more and better services, reduce administrative costs and facilitate a more balanced territorial development. The 2014 reform also had its opponents who argued that this reform was designed to favour the electoral results of the ruling coalition.

As regards fiscal decentralisation, in the early 1990s, local government taxing powers were mostly on paper. In the period 2002–2006, LGUs were given the authority to manage a good portion of public revenues and received freely disposable unconditional grants allocated through a formula based on universal criteria. Over time, the frequent amendments of local government revenues were accompanied by conflicting priorities, major policy inconsistencies and confusion regarding implementation. All this created an inadequate baseline for the effective implementation of local governments' increasing functional responsibilities. Defining the political economy arguments for such frequent legal amendments is not an easy task. However, the fact that local governments' tax powers, revenue raising options, and intergovernmental transfers have been reduced so frequently, while their functional responsibilities have remained unchanged or even increased, suggests that local interests are too frequently sacrificed to serve the interests of national policy; or even worse, to serve the interests of the respective political forces in power. Either way, the efficiency and optimal allocation of responsibilities and funds (considerations and arguments of the first-generation theories of fiscal decentralisation) have largely been abandoned as guiding principles, while political interests (considerations of the second-generation theories) have often prevailed in discussing and shaping Albanian decentralisation policies.

The fiscal decentralisation measures that have accompanied recent decentralisation reforms are expected to address some of the challenges that local governments face in delivering public services. However, many challenges remain as local governments continue to be hampered by inadequate conditional transfers from the central government, by incomplete systems for managing their tax powers, and by restraints imposed on various revenue-generating options, such as local borrowing and asset management.

As with many other countries in the region and beyond, Albania is struggling with hard budget constraints and high levels of public debt, in the context of a slow economic recovery. These factors make discussions about greater increasing the level of fiscal decentralisation difficult. On the other hand, the very implementation of the TAR, the LLSGF, and the property tax reform seems to show that decentralisation remains high on the political agenda. Therefore, there is still much room for improvement in the fiscal dimension of the decentralisation process. Everyone should be aware of the need for interventions and improvements in this area of public policy.

To circumvent the short-term political interests that might hinder long-term strategic objectives, decentralisation policy should be a subject of public discussion among all relevant stakeholders.

Notes

1. Law no. 7572, dated 10 June 1992 on the Organisation and Functioning of Local Government, Official Gazette, No. 3/1992.
2. Program on Reinforcing Local and Regional Government Structures in Albania, implemented by the Council of Europe with the support of the Swiss Agency for Development and Cooperation, in partnership with the Ministry of Interior and Local Government Associations, April 2011, Albania Baseline Assessment Report on Inter-Municipal Cooperation in Local Governance, p. 5.
3. Law no. 7570, dated 03 June 1992, on Some Amendments to Law no. 7491, dated 29 April 1991, on the Constitutional Dispositions, Official Gazette, No. 3/1992.
4. Law no. 7572, dated 10 June 1992 on the Organisation and Functioning of Local Government Official Gazette, No. 3/1992.
5. Decision of the Council of Ministers no. 269, dated 25 June 1992, on the Administrative and Territorial Division of the Republic of Albania.
6. Law no. 7608, dated 22 September 1992 on the Prefectures, Official Gazette, No. 9/1992, mandated the establishment of 12 Prefectures as the largest territorial units, headed by the Prefect which is appointed and is acted as the representative of the Council of Ministers with the aim of monitoring the implementation of legal framework from LGUs.
7. Law no. 7548, dated 08 January 1992, on the Tax System in the Republic of Albania, Official Gazette, No. 1/1992.
8. Law no. 7776, dated 22 December 1993, on the Local Budget, Official Gazette, No. 15/1993.
9. Law no. 7805, dated 16 March 1994, on the Property Tax in the Republic of Albania, Official Gazette, No. 3/1994.
10. Local borrowing was only mentioned in this law as a possible source, but it was not regulated and implemented until 2008.
11. Albania signed the European Charter of Local Self-Government on 27 May 1998 and fully ratified it on 4 April 2000, with entry into force on 1 August 2000.

12. Law no. 8417, dated 21 October 1998, The Constitution of the Republic of Albania, Official Gazette, No. 28/1998.
13. Law no. 8652, dated 31 July 2000, on the Organisation and Functioning of Local Governments, Official Gazette, No. 25/2000.
14. Law no. 8653, dated 31 July 2000, on the Territorial and Administrative Division of Local Governments, Official Gazette, No. 26/2000.
15. Law no. 8982, dated 12 December 2002, on the Local Tax System, Official Gazette, No. 82/2002.
16. Law no. 8744, dated 22 February 2001, on the Transfer of the State Immovable Properties to Local Governments, Official Gazette, No. 9/2001; Law no. 9352, dated 03 March 2005, on Some Amendments to Law no. 8102/1996; on the Regulatory Framework of the Water Supply and Wastewater System, Official Gazette, No. 19/2001.
17. The main shared functions were broadly defined as pre-school and pre-university education; primary health service and public health protection; social assistance and poverty alleviation; public order and civil protection and environmental protection.
18. Law no. 8549, dated 11 November 1999, on Civil Service, Official Gazette, No. 36/1999.
19. Law no. 8653, dated 31 July 2000, on the Territorial and Administrative Division of Local Governments, Official Gazette, No. 26/2000; The communes of Barbullush and Bushat voluntary merged to create a single commune, leading to 308 communes.
20. Law no. 8982, dated 12 December 2002, on the Local Tax System, Official Gazette, No. 82/2002.The Law was thoroughly revised in 2006 with Law no. 9632, dated 30 October 2006, on the Local Tax System. Following this law, the most important local taxes were: the small business tax; the property tax on buildings and agricultural land; the hotel tax; the tax on the infrastructure impact of new buildings; the property transfer tax; the annual tax on vehicle registration; the public space occupation tax, and the billboard tax.
21. Law no. 10190, dated 26 November 2009, on the State Budget 2010, Official Gazette, No. 26/2009.
22. Decision of the Council of Ministers no. 135, dated 03 February 2010, on the Definition of the Criteria for the Distribution of the Regional Development Fund, Official Gazette, No. 25/2010; Decision of the Council of Ministers no. 2, dated 11 March 2011, on the Criteria for Allocating the Regional Development Fund.

23. Decision of the Council of Ministers no. 691, dated 29 July 2015, on the National Crosscutting Strategy for Decentralisation and Local Governance, 2015–2020, Official Gazette, No. 137/2008 p. 17; https://www.reporter.al/shkodra-jashte-rilindjes-urbane-merr-me-pak-fonde-se-maliqi-dhe-roskoveci/; http://aam.org.al/qendrimi-dhe-shqetesimi-i-shoqates-se-bashkive-lidhur-me-ndarjen-e-fondeve-nga-komiteti-per-zhvillimin-e-rajoneve/.
24. Law no. 9869, dated 04 February 2008, on Local Borrowing, Official Gazette, No. 18/2008.
25. Law no. 10117, dated 23 April 2009, amending the Law No. 9632/2006. on the Local Tax System, Official Gazette, No. 62/2009.
26. Law no. 10025, dated 27 November 2008, on the 2009 Budget, Official Gazette, No. 182/2009; and Law no. 10190, dated 26 November 2009, on the 2010 Budget, Official Gazette, No. 175/2009.
27. Law no. 10340, dated 28 October 2010, on the Past Due Obligations towards Third Parties of the Public Utilities Owned by Local Governments, Official Gazette, No. 159/2010.
28. Law no. 10025, dated 27 November 2008, on the Year 2009 Budget, Official Gazette, No. 182/2009; Law no. 10190, dated 26 November 2009, on the Year 2010 Budget, Official Gazette, No. 175/2009 and PLGP/USAID, Statistical Brief: Local Government Finances in Albania 2002–2015.
29. Law no. 115/2014 dated 31 July 2014 on the administrative and territorial units of local government in the Republic of Albania, Official Gazette, No. 137/2014. The second-level local governments, the 12 Regions were not reorganised by the TAR.
30. Decision of the Council of Ministers no. 691, dated 29 July 2015, on the National Crosscutting Strategy for Decentralisation and Local Governance, 2015–2020, Official Gazette, No. 137/2008.
31. Law no. 139/2015, dated 17 December 2015, on Local Self-Government, Official Gazette, No. 249/2015.
32. Law no. 152/2013, dated 30 May 2013, on Civil Service, Official Gazette, No. 95/2013. It replaced the previous Law no. 8549, dated 11 November 1999 on Civil Service.
33. Under the Project "Strengthening Local Government Structures and Cooperation of Local Elected Representatives in Albania—Phase II (2012–2015)", implemented by Council of Europe with support of the Swiss Agency for Development and Cooperation (SDC), unpublished, with authors Xhumari, M. & Dollani, P., 2013.

34. Law no. 68/2017, dated 27 April 2017, on Local Self-Government Finance, Official Gazette, No. 113/2017.
35. Ministry of Finance of Albania http://www.financa.gov.al/al/raportime/buxheti/buxheti-i-pushtetit-vendor/viti-20161483103977.
36. Law no. 106/2017, dated 30 November 2017, on Some Amendments to Law no. 9632, dated 30 October 2006, on the Local Tax System, as amended, Official Gazette, No. 222/2017.

References

Bahl, W. R., & Linn, F. J. (1992). *Urban public finance in developing countries*. Oxford: Oxford University Press.

Banks, C., & Pigey, H. J. (1998). *Republic of Albania opportunities and issues for municipal reform*. East European Regional Housing Sector Assistance Project 180-0034. Washington, DC: USAID.

Brahimi, F., Baholli, F., Haldeda, N., & Dika, I. (2013). Decentralisation reform, case of Albania. *Mediterranean Journal of Social Sciences, 10*(4), 524–531.

Council of Europe. (2011). *Albania baseline assessment report on inter-municipal cooperation in local governance*.

Hoxha, A. (2002). *Local self-government and decentralisation: Case of Albania: History, reforms and challenges*. Tirana: Institute for Contemporary Studies.

Hoxha, A. (2007). *Does decentralisation support good governance? Decentralisation in Albania—A top down perspective*. CIS Working Paper, No. 31.

Ministry of Finance of Albania. (2015). *Macroeconomic and fiscal indicators*.

Ministry of Finance of Albania. (2017). *Consolidated fiscal indicators of the general government*. Retrieved from www.financa.gov.al/al/raportime/programimi-ekonomiko-fiskal/raporte-dhe-statistika-fiskale-mujore/statistika-fiskale-mujore

Network of Associations of Local Authorities in South-East Europe (NALAS). (2015). *Fiscal decentralisation indicators for Southeast Europe, 2006–2014*. Retrieved from www.nalas.eu/Publications/Books/2016_FD_Report

Oates, W. E. (1993). Fiscal decentralisation and economic development. *National Tax Journal, 46*(2), 237–243.

Oates, W. E. (1999). An essay on fiscal federalism. *Journal of Economic Literature, 37*(3), 1120–1149.

Oates, W. E. (2005). Toward a second-generation theory of fiscal federalism. *International Tax and Public Finance, 12*, 349–373.

Oates, W. E. (2008). On the evolution of fiscal federalism: Theory and institutions. *National Tax Journal, LXI*(2), 313–334.

USAID Planning and Local Governance Project (PLGP) in Albania. (2015). *Creating an equitable, transparent and predictable unconditional grant formula.* Retrieved from www.plgp.al.

USAID Planning and Local Governance Project (PLGP) in Albania. (2016a). *A profile of municipal finance system in Albania: The need for a framework law on local finances.* Retrieved from www.plgp.al

USAID Planning and Local Governance Project (PLGP) in Albania. (2016b). *Key recommendations for the development and discussion of the law on local government finances.* Retrieved from www.plgp.al.

USAID Planning and Local Governance Project (PLGP) in Albania. (2016c). *Local government finances in Albania 2002–2015.* Retrieved from www.plgp.al

USAID Planning and Local Governance Project (PLGP) in Albania. (2017). *After territorial administrative reform and on the eve of the implementation of the law on local government finance.* Retrieved from www.plgp.al

Weingast, B. R. (2009). Second generation fiscal federalism: The implications of fiscal incentives. *Journal of Urban Economics, 65*, 279–293.

Weingast, B. R. (2014). Second generation fiscal federalism: Political aspects of decentralisation and economic development. *World Development, 53*, 14–25.

World Bank. (1994). *Fiscal decentralisation and intergovernmental finances in the Republic of Albania.*

World Bank. (2008). *Albania local finance policy note: Programmatic public expenditure and institutional review.*

Part V

Conclusions

10

Conclusions: Policy Changes and Policy Reversals

Katarina Đulić, Sanja Kmezić, and William Bartlett

Decentralisation of the delivery of public goods and services has been considered one of the crucial pillars of reforms in countries in transition after 1990 (Bartlett, Maleković, & Monastiriotis, 2013; Kmezić, Đulić, Jocović, & Kaluđerović, 2016; The World Bank, 2008). These socio-economic reforms were spearheaded primarily by the international donor community and development agencies. Their programmes and technical assistance focused heavily on the decentralisation processes. For instance, the main economic rationale of the World Bank was that decentralisation improves efficiency in resource allocation and local public service provision, following the ideas of the first-generation theories of fiscal

K. Đulić
Faculty of Economics, Finance and Administration, FEFA, Belgrade, Serbia
e-mail: kdjulic@fefa.edu.rs

S. Kmezić (✉)
University of Graz, Graz, Austria

W. Bartlett
London School of Economics and Political Science, European Institute, London, UK

W. Bartlett et al. (eds.), *Fiscal Decentralisation, Local Government and Policy Reversals in Southeastern Europe*, https://doi.org/10.1007/978-3-319-96092-0_10

federalism (Musgrave, 1959; Oates, 1972; Tiebout, 1956). In addition, the politics behind this trend was to strengthen democracy and improve accountability by increasing citizen participation in local decision making (The World Bank, 2008). In addition to the World Bank Group, the main donors in the region of Southeastern Europe were USAID, UNDP, and the Open Society Institute (now the Open Society Foundations), which provided substantial technical and financial assistance to support fiscal decentralisation and local government capacity-building efforts with the same justifications.

Simultaneously, the EU has played a very important role in the region, as the observed countries have all taken part in the European integration process. The EU has also put an emphasis on decentralisation, but with somewhat different objectives. During the first years of its technical and financial support to the region, the European Commission concentrated on creating and developing regional structures that would be responsible for managing the pre-accession and cohesion funds (Avlijaš & Bartlett, 2011). Later, the EU shifted its attention more towards improving the capacities of local governments to manage local investment projects. While the economic rationale was similar to that of the donor community, the European politics behind the EU's support for decentralisation has been more complex and guided by the principle of subsidiarity. The goal of the European Commission has been to bring the somewhat detached supra-national bureaucracy in Brussels closer to local communities and to engage citizens at the grassroots level, as well as to support regional economic development policies. Cities and municipalities play an important role in implementing these policies, thus requiring strong administrative capacities and substantial resources. Overall, sub-national levels of government are responsible for the implementation of as much as 60–70% of EU legislation (A New Treaty, 2010; Local and Regional Governments, 2016).

While decentralisation has been strongly promoted by the EU, it is not a formal criterion for accession. However, the level of (fiscal) decentralisation and the state of local government (finance) represent an informal political sub-criterion, which has been regularly examined as part of the assessment of the stability of institutions safeguarding democracy and the rule of law. In particular, the progress reports for (potential) candidate countries monitor the level of decentralisation, the state of municipal finance, the administrative capacity of local governments, and the quality of all institutions that play a role in the decentralisation processes. The EU evaluates these aspects of governance to ensure that municipalities have sufficient capacities to meet the obligations stemming from the *acquis communautaire* and to manage the pre-accession funds. In sum, the EU perceives decentralisation primarily as an instrument for democratisation and (regional) economic development.

Besides the EU, another European player that has also been active in the countries covered by this book is the Council of Europe. This organisation has facilitated the ratification of the European Charter of Local Self-Government and the further implementation of its provisions that protect the political, administrative, and financial autonomy of local authorities. Over the time period we have covered, all eight countries have incorporated the principles and provisions of the Charter into their national legislation.

These two main groups of donors, together with some other foreign development agencies, have been the key drivers of the decentralisation process in the region of Southeastern Europe over the period 1990–2017. Yet, the main political force in the region is naturally the process of European integration, upon which all of the eight countries have embarked. Croatia and Slovenia are already EU member states, while the other six countries remain on the EU periphery; Albania, Macedonia, Montenegro, and Serbia are EU candidate countries, while Bosnia and Herzegovina and Kosovo are potential candidate countries. Thus, in the region of the Western Balkans, decentralisation has been draped within Europeanisation.

The countries studied in this book have emerged from two different historical and political-economic contexts. The first context—the Yugoslav federation—was highly decentralised and shaped the foundations of seven of the observed countries that were established after the dissolution of the former country. The erstwhile system was so decentralised that at one point in time it had more than 9000 different fiscal authorities—the federal level, six republics, two autonomous provinces with similar fiscal powers as the republics, eight cities and 540 municipalities, and thousands of self-managed interest communities. The latter were parastatal funds for the provision of social services (Popović, 1996; Stojanović, 2005). In addition to this plethora of budgets of the different entities, the previous fiscal framework further included the budgets of several social security funds. This administrative fragmentation was a reflection of the then political-economic system, which was rather open and liberal for a socialist country. Furthermore, the Yugoslav federation was very geographically, culturally, and ethnically diverse. In contrast, the second—Albanian—context was different in two important aspects. First, the country was highly centralised and isolated from the rest of the (broader) region. Its political-economic system suffered from severe totalitarianism and a half century-long extreme centralisation that did not accept or have the concept of local self-governance. The Albanian central government only had de-concentrated branches across the country, and the first local government units were established as late as in 1992. Second, Albania was much smaller in terms of its size, population, and diversity. This natural juxtaposition represents a good basis for comparison of the outcomes of similar decentralisation approaches implemented in the eight countries since the beginning of the transition process.

The 27-year time frame of this book has covered a period of dynamic, even "tectonic" changes in the region, which have included wars and the economic collapse caused by conflicts in almost all of the countries during the 1990s, as well as deep structural reforms that marked their political and economic transitions afterwards. In comparing the decentralisation processes in the eight countries, the book has identified three distinct phases that have triggered accompanying policy changes. In the first phase, which lasted from the early 1990s until the early 2000s, most of the countries of the former Yugoslavia slipped from decentralised systems into heavily centralised governance of public and economic affairs during the conflicts. Only Slovenia did not experience this policy change in the first phase, since it avoided the major conflict and was the first to launch transition reforms that straight away continued in the direction of decentralisation policies. The direction of change in Albania was the opposite—a heavily centralised country made its initial decentralisation steps by reforming its territorial organisation and establishing the first real local self-government entities in 1992. Although applied in two different contexts—in the most and in the least developed country in the region—

the decentralisation policies were rooted in similar rationales. These were economic development through a transition from a planned to a market economy accompanied by the democratisation of society. The former reason was more dominant in Slovenia and the latter in Albania.

The second phase started in the early 2000s and lasted until the outbreak of the global economic crisis in 2008. This phase was marked by intensive political, economic, and societal changes, which shifted the pendulum from centralisation to decentralisation. As mentioned earlier, these reforms were heavily supported by the international donor community. The scope of the decentralisation reforms was threefold. It included territorial-administrative reorganisation, changes in political institutions, and processes at the local level, as well as devolution of new responsibilities and financial resources to local governments. While the first two aspects of decentralisation are also important from the transition perspective, the heart of the decentralisation process has undoubtedly been the reform of fiscal relationships between the central and local governments. The context and motivation in each country have delineated the specific *raison d'être* of decentralisation. Three specific objectives can be identified: (1) post-war reconciliation in ethnically divided countries, (2) political democratisation, and (3) (balanced) economic development. Furthermore, the decentralisation process has been underpinned by a simultaneous process of integration of Southeastern Europe into the EU.

The outbreak of the global financial crisis shifted the policy course again and led to a major policy reversal in the region, initiating a new, third phase that is still ongoing. This phase is marked with strong centralising and pseudo-decentralising policies in all eight countries linked to the Eurozone crisis that spilled over into the region in 2009, halting growth, provoking a financial downturn, and generating significant fiscal stress (Bartlett & Prica, 2018). As an immediate response to the crisis, central governments started consolidating national budgets by introducing tight political control over public finance and various fiscal measures, most often at the expense of budgets of all other public entities. A new course of centralisation policies, together with the effects of the crisis, reverberated across all levels of government in all eight countries. This fiscal stress eventually materialised at the local level in the form of significant vertical and horizontal imbalances, liquidity problems, accumulation of arrears and excess local borrowing, which all led to an enormous growth in local indebtedness. Whereas the EU mitigated and overcame the effects of the crisis without abandoning its commitment to the decentralised management of public affairs and regional policy goals, Southeastern Europe experienced a serious financial setback. In fact, the effects of the Eurozone financial crisis were exacerbated due to the abysmal structural problems of local economies caused by uncompleted transition (except partially in Slovenia). Hence, the crisis in the region was not just a matter of the normal economic cycle, but rather an expression of deep structural and institutional imbalances, which permeated into the lowest levels of government and jeopardised local service delivery and further economic development.

While all the countries share the same political and economic goals of decentralisation policies—democratisation through greater citizen participation in local decision making and economic development through more efficient resource allocation—each country in the region has been burdened with a specific issue that has flavoured its respective decentralisation approach. Based on these specific issues, we can classify the countries into four groups. The first group includes Croatia and Slovenia. It focuses on the political economy of Europeanisation by analysing the absorption of EU funds at local level by the decentralised structures to mitigate the effects of the crisis and achieve balanced economic development. The second group includes Bosnia and Herzegovina, Montenegro and Serbia, all of which have faced serious consequences brought on by the global crisis, coupled with significant fiscal stress and high local indebtedness that have led to drastic and uniformly reactionary policy reversals partially provoked by a lack of fiscal data transparency. The third group includes Macedonia and Kosovo. In addition to dealing with challenges of transition, the major issue in these countries has been the political economy of ethnic relations. In Macedonia and Kosovo, decentralisation has been used as a policy of post-conflict reconciliation of ethnic communities, which has sought to appease and protect large minorities with strong enough centrifugal force to shake the processes of political and economic governance. In contrast one country, Albania, faces a very different issue—the legacy of half a century-long isolation, extreme centralisation, and absence of real local self-government. Thus, it remains alone in the fourth group. In addition to the typical challenges of decentralisation, this country has faced the rudimentary task of building grassroots institutions and equipping them with basic capacities and resources so that they may be able to develop local self-governance ab initio.

Within the studied period (1990–2016), fiscal decentralisation has been the essence of all the decentralisation processes and local government strengthening in the region. First, it has been instrumental in giving local governments a new role in providing public goods and services through the delegation of functions and responsibilities. Second, it has empowered them financially by establishing their fiscal autonomy and equipped them with sufficient revenues to be able to fulfil their new mandates. However, this process has involved intense political struggles over the control of fiscal resources and public financial management.

The political economy of decentralisation in the four groups of countries can be seen through the prism of (1) the key contextual determinant of, and the major motivation for, the decentralisation process; (2) the interests, behaviours, developments, and special issues that have determined the course and dynamics of the process; and (3) the current stage of fiscal decentralisation and its outcomes.

The first group includes the two countries of the region that succeeded in joining the EU in the observed period—Slovenia in 2004 and Croatia in 2013. For these two countries, the political economy of decentralisation has been enveloped in their Europeanisation processes. Unlike the other countries in the region, Slovenia and Croatia obtained access to larger European funds that they could use to achieve balanced economic development and mitigate the effects of the crisis on municipal budgets after 2009.

At the beginning of the period, in the 1990s, the Slovenian position was far better than that of the other seven studied countries. It managed to avoid a serious conflict in 1991 during the process of the Yugoslav dissolution. Also, this has always been the country with the highest economic development in the region. These two facts shaped the initial context in which Slovenia started its transition reforms. Unlike Slovenia, Croatia experienced a war from 1991 until 1995, which left the country with severe economic and political consequences. A part of its territory was devastated and ruined, which would later lead to unbalanced regional development and, thus, to an asymmetric fiscal decentralisation approach. Yet, despite similar preconditions in the other war-affected countries in the region, Croatia managed to join the EU in 2013.

Slovenia started its first decentralisation reforms in 1994 focusing on territorial reorganisation. It established 147 municipalities; however, in the years that followed, it opted for further fragmentation, ending up with 212 municipalities. Such significant fragmentation in a rather small country contributed to challenges with fiscal capacities in the majority of municipalities, leading to horizontal and vertical imbalances. It also affected the management and absorption of the EU structural and cohesion funds. Similar to Slovenia, Croatia also decided to establish a large number of municipalities on its territory, fragmenting it into 556 local governments. In addition, a Croatian specificity is that it simultaneously established an intermediate, second tier of government—21 regional self-governments (counties). Such great fragmentation left the majority of municipalities with quite limited fiscal capacity. The situation was further aggravated by the fact that certain areas were devastated by the war, which later became the basis for their special fiscal status. Moreover, the central government also gave a special financial status to underdeveloped mountainous municipalities and certain islands for their economic development projects. All these circumstances and a combination of different factors have further hindered efforts to decrease regional disparities and achieve more optimal horizontal and vertical balances.

Although Slovenia was the first in the region to initiate and implement intergovernmental fiscal reform, at the end of the observed period its basic fiscal decentralisation indicators show that the levels of local government revenues and expenditures are still low. Bearing in mind the Slovenian much better macroeconomic situation and the fact that the municipal revenues and expenditures are, in absolute terms, a few times greater than in the rest of the region, it comes as a surprise that Slovenian relative indicators are more or less the same as in the other observed countries. For instance, in 2003, the share of total local revenues in the GDP was 4.8%, while in 2015, this share was 5.8%. Analogously, the shares were more or less the same on the expenditure side (with 5.7% in 2015). Slovenian municipalities primarily rely on the elastic pro-cyclical personal income tax. The lack of diversity of municipal sources of revenues made Slovenian municipalities fiscally vulnerable when the crisis hit, affecting salaries and employment. Similar to the majority of other countries in the region, Slovenia decentralised the property tax and made it the primary own-source revenue for local governments. During the observed period, specifically after 1999, the purview of municipal responsibilities doubled, at least. Yet, the level of municipal expenditures has increased at much a slower pace (by less than 20% from 2003 until 2015). This created significant vertical imbalances. However, the dependency of Slovenian municipalities on the equalisation funds has diminished over time. Since the legislative changes in 2007, the percentage of municipalities that receive these funds dropped from 90% (2002–2006) to 50% at the end of the observed period.

When it comes to dealing with imbalances in Croatia, mechanisms for both horizontal and vertical equalisation have been distorted due to the influence of political factors. At the beginning, the central government had legitimate reasons for giving a special fiscal status to the war-affected and underdeveloped areas. However, once these areas gained this preferential status, it became almost impossible for them to lose it regardless of the achieved economic development. Over time, it has become evident that the political (partisan and coalitional) alignment between central and local governments heavily affects this favoured treatment. As in Slovenia, Croatian municipalities rely on revenues from the personal income tax to the largest degree. This weakens their fiscal autonomy since the central government determines all elements of this source of revenue, also making it an instrument for various political purposes—from equalisation to financing local capital projects. The excessive reliance of Croatian municipalities on the personal income tax (it makes up almost 90% of all municipal tax revenues) is troublesome for several different reasons. First, a lion's share of the intergovernmental transfers represents the shared personal income tax. Second, one of the primary municipal own-source revenues in Croatia is the personal income surtax. Third, the heavy reliance on this elastic type of taxation was particularly problematic after 2008, as the effects of the crisis on municipal budgets were immediate. Thus, the lack of diversified sources of revenues makes Croatian municipalities quite vulnerable.

Furthermore, although the level of local debt in Croatia is relatively low and within the regulatory limits, municipalities face serious fiscal risks due to off-balance-sheet liabilities. Debt reached 700 million EUR (in 2015). However, the guarantees to local utility companies grew to as much as 400 million EUR (in 2010) and then started falling gradually, dropping to 230 million EUR (in 2014). In Croatia, like in the other countries in the region, there is a lack of systemic, consolidated fiscal risk monitoring. Slovenia, on the other hand, represents a good example for the entire region. Namely, Slovenian municipalities are obliged to conduct consolidated debt management when calculating the total amount of the legally allowed borrowing. The borrowing ceiling includes fiscal risks and liabilities often neglected in other countries, such as the guarantees given to local utility companies and indirect budgetary users, financial leases, and other obligations that are not direct loans. These tight borrowing rules impose harder budget constraints relative to the other countries in the region, which still struggle to monitor and control accumulating arrears and off-balance-sheet liabilities.

In the period before the crisis, Croatian municipalities allocated approximately one-fourth of their budgets to capital investments. After 2009, this share dropped to 16% and stayed at this level despite the economic recovery over time. Some municipalities managed to compensate this gap by resorting to European Structural and Investment Funds. Until 2011, the absorption and utilisation of the funds were very low and unevenly distributed between fiscally stronger and weaker municipalities. Faced with a prolonged loss of revenues due to the crisis, certain Croatian municipalities consolidated their capacities and started pulling resources from the EU funds. Interestingly, the utilisation of the funds increased almost 20 times in only four years (2011–2015). However, during this period, the weaknesses of municipalities in absorbing the funds became evident. First, considerable territorial fragmentation created a large number of small municipalities with weak administrative and fiscal capacities. This restricted their potential for co-financing, which is required by the EU for the utilisation of funds. Second, local governments were unprepared to benefit from the EU funds because the central government failed to provide a transparent investment master plan with the prepared municipal capital projects. Third, although the degree of fiscal decentralisation has increased since 2001, the fiscal decentralisation indices in Croatia are still low compared to the EU average. Local government budgets made up only around 12% of the general government budget at the end of the observed period. In order to increase the co-financing and absorption capacity of municipalities, their fiscal capacity needs to be increased too. This means that the country needs to continue its fiscal decentralisation process. Slovenian municipalities also tapped into the EU funds and managed to neutralise the drop in state and local funds for investments, thus mitigating the effects of the crisis to a significant extent, despite the fact that the 2014–2020 EU Financial Framework resources were rather limited.

In assessing the current decentralisation trajectory of these two countries, one can conclude that Slovenia and Croatia have done a lot of work on intergovernmental fiscal reforms. However, if one examines the fiscal decentralisation indicators only, it seems that, despite more favourable economic conditions in these two countries, their progress has been less impressive. They ended up at a similar level of the shares of local government revenues in total government revenues and in the GDP as the rest of the region (with the exception of Albania and Kosovo), but these shares are still significantly lower than the EU average (Levitas et al., 2016). It seems that municipalities in both Slovenia and Croatia have benefited more from Europeanisation than from the decentralisation process. Access to EU funds has allowed these municipalities to mitigate the effects of the crisis faster and better than the municipalities in the neighbouring EU periphery. Yet, great fragmentation, coupled with low fiscal decentralisation, prevents the majority of municipalities in these two countries from fully taking advantage of this privilege. Smaller and less developed municipalities lack capacities to mobilise EU funds, which leads to a situation in which only stronger local governments can utilise these funds. This skewed absorption of the funds further deepens the development gap between richer and poorer municipalities, actually hampering the countries in achieving balanced regional development, which was one of the initial and major goals of decentralisation. To conclude, the key challenge in these two countries (primarily in Croatia) is to optimise the number of sub-national government units, in order to allow them to attain economies of scale and more balanced economic development. However, merging and consolidating municipalities assumes that some of them have to be abolished. This would be the most difficult task since it requires the readiness of all parties to give up their party-related preferential status and personal benefits in government structures in order to achieve public interest. The alternative approach would be the development of inter-municipal cooperation, which carries its own political and partisan challenges and bureaucratic bottlenecks.

The second group includes the countries that were most severely marked by the global financial crisis, local government fiscal stress and indebtedness, and sharper policy reversals—Bosnia and Herzegovina, Montenegro, and Serbia. Although the initial context of the launched decentralisation reforms in Montenegro and Serbia, on the one hand, and Bosnia and Herzegovina, on the other, was quite different, they ended up facing similar economic challenges, albeit to different degrees. In Bosnia and Herzegovina, decentralisation policy was implemented through the post-war Dayton Agreement with the aim of ethnic conflict resolution. Hence, the imposed territorial arrangement has not been a reflection of the economic-geographic optimisation, but has instead primarily been based on ethnic administrative boundaries. Such constitutional organisation has burdened the country's fiscal structure and introduced an atypical fiscal asymmetry, which has aggravated meaningful intergovernmental reforms and the fiscal decentralisation process. Although the vogue of fiscal decentralisation has also affected Bosnia and Herzegovina, the speed and the success of the process were weak, and attention given to local government reform was rather superficial, leading to an absence of drastic policy reversals. The objectives of decentralisation in Serbia and Montenegro were different—to promote democracy through the improvement in local political accountability and citizen participation, and economic development through a more efficient allocation of resources and better service delivery. These two countries have not embarked on territorial-administrative decentralisation, albeit for two different reasons. Serbia wanted to avoid further fragmentation of the country after the 1999 war in Kosovo, while the size of Montenegro did not generate such a need. When it comes to fiscal decentralisation, the strength of commitment and the behaviour of political and bureaucratic elites in Montenegro and Serbia were very different. The motivation of key stakeholders in Montenegro was stronger. This was confirmed by several reactionary policy measures adopted to stabilise local public finance after the 2008 crisis. In contrast, a lack of intrinsic political commitment to fiscal decentralisation in Serbia led to a sharp policy reversal when the country was faced with its first external shock. By consolidating its own national budget to deal with the crisis, the central government adopted a series of ad hoc measures that further deteriorated local public finance instead of stabilising it. Interestingly, both Montenegro and Serbia displayed the same inconsistency in approach to political decentralisation and the reform of political institutions at the local level. Both countries first introduced the direct election of mayors and, only a few years later, repealed the system, when political elites realised that their parties could lose local elections because they did not have politically strong enough, party-affiliated leaders who could ensure victory. On the other hand, Bosnia and Herzegovina decided to preserve the direct election of mayors, which led to higher local political accountability.

In these three countries, the common denominator was the deep impact of the 2008 crisis, which disturbed the decentralisation discourse leading to notable fiscal stress, high local indebtedness, and a sharp decline of local capital investment. Serbia additionally suffered from more drastic and uniform reactionary policy reversals, aggravated by the external and internal lack of fiscal data transparency. The effects of the crisis were the most evident on the revenue side of municipal budgets in all three countries, which, coupled with strong pressures to maintain the same level of expenditures, led to serious vertical imbalances. Before the crisis, local governments in Serbia and Montenegro primarily generated their funds through own-source and other real estate-related revenues. These suffered a sharp decline after 2008 because the real estate and the construction sectors were the first to take a hit from the crisis. On the other hand, the reason for the decline of local revenues in Bosnia and Herzegovina was a dramatic fall in consumption. Unlike local governments in all other countries in the region, Bosnia and Herzegovina's municipalities relied primarily on the value-added tax (VAT) and other indirect taxes, which were consequently strongly affected. Thus, we can conclude that a lack of diversity of sources of revenues makes local governments in these countries very vulnerable to external shocks. During the period of strong growth, which preceded the crisis, municipalities in all three countries used the increase in their revenues to increase employment in local authorities, regardless of real need. When hit by the crisis, they were pressured to maintain the same level of current employee expenditures, obliged by collective bargaining and unions as well as by ruling party-related patronage networks. The direct consequences of such developments were the sacrifice of capital investment, the deterioration in the quality of local public services, and a drastic increase in local borrowing. The factor that further contributed to vertical imbalances was the Serbian and Montenegrin central governments' decision to promote good business climate, after the onset of the crisis, by reducing the fiscal burden on businesses almost exclusively at the expense of local municipal revenues. In addition, the Serbian government adopted more than 15 different fiscal measures that all further aggravated the situation in local budgets. This density and ad hoc character of measures in a relatively short period of time are a peculiarity of Serbia's intergovernmental fiscal governance.

Besides vertical imbalances, the three countries also faced large horizontal disparities, which fiscal decentralisation per se was not able to resolve. In Montenegro, there is a deep divide between the southern, coastal municipalities, which experienced strong economic development over the last two decades, and the northern, mountainous municipalities, which became underdeveloped and underpopulated. The horizontal imbalances remain primarily due to the regional economic disparities and strong urbanisation around the capital city and the coastal area; thus, these could not be addressed by fiscal equalisation mechanisms only. In Bosnia and Herzegovina, the VAT revenue-sharing formula, as well as other revenue-sharing schemes, primarily takes into account the size of the municipal population. However, Bosnia and Herzegovina was unable to conduct a census for more than 20 years, due to a lack of political agreement of nationalistic party elites. The (also disputable) 2013 census revealed the shortcomings of the existing revenue-sharing mechanisms, as the population was severely underestimated in the majority of local municipalities. Bosnia and Herzegovina still needs to tackle and remedy these flaws in the local finance system.

When it comes to the assessment of the current stage of fiscal decentralisation trajectory and the outcomes of the whole process of decentralisation, Bosnia and Herzegovina has attained positive results when compared to the early post-war years. First, the decentralisation framework set by the 1995 Dayton Agreement has managed to lessen ethnic cleavages, while at the same time supporting the process of post-conflict reconciliation and maintaining peace in the country for more than 20 years. Although this constitutional arrangement did not acknowledge and regulate local self-government, cities and municipalities became the focus of further decentralisation processes in the years that followed. Second, political decentralisation has also brought on positive results. At the local level, higher democratisation has been achieved through the direct election of mayors—a system that has ensured higher local accountability and citizen engagement in local politics. Third, the answer to the question of whether (fiscal) decentralisation has resulted in better local service delivery and stronger economic development has been ambiguous and the results mixed at best. On the one hand, local government budgets were two to three times bigger in absolute terms in 2016 when compared to the baseline year 2003. Yet, on the other hand, the shares of local government revenues/expenditures in the total government revenues/expenditures and in the GDP have remained more or less the same relative to 2003. As local revenues increased, as a result of both fiscal decentralisation measures and the years of economic growth, expenditures analogically started to rise, particularly expenditures for employees. When the first effects of the crisis occurred in 2009, revenues were used for maintaining and further increasing employment in local public authorities for four different reasons: (1) the country faced deep structural economic problems leading to structural unemployment; (2) thus, the private sector was too weak; (3) nepotism employment became too widespread due to strong patronage networks and party-related favouritism, which was additionally accentuated by an ethnic component; and (4) laying off civil servants was politically unpopular and difficult for social reasons. The pressure to service the increasing current expenditures for employees adversely affected capital expenditures and increased local indebtedness. Hence, fiscal decentralisation also brought on negative side effects, expressed not only as excessive local borrowing, but also through the rise of arrears. Although it is evident that local borrowing has dramatically increased compared to the baseline year 2003 (when debt was virtually non-existent), non-transparent reporting and accounting prevent us from determining how this money has been spent. To curb debt and outstanding arrears, Bosnia and Herzegovina must introduce harder budget constraints together with more transparent and accurate financial reporting. To conclude, despite some improvements in strengthening local governments, fiscal decentralisation in Bosnia and Herzegovina seems to have failed to yield notable economic development results and achieve efficiency in resource allocation.

In Montenegro, the goal of local democratisation was only partly met, if we use the direct election of mayors as a criterion for achieving higher political accountability and citizen engagement. By revoking the direct election of mayors in 2009 (after only six years), Montenegro left this political decentralisation discourse. Similar to Bosnia and Herzegovina, Montenegro ended up in 2015 with humongous local debt, with arrears comprising more than 55% of it. Arrears accumulated primarily due to the failure to pay taxes and social contribution for civil servants employed in local authorities for a number of years. Like in Bosnia and Herzegovina, municipal budgets in Montenegro grew significantly from 2002 until 2016—both in absolute (more than four times) and relative terms (a bit better in 2016 than in 2002, but way lower than at the peak of decentralisation in 2007–2008). The pattern of employing and spending for local employees that was identified in Bosnia and Herzegovina was also present in Montenegro. However, Montenegro approached the problem differently. Its central government addressed the problem of vertical imbalances and increased indebtedness with several diverse policy measures. It consolidated local finance by increasing municipal revenues, while at the same time introducing hard budget constraints, debt restructuring programmes, and additional fiscal restrictions aimed at overseeing the local budgetary process. While this approach helped put local debt under control, it also diminished local fiscal autonomy. In order to fully resolve the problem of municipal outstanding debt and arrears, political will at the central level will be crucial, but this is also highly dependent on future election outcomes and coalition agreements. Although these challenges look the same in Montenegro and Bosnia and Herzegovina, the latter is additionally burdened with one more pre-condition—the political consensus of ethnic elites. Pressured with the need to maintain the high level of current expenditures for employees and to service the growing debt and outstanding arrears, Montenegro has had to make serious cuts of expenditures for capital investments. While it is true that at the end of the observed period capital investments were highly compromised at the local level, the blend of peaks of economic growth and the fiscal decentralisation process in 2007 and 2008 allowed Montenegrin municipalities to undertake large investment and development projects. Thus, the answer to the question of whether fiscal decentralisation has led to good economic development and efficiency outcomes in Montenegro is rather mixed, with the current stage failing to fully realise the benefits of the process.

The fiscal decentralisation trajectory in Serbia today is close to its initial levels in the early years of the process (2004–2005), measured as the total local government revenue (or expenditure) in general government revenue (or expenditure) and in the GDP. Hence, the process has reverted to a centralistic course and is below its pre-crisis peak. This trend is worrying since, in this category of countries, only Serbian local governments have become responsible for a wider spectrum of local functions, including some social sector services. When assessing the outcomes of decentralisation policy vis-à-vis democratisation, and by using the same criterion of the direct election of mayors, Serbia has encountered the same setback as Montenegro. In order to raise political accountability and citizen participation in local decision making, Serbia empowered citizens to elect the heads of their local communities directly in 2002. However, confronted with the loss of control at the local level, political parties made the Parliament revoke the system as early as in 2006. Still, the situation is far better than during the autocratic regime of the 1990s. Unfortunately, political parties also preserve and further contribute to non-transparency of fiscal data, which hampers evidence-based decision making in public finance. A lack of transparent, complete, and accurate fiscal databases is an impediment for efficient and optimal fiscal decisions and outcomes. Ruling political parties hide the data to preserve their power and short-term clientelist interests, thus sacrificing long-term development and public interest. Fiscal decentralisation in Serbia has never been reflected in stable, local fiscal autonomy. While the central government does not interfere directly in municipal budgeting, as is the case in Montenegro today, it undermines local fiscal management by incessant meddling through adhocratic measures. Finally, a similar relationship between current and capital spending is also evident in Serbia. This is particularly highlighted in the capital city of Belgrade, which is supposed to be the driver of economic development and where investments in 2014 were more than twice below the level in 2006 and more than four times below the level in the period 2007–2011.

To conclude, the most important trend in this category of countries is the reversal of the decentralisation discourse, as a centralistic trajectory has been present in the final years of the observed period. In addition, the drastic drop in capital investment and the uncontrolled rise in liabilities (particularly in arrears), accompanied by the fall of local revenues, have become a ticking time bomb. In order to prevent a deeper economic crisis, the central governments need to adopt harder budget constraints, raise the level of fiscal transparency, and improve the fiscal autonomy and capacity of local governments. Here, the EU should be the key partner leading and supporting the process within the Europeanisation framework.

The third group of countries faced the most difficult task—to resolve deep ethnic cleavages and organise themselves to function in the post-conflict context with high ethnic tensions. Similarly as in Bosnia and Herzegovina, decentralisation has been the principal instrument for appeasing nationalistic forces, ensuring participation and integration of ethnic minorities, and facilitating the completion of state-building processes in Macedonia and Kosovo. Decentralisation in Kosovo commenced immediately after the 1999 war within the post-conflict, peace-keeping framework of the United Nations Mission in Kosovo (UNMIK) administration, in accordance with the UN Resolution 1244. The main goals of the decentralisation policies were to ensure local trust building between Serbs and Kosovo Albanians, to integrate the Serbian minority into the newly established Kosovar institutions, and to legitimise the state-building process. In 2001, Macedonia as well experienced the ethnic conflict. The tensions between Macedonians and Albanians ended with signing the Ohrid Framework Agreement in

2001. Thus, the focus of the earlier 1990s decentralisation initiatives was changed—instead of achieving higher efficiency in local governance, the principal objective of decentralisation became ensuring peace and cooperation.

For the purpose of protecting and satisfying minority interests, the territorial organisation of both Macedonia and Kosovo was designed to accommodate the geographic distribution of ethnic communities, not taking into account the economies of scale. While in Macedonia the size of the municipality became an issue over time, in Kosovo, the process continued on the course of further fragmentation. After the centralistic early 1990s, Macedonia reorganised the country in 1996 for political-ethnic reasons, by increasing the number of local government units from 34 to 123. Due to sub-optimal service delivery, and within the new context of the post-conflict agreement, Macedonia restructured the territorial organisation twice—in 2004 and 2013. In order to also take into account the economies of scale, the country merged and streamlined local government units to 84 and 80, respectively. In Kosovo, the 2000 UNMIK regulation established 30 municipalities. Later, eight new municipalities were founded for two different reasons—(1) to accommodate ethnic interests and (2) to bring decision making closer to citizens. When it comes to the second reason, there is increasing pressure to form additional local government units. The population of 11 villages claims that their local preferences are neglected, since there is a lack of capital investment and of sufficient level of municipal services in their communities. The current model of municipal financing further aggravates this issue and makes it less resolvable. The low share of own-source revenues in total local revenues, as well as the fixed annual amount of intergovernmental transfers, seriously limits fiscal autonomy and capacity of local governments. It means that the existing municipalities would be worse off if new local governments were established. To allow the expression of local preferences and, thus, further fragmentation, it is necessary to create a new system of intergovernmental grants and own-source revenues, while taking into consideration the economies of scale and efficiency of public service delivery.

The approach to fiscal decentralisation in Macedonia and Kosovo was quite similar. On the expenditure side, local governments obtained almost the same set of functions. In Macedonia, the delegation of expenditure assignments was gradual. In the first phase, municipalities got the right to build and manage facilities in the social sector. In the second phase, they were assigned the financing of salaries of teachers and social sector personnel through block grants. The largest portion of local expenditures was allocated for education, particularly for salaries and other related costs for teachers. The municipalities in Kosovo got a quite similar scope of functions through the UNMIK regulation in 2000. The competences were further broadened in 2007 and 2008 with the UNMIK regulation and the Law on Local Self-Government, respectively. An approximately equal share of expenditures was allocated for education—almost half of the total local budget. In 2008, the Serb-majority municipalities got an enhanced purview of powers related to secondary health care, higher education, selection of local police commanding officers, and so on.

During the years of fiscal decentralisation, municipalities in Macedonia (in 2005) and in Kosovo (in 2008) got the right to determine and administer the property tax entirely. Like in Montenegro and Serbia, the property tax has become major own-source revenue over the years. However, the share of own-source revenues in total local revenues, as well as the share of total local revenues in the GDP, remains very low in both countries. Due to the limited fiscal autonomy and the fact that municipalities are funded mainly via intergovernmental transfers (shared revenues and grants), the fiscal relations in Macedonia mirror de-concentration more than decentralisation of resources. Despite the goal to decentralise power from the central to the local level in Kosovo, the transfer of sufficient financial resources has been neglected. This hampered financial autonomy and sustainability, thus compromising the results of the decentralisation process. Similar as in Macedonia, the decentralisation process has been directly affected by local ethnic patronage networks. The fiscal dimension of the decentralisation process has been a peculiarly politically sensitive issue, as the Serb-majority municipalities in the north of the country have developed parallel institutions and access to two sources of financing—from the budget of the Republic of Serbia and from the budget of Kosovo.

When assessing whether fiscal decentralisation has attained its major objective in Macedonia—the reconciliation of ethnic tensions—one can conclude that the goal has been partly achieved. Interethnic conflict has ceased, but it is questionable whether the outcome is sustainable. Over the years, it has become evident that reconciliation cannot be secured by relying on decentralisation alone. In Macedonia, the decentralisation policy has managed to satisfy minority demands by delegating them certain public affairs and resources. Still, it failed to ensure political accountability for and economic efficiency in providing public services. This is due to the general clientelistic practices in Macedonia at the local level, which have become even more aggravated by the ethnic component involved. In such cases, decentralisation further legitimises and strengthens ethnic divisions because local ethnic political elites want to maintain their preferential status and political benefits. Furthermore, it also becomes questionable whether democratisation has been achieved in such a political setting. The municipalities where mayors are not of the same political affiliation as the ruling party at the central level are disadvantaged and face serious political obstacles in conducting local public affairs. These developments have shadowed the economic aspects of decentralisation policies, putting aside the goal of achieving an efficient allocation of resources and optimal provision of local public services. Decentralisation in Kosovo has been one of the major issues in the process of international state building and calming ethnic tensions. From the early 2000s, the UNMIK administration insisted on a bottom-up approach to institutional building. The main part of this grassroots endeavour was the empowerment of mayors, who have become key political figures that cannot be dismissed by municipal assemblies or by the simple majority of local votes. They can be removed from office only if more than 50% of all registered voters opts for their dismissal. Due to these excessive powers, their political accountability is distorted. The main goal of decentralisation and its role in peace building and democratisation in Kosovo is yet to be tested, particularly in relation to the status of the Association of Serb Municipalities.

Although the focus of decentralisation in these countries was placed on calming ethnic tensions, one should not overlook their significant achievement in fiscal decentralisation. Both countries have made progress that dominates trends in the region. In Macedonia, the relative growth of the share of local government revenue in the GDP was the greatest over the observed time frame, although at the end of the period, it reached more or less the same level as the other countries. The data show that Macedonia was actually at the lowest starting position in the region at the beginning of the decentralisation process—at only around 2% in 2006 (Levitas et al., 2016). Kosovo, on the other hand, was supported by the UNMIK decentralised approach to institutional building, and it started from a much higher baseline—at around 7% in 2006. It ended up with fiscal decentralisation indicators highest in the region (9.1%) closest to the EU average (11.3%) in 2014 (Levitas et al., 2016). Yet, local governments in both countries still lack the necessary fiscal capacity. This means that fiscal decentralisation has to remain the main instrument for securing the necessary financial autonomy and resources for local communities so that they can carry out the assigned tasks and fulfil their new roles in both Macedonia and Kosovo.

In the fourth category, there is only one country—Albania. As explained earlier, the Albanian decentralisation process emerged from an entirely different context. The 50-year-long centralism and totalitarianism left the country deprived of the real local self-government. The central government administered the country through a network of its 642 local (de-concentrated) offices, not establishing lower tiers of government. The long isolation kept the country at a very low level of economic development with an overwhelming prevalence of a rural population. A peculiarity of the decentralisation process in Albania is that it has occurred in parallel with a dramatic urbanisation and migration triggered by the opening of the country in the early 1990s. The capital city of Tirana grew threefold between 1991 and 2011, and the share of the urban population increased to more than 50%.

In 1992, Albania started to build its grassroots institutions, organising the country into 393 local self-governments, out of which almost three-fourths were small rural communities. However, all local government units received the same purview of responsibilities, regardless of their size and fiscal capacity. This system was the root of a latent problem, which led to a significant accumulation of arrears during the course of 25 years. Although it seems that the country followed an adequate sequencing of the decentralisation processes over the 25-year-span, it ended up with loopholes and results similar to those of the other countries in the region.

In 2009, Albanian local governments got a wider scope of responsibilities—the management of utilities and some expensive social service functions. The timing of this delegation was unfortunate, since it coincided with the onset of the global financial crisis, which negatively affected municipal revenues. Interestingly, despite a very different context in Albania, the central government employed the same package of measures towards local governments as some other countries in the region (e.g. Serbia and Montenegro) in order to react to the crisis. This reflects the cookie-cutter approach of international donors, which further aggravated the situation. On the one hand, they spearheaded decentralisation efforts, particularly fiscal decentralisation, while on the other, they pushed for the regulatory "guillotine" aimed at cutting the administrative burden of doing business. To spur local economy and stimulate businesses, central governments primarily reduced and/or abolished a number of local fees and charges for businesses. Similar to Montenegro, Albania protected certain groups of investors at the expense of local budgets. Not only did the central government interfere in these own-source revenues, but it also continuously changed downwardly shared revenues and grants. After 2009, from year to year, the central government reduced the size of unconditional (non-earmarked) grants used for financing delegated functions, while it increased earmarked grants for capital projects. However, ministers and government appointees allocated these grants arbitrarily, based on their political interests. These developments demonstrate the strong political grasp of local fiscal autonomy, where local interests are often sacrificed to serve either the central government's or party-financial interests. These trends on expenditure and revenue sides created vertical imbalances. To tackle demographic changes and horizontal imbalances, and to attain more optimal economies of scale, Albania reformed its territorial organisation for the second time in 2014. It reduced the number of local government units from 393 to 61. These newly created municipalities absorbed both assets and liabilities of the previous communities, including their arrears. These presented a serious burden despite the fact that Albanian local governments are still not allowed to borrow. While the prohibition to assume debt curbs outstanding liabilities, it further cripples capital investment capacities at the local level. Currently, the only advantage is that Albania can learn from its neighbours and introduce stricter borrowing rules and harder budget constraints, once it allows its municipalities to incur debt.

To assess the decentralisation trajectory in Albania, one should take into account both the initial context and the current developments. Albania has achieved dramatic progress in all aspects of decentralisation and local government reform, thus securing democratisation and economic development. At the beginning of the observed period, in 1990, local self-government almost did not exist. In 2017, Albania reformed local finance by introducing a serious system of municipal financing including the decentralisation of property taxation. However, as in the other countries in the region, Albanian municipalities were not spared certain post-crisis policy reversals and centralistic measures. Namely, like in Serbia, the central government has been interrupting the decentralisation process with frequent, ad hoc legal amendments that express inconsistencies and conflicting policy priorities. Although Albania looked to be the counterpoint to the countries that emerged from the former Yugoslavia at the beginning of the process, the trend of convergence is evident at the end of the period. The Albanian local governments today face similar challenges as the ones in the region. The central governments' responses to these challenges are also quite similar. While there are variations, this implies that the donor-led reforms involved the transplantation of almost identical programmes and policies.

* * *

In observing where the eight countries of Southeastern Europe studied in this book stand after the whole period of transition and decentralisation from 1990 until today, the following conclusions can be drawn. One of the most important observations is that decentralisation has been one of the key instruments for keeping peace and calming ethnic tensions in countries previously affected by conflicts. Municipalities in the region have achieved dramatic progress since the early 1990s. They have gained a new role in the public sector and have become important political and economic players. In the period after 2000, cities and municipalities obtained a far wider purview of responsibilities and functions, including important social sector services. They also became a relevant partner in the process of European integration, bearing in mind the competences they receive with the adoption of the *acquis communautaire* in countries that succeeded in EU accession. At the end of the period, local governments now have much greater fiscal autonomy and sources of funding. If one looks only at the fiscal decentralisation aspect, indicators are far better than in 1990 and 2000. However, the shares of local government revenue (and expenditure) in total government revenue (and expenditure) and their shares in GDP are today only at the pre-crisis levels, and half of the countries have still not fully recovered to reach the 2007–2008 indices. Moreover, the fiscal decentralisation indicators for the region are still well below the EU average. This fact is rather worrying considering the portfolio of responsibilities and expenditures assigned to local governments. This vertical imbalance has led to extensive borrowing and to the rapid accumulation of arrears. The lack of transparent consolidated financial reporting has prevented both local and central governments from effectively controlling their total fiscal risks. Thus, the immediate goal of the central governments should be to impose harder budget constraints for local governments, with consolidated financial reporting and transparent presentation of all liabilities, as well as to adopt rules on general transparency of fiscal data to enable sound public financial management. The EU should be the key partner in supporting these endeavours within the EU accession process. The lessons from Slovenia and Croatia show that EU funds can be crucial for mitigating external economic shocks. Yet, significant territorial fragmentation weakens the fiscal capacity of municipalities, reducing their potential to absorb these funds. The large number of small municipalities also aggravates the efforts to attain more balanced regional development. Finally, small municipalities have difficulties in providing local public services efficiently since they cannot achieve economies of scale. The main obstacle to consolidating and merging municipalities and to establishing inter-municipal cooperation remains the political patronage networks (particularly when an ethnic component is involved). It will be very challenging to convince political elites to abandon their quasi-rents and privileges, to stop the waste of scarce resource, and to achieve greater public welfare. It seems that the wave of fiscal decentralisation in the studied countries slowly receded after the post-2008 economic crisis. It may take a combination of the current economic upswing, a political revival of the idea, and stronger EU leadership to support a renewed surge in fiscal decentralisation in the region.

References

A new treaty: A new role for regions and local authorities. (2010). Brussels: European Union, Committee of the Regions.

Avlijaš, S., & Bartlett, W. (2011). *The political economy of decentralisation and regional policy in Serbia: Choices and outcomes.* LSEE papers on Decentralisation and Regional Policy.

Bartlett, W., Maleković, S., & Monastiriotis, V. (2013). *Decentralization and local development in South East Europe.* Basingstoke: Palgrave Macmillan.

Bartlett, W., & Prica, I. (2018). Debt in the super-periphery: The case of the western Balkans. *Third World Thematics.* https://doi.org/10.1080/23802014.2017.1438850

Decentralization in client countries—An evaluation of World Bank support 1990–2007 by independent evaluation group IEG. (2008). Washington, DC: The World Bank.

Kmezić, S., Đulić, K., Jocović, M., & Kaluđerović, J. (2016). *Fiscal decentralisation and local government financing in Serbia and Montenegro.* Maribor: Institute for Local Self-Government and Public Procurement—Lex Localis.

Levitas, A., et al. (2016). *Fiscal decentralization indicators for South-East Europe: 2006–2014.* Skopje: Network of Associations of Local Authorities of South-East Europe (NALAS).

Local and regional governments in Europe—Structures and competences. (2016). Brussels: CCRE CEMR.

Musgrave, R. A. (1959). *The theory of public finance.* New York: McGraw-Hill.

Oates, W. E. (1972). *Fiscal federalism.* New York: Harcourt Brace Jovanovich.

Popović, D. (1996). *Poluvekovni razvoj fiskalnog sistema u Jugoslaviji.* Beograd: Zadužbina Miloša Crnjanskog.

Stojanović, S. (2005). *Fiskalni federalizam.* Beograd: Institut za uporedno pravo, Centar za antiratnu akciju.

Tiebout, C. M. (1956). A pure theory of local expenditures. *The Journal of Political Economy, 64*(5), 416–424.

Index[1]

[1] Note: Page numbers followed by 'n' refer to notes.

W. Bartlett et al. (eds.), *Fiscal Decentralisation, Local Government and Policy Reversals in Southeastern Europe*, https://doi.org/10.1007/978-3-319-96092-0